Chapters in a Mythology

The Disquieting Muses, 1917, by Giorgio de Chirico.

Chapters in a Mythology
The Poetry of
Sylvia Plath

JUDITH KROLL

HARPER & ROW, PUBLISHERS

New York, Hagerstown, San Francisco, London

(*continued on next page*)

Library of Congress Cataloging in Publication Data
Kroll, Judith, date
    Chapters in a mythology.
    "Selected bibliography of sources cited from the work of Sylvia Plath": p.
    Bibliography: p.
    Includes index.
    1. Plath, Sylvia—Criticism and interpretation.
I. Title.
PS3566.L27Z75   1976   811'.5'4   75-6344
ISBN 0-06-012457-1

76 77 78 79 80 10 9 8 7 6 5 4 3 2 1

Only when all our hold on life
   is troubled,

Only in spiritual terror can
   the Truth

Come through the broken mind—

—*W. B. Yeats,* The Hour-Glass

Contents

Preface

The focus of this book is on the thematic meaning of Plath's late poems. It deals with their rhetoric and analyzes them individually primarily insofar as that is relevant to a demonstration of her deep and complex vision.

Of Plath's discernible sources, drawn from her very wide and very completely assimilated reading, I have dealt in detail with the ones that seem to me crucial in revealing her artistic purposes. Foremost among these are Graves and Frazer. There is a great deal more to be said of the uses she made of Eliot, Lawrence, Woolf, and others, and of the effect of her collaboration with Ted Hughes. But further elaboration of these influences will I trust prove consistent with what I have argued about the meaning of her work as a whole.

The impetus for this book was an interest that began in 1961. While I was an undergraduate at Smith College I was introduced to some of Plath's poems by Professor Alfred Young Fisher, with whom she had worked on her writing during her senior year. This study was begun in 1967 and submitted in an earlier version as a doctoral dissertation at Yale in April 1974. Ted Hughes subsequently read that version, and when I discussed it with him on several occasions in June 1974, he substantially confirmed the inferences I had drawn about Plath's sources and related matters. Because it is important to know the extent to which Plath's meaning can be established on internal evidence, I have clearly indicated these external confirmations. Although, as will be evident, I have added some material (including some based on access to Plath's library), mostly in the way of confirmation or additional detail, my reading of Plath has been substantially modified only in one or two cases, notably that of "Stopped Dead," where I have added an alternative interpretation. This, too, might have been inferred from internal evidence. I am grateful to Ted Hughes for reading my dissertation and discussing it with me, and for giving me access to some of the items in Plath's library.

I owe thanks to Olwyn Hughes for permission to quote from Plath's published and unpublished work, and for the opportunity to study manuscripts of the poems in 1972, while I was at work on the final draft of my dissertation, at a time particularly useful for adding detail to the argument I had mapped out.

I was extremely fortunate to have Cleanth Brooks as my dissertation adviser. Although he should not be held responsible for any of my critical excesses or defects of scholarship, I am indebted to him for the balanced skepticism and openmindedness of his response to my ideas, for his suggestions, and for his encouragement.

I owe a number of other debts of gratitude. Margaret Cardwell Higonnet read two versions of this study and made many valuable criticisms. Marie Borroff, Sheila Cobb Ewing, Albert Rothenberg, and Margaret Wimsatt also made helpful suggestions. Susan Meserve Driscoll, for three years my student assistant at Vassar College, helped me with bibliographical research. Beverly Owen shared with me the material she had collected for her master's thesis on Plath. Laura (Riding) Jackson communicated several points of information about a radio broadcast of hers. Ann Hummel of the BBC provided me with a 1968 script of *Three Women;* Kathleen Hutchings sent me a script of Ted Hughes's "Difficulties of a Bridegroom."

Mildred Tubby produced, from a chaotic draft, the typescript of my dissertation, which was a great help in preparing this book. Vassar College provided research assistance.

Frances McCullough, my editor at Harper & Row, knows a great deal about Sylvia Plath's life and work, and her help has substantially benefited this book.

The text of Plath's poems in this study agrees with the manuscript of her (forthcoming) *Collected Poems,* which differs in a few cases from various published versions. For the convenience of the reader, however, the list of Plath's poems included in my bibliography gives page references to presently available (U.S. and British) editions of her work, and, where the poems are not yet in readily accessible book editions, to magazine versions.

J. K.

June 1975

Chronology

1932   October 27: Sylvia Plath born to Aurelia Schober Plath and Otto Emil Plath, of Jamaica Plain, Massachusetts.

1935   April 27: birth of Warren Plath.

1936   Move to Winthrop, Massachusetts.

1940   October 12: Otto Plath's leg amputated.

        November 5: Otto Plath dies from pulmonary embolism.

1942   October: move to Wellesley, Massachusetts.

1950   September: Sylvia Plath begins freshman year at Smith College, Northampton, Massachusetts.

1952   August: prize-winning story, "Sunday at the Mintons'," published in *Mademoiselle* magazine.

1953   June: Guest Managing Editor for *Mademoiselle*, New York City.

        August 24: disappearance and suicide attempt in Wellesley; subsequent hospitalization at McLean Hospital, Belmont, Massachusetts.

1954   Winter: returns to Smith College for second semester.

        Summer: lives in Cambridge, Massachusetts, and attends Harvard Summer School.

1955   January: submits English honors thesis, on the "double" in Dostoevsky, at Smith College.

   April: ties for first prize in the Glascock Poetry Contest (Mount Holyoke College).

   May: wins Academy of American Poets Prize and the Ethel Olin Corbin Poetry Prize, and graduates from Smith College.

   October: begins study on a Fulbright grant at Newnham College, Cambridge University.

1956   February 25: meets Ted Hughes.

   June 16: marries Ted Hughes in London.

1956–57 Second Fulbright year at Newnham College.

1957   Submits poetry manuscript, "Two Lovers and a Beach-comber," for English Tripos (and M.A. degree) at Newnham College.

   June: returns to United States with Ted Hughes. Wins Bess Hokin Prize (*Poetry* magazine).

1957–58 Instructor in English, Smith College.

1958–59 Writing and part-time work, Boston, Massachusetts.

1959   September-November: works on poetry at Yaddo, Saratoga Springs, New York.

   December: departs, with Ted Hughes, for England; settles in London.

1960   April 1: birth of daughter, Frieda Rebecca.

   October: *The Colossus* (poems) published by William Heinemann Ltd. (London).

1961   February: miscarriage.

   March: appendectomy.

July: vacation in France (including Berck-Plage); wins first prize in the Cheltenham Festival Contest (the Guinness Poetry Award); decision to purchase house in Devon, England.

August: meets Assia Gutman. Moves to Devon.

Edits anthology of American poets, *American Poetry Now*, as a supplement to *The Critical Quarterly* (England).

November: receives Eugene F. Saxton Grant to work on *The Bell Jar*.

1962 January 17: birth of son, Nicholas Farrar.

April: hears Laura Riding broadcast on BBC (April 1). Writes "Little Fugue," "Crossing the Water," "An Appearance," "Among the Narcissi," "Pheasant," and "Elm" within a period of ten days: the first rush of late poems.

May 14: *The Colossus & Other Poems* published in the U.S. by Alfred A. Knopf.

June: Mrs. Plath arrives for a visit in Devon, and returns to the U.S. in early August.

July: learns of her husband's involvement with Assia Gutman.

August 19: *Three Women* broadcast on the BBC Third Programme.

September: trip, with Ted Hughes, to Ireland; returns alone to Devon; she and Ted Hughes separate by the end of the month, or early October.

October: at least twenty-six poems written in the first month of separation from her husband.

October 30: poems and interview recorded for the British Council in association with the Poetry Room in the Lamont Library of Harvard University.

December: moves, with her two children, to a flat in London.

1963   January: *The Bell Jar* published by William Heinemann Ltd. under the pseudonym "Victoria Lucas."

February 11: Dies by her own hand.

I

The Mythic Nature of the Poetry

Most readers of contemporary poetry in the English-speaking world are by now acquainted with the life and work of Sylvia Plath. But the particular renown she has posthumously won is not the success she intended and deserves. The reading of her work has been entangled in a fascination with her suicide and the broken marriage which preceded it, and such misreading is as widespread among her admirers as among her detractors; she has become for both a convenient symbol. To approach Plath as a poet rather than to use her as an image of a poet one must confront her work in its own terms, which is to say, as literature. In these terms, the fact, for example, that she killed herself is irrelevant to the consideration of the meaning of her work; as literature, her poems would mean what they do even if she had not attempted suicide.

Among the current classifications in literary criticism, Plath is usually assigned the category of 'confessional' poet. That view is facilitated by the obviously autobiographical element in her work and by the apparent accessibility of many of her best-known poems, in which the 'confessional' surface is sensational enough to divert the reader from seeing deeper meanings. One might even prefer to read many of her poems as one might view the bloodstains at the site of a murder, as residues of real events—for example, "Daddy" and "Lady Lazarus" as the expression by the actual Sylvia Plath of a supremely venomous attitude toward her father. The thrill this provides might easily be lessened when the more impersonal dimensions of such poems are considered.

But the very accessible confessional aspect of her work is so powerfully affecting that the thought that there might be something more, and quite different in nature, hardly arises. Nevertheless, her poetry is not primarily literal and confessional. It is, rather, the articulation of a mythic system which integrates all aspects of her work, and into which autobiographical or confessional details are shaped and absorbed, greatly qualifying how such elements ought to be viewed. Her husband Ted Hughes writes:

Her poetry has been called "confessional and personal," and connected with the school of Robert Lowell and Anne Sexton. She admired both these poets, and knew them personally, and they both had an effect on her. And she shares with them the central experience of a shattering of the self, and the labour of fitting it together again or finding a new one. She also shared with them the East Massachusetts homeland. But the connection goes no further. Her poetic strategies, the poetic events she draws out of her experience of disintegration and renewal, the radiant, visionary light in which she encounters her family and the realities of her daily life, are quite different in kind from anything one finds in Robert Lowell's poetry, or Anne Sexton's. Their work is truly autobiographical and personal, and their final world is a torture cell walled with family portraits, with the daily newspaper coming under the door. The autobiographical details in Sylvia Plath's poetry work differently. She sets them out like masks, which are then lifted up by dramatis personae of nearly supernatural qualities.[1]*

In a great deal of the work of Robert Lowell and Anne Sexton, often considered the paradigm 'confessional' poets, the voice—intensely personal and almost journalistic—is the direct voice of the author in an everyday role. In Plath the personal concerns and everyday role are transmuted into something impersonal, by being absorbed into a timeless mythic system. The poetry of Lowell and Sexton relates their narratives; in Plath—although many narrative details of her mythic system are drawn from her life—the emphasis is more on expressing the structure of her state of being. 'Confessional' poetry usually comprises a plurality of con-

---

* Notes to the chapters begin on page 213.

cerns—politics, the writing of poetry, marriage, aging, fame, and so on—that remain relatively independent. But in Plath's poetry, there is one overriding concern: the problem of rebirth or transcendence; and nearly everything in her poetry contributes either to the statement or to the envisioned resolution of this problem.

Because a mythic system accommodates the personal element, the voice of her poetry is detached from the personal in a sense that it is not in 'confessional' poets, whose strategy depends partly upon convincing the reader of a lack of such detachment. For them mundane life overflows into art, but with Plath it is just the opposite.

She has a vision which is complete, self-contained, and whole, a vision of a mythic totality, which such poets as Lowell and Sexton do not have. Much of the vitality in their poetry arises from the very incompleteness of the vision; from a sense that there exist possibilities of discovery and change; from the interest and pleasure one may have in observing the self in encounters whose outcome is not foreclosed; from confronting a future which is open-ended. Plath's late poems, on the other hand, convey the sense that the future is foreclosed, that no substantial change can be occasioned by experience, and that only rebirth or transcendence of self would be a resolution.

Both her artistic detachment from the personal and its absorption in the mythic—which, having absorbed the personal, has brought it to a different level—are suggested by a remark she made toward the end of her life about writing poetry:

I feel like a very efficient tool or weapon, used and in demand from moment to moment . . .[2]

This unselfconsciousness and detachment from the personal give Plath's late poems (the expression of the unmistakable voice announced in *Ariel*, which contains about half the late poems, all but a handful of which were written between April 1962 and her suicide in February 1963) much of their power, and suggest why they have "impressed themselves on many readers with the force of myth."[3] A further reason for this effect is suggested by Ted Hughes:

In her poetry . . . she had free and controlled access to depths formerly
reserved to the primitive ecstatic priests, shamans and Holy men, . . .[4]

Plath's vision is at that level, and the effect is that of a mythic poem
written by its protagonist.

If her poetry is understood as constituting a system of symbols
that expresses a unified mythic vision, her images may be seen to
be emblems of that myth. Red, white, and black, for example, the
characteristic colors in her late poetry, function as mythic emblems
of her state of being much as they do in the mythologies which
she drew upon. A great many other particulars of her poetry are
similarly determined by her system, and personal and historical details as well are subordinate to it. While a confessional poet might
alter certain details to make them more fitting—in the spirit of
Aristotle's observation that poetry is truer than history—Plath's
alteration of details has a deeper significance. Her protagonist in
"Daddy" says, "I was ten when they buried you," but Plath
was only eight when her father died. A magical "one year in
every ten" cycle, however, conveys the mythic inevitability necessary to define her state of being. It is precisely such details of confessional literalness that Plath most frequently alters or eliminates,
when they are not sufficiently mythic. Neither Lowell nor Sexton
writes poems in which mythic inevitability and cyclical orderli-
ness are as important, for they do not have the kind of vision to
which such considerations are relevant.

The subordination of details, in Plath's poetry, to her mythic
vision, goes beyond alterations of matters of fact, for the significance
even of apparently 'occasional' poems about small events—such
as cutting her thumb ("Cut") or seeing red flowers ("Poppies in
October")—lies in their evocation of her pre-existing primary concerns. While the details in 'confessional' poems stand on their own,
frequently unified only to the extent that they occur within a
single consciousness, there is hardly a detail in Plath's poetry that
is not connected with and does not intimate her entire vision.

To a reader unaware of this unity, Plath's poetry will seem to
contain a collection of brilliant and fortuitous images, bearing more
or less the significance they do for us in daily life. A few critics,
however, have begun to go beyond this in noting certain recurrent

patterns of association between some of these images. Annette Lavers, for example, observes that white is in some cultures a symbol of death, and that this, "coupled with the other attributes of death, makes the moon the perfect symbol for it." Therefore, "Words like 'pearl,' 'silver' or 'ivory,' which can be used to describe moonlight, always announce some untoward event." Lavers goes so far as to suggest the existence of some kind of "code" in which "objects and their qualities are endowed with stable significations."[5] But beyond that there is a mythic system that is encoded, in which virtually every image in the late poems participates.

Other misapprehensions arise if one ignores the more impersonal or mythic dimension in Plath's poetry. Without this awareness, the elements of suffering, violence, death, and decay will generally be seen as aspects of a self-indulgent stance that is merely —albeit brilliantly—nasty, morbid, and decadent, the extremist exhibitionism. Were she a 'confessional' poet, this might be the case. But her poetry is of a different order, and these details are absorbed into a broader system of concerns. To see the autobiographical details only as such is to regard Plath's vision of suffering and death as morbid, but to appreciate the deeper significance of her poetry is to understand her fascination with death as connected with and transformed into a broader concern with the themes of rebirth and transcendence.

There is a similar danger of missing the meaning of her poetry in regarding her themes and imagery as illustrations of pathological symptoms, as if what is of significance in her poetry were reducible to the presentation of a case history. To see a theme or image—for example, that of the division between one's 'true' and 'false' selves —merely as a 'symptom of schizophrenia' is to dismiss the meaning with which one is confronted. In a discussion of this sort of reductivism, Thomas Szasz mentions that

Jesus himself, according to two psychiatrists . . . was a "born degenerate" with a "fixed delusional system"; manifesting a "paranoid clinical picture [so typical] it is hardly conceivable people can even question the accuracy of the diagnosis."[6]

The final outcome of this sort of application of labels is the denial of the possibility of meaning. For it is of the same order of irrelevance as bringing to mind that acts of consciousness are chemical reactions.

To deal with the structure of Plath's poetry is primarily to deal with the voices, landscape, characters, images, emblems, and motifs which articulate a mythic drama having something of the eternal necessity of Greek tragedy. The myth has its basis in her biography, but it in turn exercises a selective function on her biography and determines within it an increasingly restricted context of relevance as her work becomes more symbolic and archetypal.

Ted Hughes, with whom she shared many interests and worked very closely, has made this germinal and somewhat cryptic statement about her poetry:

Most readers will perceive pretty readily the single centre of power and light which her poems all share, but I think it will be a service if I point out just how little of her poetry is 'occasional,' and how faithfully her separate poems build up into one long poem. She faced a task in herself, and her poetry is the record of her progress in the task. The poems are chapters in a mythology where the plot, seen as a whole and in retrospect, is strong and clear—even if the origins of it and the *dramatis personae*, are at bottom enigmatic. . . . The world of her poetry is one of emblematic visionary events, mathematical symmetries, clairvoyance, metamorphoses, and something resembling . . . biological and racial recall. And the whole scene lies under the transfiguring eye of the great white timeless light.[7]

If one first grasps the 'plot' of the myth and the dynamics of the mythic motifs and then returns to the late poems, it becomes immediately apparent that they constitute a unified body of work, and that the early poems logically and consistently progress toward the final formulation of the myth and its subsidiary motifs. All of Sylvia Plath's late poems, including even the few that seem to be out of the mainstream, can best be understood in terms of her underlying system, as can her characteristic and effortless skills— the arrestingly exact images; the language that is at once colloquial and charged with extraordinary intensity; the ritualistic and prophetic tone; the shifting perspectives, masks, and other devices —these all evolve from the same basic concerns and necessities.

In "Electra on Azalea Path" (1958), she announces some of the autobiographical events and attitudes which she later mythologizes. In terms of its relation to her mature work, one might compare it with Yeats's "The Phases of the Moon," which, though not itself expressing in final form his myth (the materials of *A Vision*), provides (precisely because it is didactic rather than symbolic) a straightforward, fairly prosy exposition of his system and a gloss on the highly evolved symbolism of the later poems.

ELECTRA ON AZALEA PATH

The day you died I went into the dirt,
Into the lightless hibernaculum
Where bees, striped black and gold, sleep out the blizzard
Like hieratic stones, and the ground is hard.
It was good for twenty years, that wintering—
As if you had never existed, as if I came
God-fathered into the world from my mother's belly:
Her wide bed wore the stain of divinity.
I had nothing to do with guilt or anything
When I wormed back under my mother's heart.

Small as a doll in my dress of innocence
I lay dreaming your epic, image by image.
Nobody died or withered on that stage.
Everything took place in a durable whiteness.
The day I woke, I woke on Churchyard Hill.
I found your name, I found your bones and all
Enlisted in a cramped necropolis,
Your speckled stone askew by an iron fence.

In this charity ward, this poorhouse, where the dead
Crowd foot to foot, head to head, no flower
Breaks the soil. This is Azalea Path.
A field of burdock opens to the south.
Six feet of yellow gravel cover you.
The artificial red sage does not stir
In the basket of plastic evergreens they put
At the headstone next to yours, nor does it rot,
Although the rains dissolve a bloody dye:
The ersatz petals drip, and they drip red.

Another kind of redness bothers me:
The day your slack sail drank my sister's breath
The flat sea purpled like that evil cloth
My mother unrolled at your last homecoming.
I borrow the stilts of an old tragedy.
The truth is, one late October, at my birth-cry
A scorpion stung its head, an ill-starred thing;
My mother dreamed you face down in the sea.

The stony actors poise and pause for breath.
I brought my love to bear, and then you died.
It was the gangrene ate you to the bone
My mother said; you died like any man.
How shall I age into that state of mind?
I am the ghost of an infamous suicide,
My own blue razor rusting in my throat.
O pardon the one who knocks for pardon at
Your gate, father—your hound-bitch, daughter, friend.
It was my love that did us both to death.

The protagonist of the late poems is a 'heroine' who has been exiled from paradise by the death of her much-loved, authoritarian father, whom she "thought . . . was God."[8] His death has left her unable to revise a sense of herself in relation to him ("You died before I had time," as she says in "Daddy"), rupturing her history and marking the point after which nothing was ever the same. Her childhood thereafter became fixed and isolated in time; as she put it, it was as if "sealed . . . off like a ship in a bottle—beautiful, inaccessible, obsolete, a fine, white flying myth,"[9] and discontinuous with the rest of her life. An image in "The Eye-Mote" conveys the inaccessibility of her psychic wound to the healing processes of time: she was "fixed . . . in this parenthesis." Her childhood now seems a different world, with a quality of existence that is closed forever, and at the same time it gives to her later life a quality of incompleteness and unreality, as if there were two unintegrated sets of parentheses, one enclosing the child and one the adult. This split in psychic time is connected with her attunement to the mythic level of existence. As Herbert Fingarette says in *The Self in Transformation:*

. . . the mythic always has a special and definite relation to time. The central events of myth always occur in a strange and distant past, a past hospitable to marvelous beings and miraculous doings. Mythic time reflects the . . . paradoxical quality . . . [that it is] both continuous and discontinuous with the present time-order. The mythic time is connected to historical time by the familiar genealogies of gods, biblical patriarchal lines, royal family descents, and other totemistic identifications. And indeed mythic beings often operate in present time, but always in conformity with their destinies and natures as established in the mythic past. Myth is dramatic yet timeless in the way that the unconscious is: "Gods moving in crystal," "for ever panting, for ever young."[10]

And it has been observed that:

. . . in all inner disturbance the time factor is a cardinal point. There is always primarily a search for past time, for the obscure and forgotten crisis or the might-have-been; it is an attempt at recapturing it and working it out differently, usually more happily, or for simply dwelling on it.[11]

Plath's father's death both caused and came to represent the fundamental division in her sense of herself: at least, this is how the 'story' of her poetry expresses it. The self that she had defined through her deep attachment to her father continued to press its claims without possibility of satisfaction or development. If her relation to her father was of central importance in her life, then life without him had the character of absence, of unreality and stagnation; and life with him, in the suspended time of childhood, was impossible of fulfillment. This is the basis of the sense of suspended time and stasis that pervades her later poetry. (When she separates from her husband, she experiences his absence in a similar manner.)

The self left back in childhood, "sealed . . . off . . . in a bottle," must be recaptured and rejoined in order for her to live fully in time. Yet because part of herself and her history has remained in parenthesis, everything that has happened to her since that rupture has, in effect, happened to an incomplete person; all subsequent experience has been added to a false foundation, happening to someone not fully integrated with her own history.

This is, in terms of the myth, the original split into false and true selves: the true self is the child she was before things went wrong; that part, as "Electra on Azalea Path" makes plain, lies buried with her father. The part which has continued to live after her father's death is, then, incomplete, a kind of false self; and the life lived by it is, to that extent, unreal. This is precisely the situation expressed in "Daddy":

> You do not do, you do not do
> Any more, black shoe
> In which I have lived like a foot
> For thirty years, poor and white,
> Barely daring to breathe or Achoo.

This tension between false and true selves, initially determined by her relation to her father, is the basis for further development, and consequently pervades all future manifestations of self, whether in relation to others or in her image of herself. (In "Daddy," for example, the figure of husband as Nazi takes over the burden of suppressing the true self.) The same structure recurs in her portrayal of female roles, which include false self-images such as the "drudge," and the veiled, submissive doll-woman in "Purdah." The false self of the heroine is ineffectual, dominated, and powerless—essentially the same kind of false self as the one who "lived like a foot."

The true self (the positive, whole, reborn self) is associated with artistic creativity, and with the autonomy possible only if one is not defined primarily in relation to an other. When the true self has emerged fully, the heroine will not be defined primarily in relation to a man—particularly since she considers her attachment to (now-absent) males to be responsible for the origin of the false self. When wifehood, daughterhood, and motherhood appear primarily as male-defined roles—when simply being a man's wife ("The Applicant"), daughter ("Daddy"), the mother of his children or his domestic overseer ("Stings") cripples a woman and makes her subservient, then these roles are negative and may be considered forms of the false self. Lady Lazarus, the lioness, and the queen bee are not male-dependent, and they represent triumph over the negative, male-defined aspects of these typical female roles.

Insofar as motherhood is part of a male-dependent and entrapping domesticity, it constitutes a negative kind of creativity. One might celebrate being devoured by art ("The blood jet is poetry") but not by self-sacrificing child-care and domestic drudgery ("for years I have eaten dust/And dried plates with my dense hair./And seen my strangeness evaporate"). But motherhood also appears, not so much an exalted form of creativity like writing poetry, as a mythic or heroic attribute. Even poems which center on an abandoned or isolated mother and child ("For a Fatherless Son," "By Candlelight," "Nick and the Candlestick") emphasize a self-sufficient maternal universe. The autonomy of the queen bee may be seen in this; so that while the mother in "Nick and the Candlestick" speaks with a note of mournfulness as she contrasts the messy complexities of adulthood with the purity of infancy ("The blood blooms clean/In you, ruby./The pain/You wake to is not yours"), she ends by stating: "You are the baby in the barn."

Motherhood and fertility are implicitly celebrated when barrenness appears as a despised or frightening quality (as in "Childless Woman," "The Fearful," and "The Munich Mannequins"), and this contrast, as will later be discussed, is a significant element in the mythic drama, where barrenness often characterizes malevolent or baleful female forces (such as the "barren" moon in "Elm"), and where biological fertility is the province of the heroine.

The true self, most often revealed in the process of awakening from or overthrowing a state of suppression, is usually seen as coexisting with the false self: the lioness masked by the doll-bride in "Purdah"; the queen bee sleeping in the guise of a drudge, a worker bee, in "Stings." This coexistence of false and true selves—the feeling of being at once helpless and trapped while truly powerful and free—is, in the late poems, the heroine's intolerable state of being.

The late poems represent various attempts to resolve the conflicts between true and false selves. In trying to assert the true self over the false self that has evolved in relation to her father's (and then husband's) absence, the heroine undertakes suicide, reunion by proxy, and, finally, exorcism through ritual 'killing,' all of which is summarized in "Daddy."

As this same poem spells out, the husband in the poetry is

sometimes perceived as a surrogate father, and the same conflict between true and false selves is reenacted in relation to him. In poems such as "The Detective" and "Purdah," the speaker has in different ways been made unreal by a man. In "The Detective," the husband is by implication the "killer"; in "Purdah," the bride describes herself as an art-object belonging to her bridegroom. Here and in other poems, the basic relationship is that of master to slave, oppressor to oppressed, torturer to victim, object to its creator. A familiar pattern directs the fate of the heroine: the true self deadened or repressed; the unreality of a life lived by the false self; the struggle of the true self for rebirth.

The rebirth which the true self sometimes achieves usually entails the ritually enacted destruction of the male. The new or reborn true self appears as a victor or rebel, as when it throws off the disguise of "drudge" and emerges as the queen bee ("Stings") or rises from its own ashes to "eat men like air" ("Lady Lazarus"). Either directly or indirectly the drama in which the true self and false self struggle for dominance is expressed by the double-sided process of death and rebirth. Conflict, transition, and resolution between true and false selves are all enacted in terms of these motifs. Where the false self appears to be dominant, there is almost always a promise of rebirth.

The pervasive imagery of suicide and personal death should be seen in light of this duality. Virtually all the apparent 'death-wishes' in her late poems have the ambiguity of a simultaneous wish for rebirth, which can only be achieved through some kind of 'death.' It is not that life itself is unacceptable, "that life, even when disciplined, is simply not worth it" (as Robert Lowell says in his foreword to *Ariel*), but that life lived on the wrong terms, a life lived by the false self, is not life but an intolerable death-in-life which can be overcome only by dying to that life. The late poems are really exploratory attempts to release the true self and to establish an authentic existence.

The crucial motifs of Sylvia Plath's myth can be identified as three sets of polarities: the male as 'god' and as 'devil,' the false self and the true self, and death-in-life and life-in-death (or death and rebirth). The motif of a dominant male figure includes the heroine's father, and other male figures—identified as husband, but sometimes as lover or bridegroom. This dominant male may appear in godlike guise as a colossus, "bag full of God," or "Lord of the mirrors," or in the guise of a "devil," Nazi, or "vampire." The protagonist, rejected by her personal 'god,' characteristically attempts to resolve the resultant death-in-life by transforming him into (or exposing him as) a devil or similar figure as a basis for rejecting him.

The motif of false and true selves derives from the heroine's relation to the male figure, from which her true self has been alienated, thus giving rise to a false self. Either the false self or the male (or both) must be killed to allow rebirth of the true self. The motif of death and rebirth also provides the terms of conflict and resolution in this matter: life lived by the false self is death-in-life, while the rebirth of the true self promises life-in-death, expressed in the poetry in images of purgation, purification, and transcendence.

The central motifs of Sylvia Plath's myth are so closely parallel to motifs that occur universally in the history of myth, religion, and literature (and, according to Jung, do so because they are expressive of structures that are constituents of the human psyche), that they might be identified as archetypes. It is not surprising that this should be the case, given Plath's personal and poetic history. In respect to the theme of the father as 'god' or 'devil,' for example, one might point out that Plath was, after all, writing about an elemental relationship, in her case made critical by the fact of her father's untimely death; one would expect such a relationship to be prefigured in universal structures of meaning. Further, she was familiar with literary and psychoanalytic archetypes and symbols, both through the psychotherapy she had undergone and through her readings, which included Jung, Frazer, Rank, Freud, and Graves, and her college honors thesis on the "double personality" in Dostoevsky. (Undoubtedly her psychiatric experience was connected with her choice of topic.) This multitude of similarities between universal archetypes and the major motifs of her work helps to explain the power of her late poems.

II

The Structure of the Imagery

Plath's organizing myth determines not only the motifs, but also the rhetorical forms through which it finds concrete embodiment. Her poetic techniques (and her imagery in particular) derive from and in part constitute the central meaning of her poetry, much in the way that Eliot's technique of juxtaposition communicates on its own, apart from its particular content, an aspect of the meaning of *The Waste Land.*

A. Alvarez, in a memorial broadcast on Sylvia Plath, noted that

In 'Poppies in October' . . . what starts as a description finishes as a way of defining her own state of mind. This, I think, is the key to the later poems; the more vivid and imaginative the details are, the more resolutely she turns them inwards. The more objective they seem, the more subjective they, in fact, become.[1]

This is the poem to which Alvarez refers:

POPPIES IN OCTOBER

Even the sun-clouds this morning cannot manage such skirts.
Nor the woman in the ambulance
Whose red heart blooms through her coat so astoundingly—

A gift, a love gift
Utterly unasked for
By a sky

Palely and flamily
Igniting its carbon monoxides, by eyes
Dulled to a halt under bowlers.

O my God, what am I
That these late mouths should cry open
In a forest of frost, in a dawn of cornflowers.

The imagery in this and other late poems has an even deeper relation to Plath's central meaning than Alvarez's observation acknowledges. Two related points are, in particular, worth noting. The first is the absence of any true process in the poem, which does not, in any clear-cut way, begin with objectivity and then travel inward. In fact, the only "objective" reference to poppies is in the title; the subjectivity is there from the beginning. The second point is that the remark about her "state of mind" involves some inexactitude, since a state of mind might be something contingent, evanescent, and never experienced again; but the imagery—or "details"—in this and other late poems is the consistent expression of a myth which exists prior to any particular poem, and with reference to which the details are determined. What is expressed in "Poppies in October" might therefore more accurately be called a *state of being:* in this case, the state of being is death-in-life, or the dominance of the false self, which coexists with the suppressed true self. There is, then, no encounter with an objective reality distinctly different from the speaker's inner reality; no case of an objective reality becoming, in the course of the poem, colored and transformed by an emotional condition. Rather, from the opening line where the poppies are unmanageable skirts and in which they sympathetically evoke her true self, the poem reflects a state of being, though of course this state is increasingly revealed as the cumulative weight of the poem gathers.

In general, the "subjective" details of Plath's late poems have not only been turned inward from the start, they are urged upon us as the direct content of her experience; they are not mere conceits approximately embodying her states of mind. Her experience, she suggests, *is* things perceived in a subjective or metaphorical way, so much so that the details often have the force of hallucination.

Perhaps this is why among her figures of speech metaphors are so strikingly frequent, and similes have the immediacy of metaphor. Poppies appear not just "like" mouths, but *as* mouths; and red flowers appear directly *as* "blood clots," not "like" blood clots. She creates the impression that her direct experience is metaphorical and that its form is dictated by her prior state of being. "Poppies in July," however, is not merely a freakish surrealist landscape in which poppies are bloody mouths. It is the qualities of unnatural vitality and autonomy, elemental savagery and frank violence of the poppies that are perceived directly and that are properly expressed in metaphorical terms. Such qualities strike the speaker's eye in precisely the way that the redness, shininess, and fluted shape of poppies might strike the eye of the ordinary observer.

Such details result from an encounter between the underlying myth (a unitary, pre-existing structure of meanings) and those objects which perfectly embody that myth. Adapting a term from ethology, one might say that the referents of Plath's images—in this case the poppies—function as *releasers* of predetermined themes that are constant throughout the poetry.

One may consider in this light the constant meaning throughout her late poetry of red flowers (and other red objects) against a pale background, whether this background is the landscape or the persona's frame of mind, or both. Red is a dominant color which forces itself to the foreground and invades and usurps the attention; it is a color naturally associated with blood, danger, and violence, as well as with vitality. No flowers of another color, no yellow tulips, would have for her the deep significance of red ones (in "Tulips") and become the occasion for a more or less similar poem. The notion of a 'releaser' suggests why, out of the thousands of stimuli of daily life, all of apparently equal triviality and ordinariness, a field of red poppies or a cut thumb rather than something else should become the subject of a poem. They have an inherent kinship with the speaker's state of being.

This state of being has been described as the unresolved conflict between true and false selves, between death or death-in-life, and rebirth or life-in-death. These antagonistic elements appear in "Poppies in October" (and in "Poppies in July," "The Bee Meeting," "Cut," as well as in other poems). The almost animal vitality of the poppies rebukes the deadened men with "eyes / Dulled to a halt under bowlers"; the chilly landscape; and the benumbed speaker herself. The poppies call to their counterpart in the speaker, who has within her a sleeping or incipient true self, a vital center which the poppies awaken through a natural sympathy, related as they are to their frozen surroundings in a way parallel to the relation of the submerged true self to the encompassing numbness of the false self. Their redness "talks" to her true self, just as in "Tulips" the redness of the flowers "talks" to the wound of the patient.

In comparison to the red flowers, and in comparison to the dormant and vital true self, the self depicted in the late poems often is pale and ineffectual. The flowers, more animal than she, are associated with raw, living flesh: they are "blood clots," bloody mouths, "bloody skirts"; in "Tulips," they breathe, turn, talk, eat, and watch. All of these images are expressions of the death/rebirth motif. In "Cut," "Ariel," and "Stings," among others, there is the same structure, in which her red blood, "the red / Eye, the cauldron of morning," and the "lion-red" queen bee, all in the same way call forth or 'release' the speaker's incipient true self.

"Poppies in July" presents these themes more explicitly than "Poppies in October":

> Little poppies, little hell flames,
> Do you do no harm?
>
> You flicker, I cannot touch you.
> I put my hands among the flames. Nothing burns.
>
> And it exhausts me to watch you
> Flickering like that, wrinkly and clear red, like the skin
>   of a mouth.
>
> A mouth just bloodied.
> Little bloody skirts!
>
> There are fumes that I cannot touch.
> Where are your opiates, your nauseous capsules?

If I could bleed, or sleep!—
If my mouth could marry a hurt like that!

Or your liquors seep to me, in this glass capsule,
Dulling and stilling.

But colorless. Colorless.

The poppies 'release' the conflict in her state of being by suggesting two possible kinds of death related to the polarities of the death/rebirth motif: "If I could bleed, *or* sleep!" One is the impulse toward a vital, gaudy, and bloody physical death, a natural affinity with the poppies as "hell flames" and "bloody skirts." In this case, the redness stimulates the hidden true self, the emergence of which would resolve in one way her state of being. The other possible resolution, a kind of death opposed to the first and symbolized by paleness or colorlessness, is also embodied in the poppies. This second death is promised by the poppies' opium: a colorless, rather than a bloody death; the achievement of even greater stasis, not a violent catastrophe; a death of consciousness which does not necessarily entail physical injury. The "dulling and stilling" qualities of the opium would penetrate the "glass capsule" of the speaker's life, in which she is already dulled and stilled, and would obliterate her awareness of suffering.

The meanings encoded in contrasting colors recur elsewhere in diverse and ingenious forms. The blood-red flowers are only one concrete visual embodiment of the contrast of the energy and vitality of the true self with the stasis, passivity, and numbness of the false self. These opposed forces appear in a poem such as "Purdah," in which the placid, sedentary, doll-like woman, entombed in a luxurious harem, reveals her hidden center of violence:

> Jade—
> Stone of the side,
> The agonized
>
> Side of a green Adam, . . .
> . . .
> I am his.
> Even in his

Absence, I
Revolve in my
Sheath of impossibles,

Priceless and quiet
Among these parakeets, macaws.
. . .
And at his next step
I shall unloose

I shall unloose—
From the small jeweled
Doll he guards like a heart—

The lioness,
The shriek in the bath,
The cloak of holes.

In this case the threat to destroy the oppressive bridegroom pre-figures relinquishing the false self and liberating the true one. The poem may have been sparked by seeing or imagining a jade figurine; if so, this 'occasion' could be said to 'release' the same forces and thematic concerns that the red flowers 'release' in other poems, that the experience of riding a horse sets off in "Ariel"; and similar forces are 'released' in other poems, such as "Years," "Getting There," and "Contusion," to name only a few.

This is why there is no real temporal development in the late poems; for since the objects in these poems function as 'releasers' of a predetermined meaning, there is no real openness to possibilities (though there is sometimes an apparent temporal development, as in "Kindness" or "The Bee Meeting," for the sake of drama). The object encountered by the persona does not have the potential for determining an outcome, and therefore a certain tension between object and subject is lacking. The tension in Plath's poetry is located instead in the pre-existing oppositions constituting the state of being which is 'released' by certain objects and situations through their inherent relevance to it, in a reenactment of her timeless myth.

In this respect, an extreme contrast to Plath's poetry can be found in that of Wallace Stevens. In poems such as "Sea Surface Full of Clouds," "Thirteen Ways of Looking at a Blackbird," and "The

Man with the Blue Guitar," the object is a group of potential meanings elicited from or constructed by the imagination. The possibilities for development are not limited by a prior myth, for the myth of the imagination, which for Stevens is supreme, allows for infinite possibilities, and most of Stevens' poems are in some sense demonstrations of this. Whereas Stevens recognizes an infinity of meanings that the imagination can receive from or attribute to objects, such meanings are limited in Sylvia Plath; but the very limiting demonstrates and reinforces the power of her myth.

III

The Central Symbol of the Moon

The moon as image and symbol is one of the most striking elements in Plath's mythic system. The moon's role in the "chapters in a mythology" illuminates the nature of the entire mythology, because it is a shorthand symbol or emblem of the whole vision, rather than a detachable and purely local image (as it was, typically, in most of the earlier poems). There are more than one hundred direct references to the moon in Plath's poetry, and they divide along precisely these lines: the early extraneous references and the late symbolically integrated ones.

The moon in Plath's poetry functions, more particularly, as her emblematic muse—her Moon-muse—which symbolizes the deepest source and inspiration of the poetic vision, the poet's vocation, her female biology, and her role and fate as protagonist in a tragic drama; and, through the use of a lunar iconography, it gives concrete form to the particular spirit of the mythicized biography. Most of these meanings—and others as well—should be apparent as aspects of what Ted Hughes called

. . . a strange muse, bald, white and wild, in her 'hood of bone,' floating over a landscape like that of the Primitive Painters, a burningly luminous vision of a Paradise. A Paradise which is at the same time eerily frightening, an unalterably spot-lit vision of death.[1]

THE DISQUIETING MUSES: AN IMAGE
AND A LANDSCAPE

The Moon-muse which haunts the super-real, often hallucinatory landscape of Plath's late poems, and the landscape it illuminates, have roots in the "metaphysical" paintings of Giorgio de Chirico. His *Disquieting Muses* is particularly important in this respect. It is the painting from which Plath, in a poem probably of 1958, borrowed title, atmosphere, and visual imagery—particularly the imagery of the "muses."

This poem represents an early attempt to express, partly in the form of dramatic myth, some of her central concerns. It provides in a clear though incipient form a glimpse of certain images, meanings, and relationships which were later to be absorbed, modified, and transformed by the power of a unified poetic vision. In "The Disquieting Muses," however, Plath had not yet developed her own mythology; she was instead borrowing from a ready-made vision. That she took up, at this point in her life, one borrowed vision after another (not only that of de Chirico, but also of Radin, Rousseau, and others as well) indicates that she was searching for a unifying vision and an authentic voice.

"The Disquieting Muses" was not the only poem that she derived from a particular de Chirico painting. In "On the Decline of Oracles," written at about the same time, Plath describes de Chirico's *The Enigma of the Oracle* and uses as an epigraph to the poem a quotation from his poetic essay "The Feeling of Prehistory," and she refers to details from the life of Böcklin, de Chirico's master. Reproductions of the two paintings mentioned, as well as the details from the biography of Böcklin, and the essay on "Prehistory," are all included in James Thrall Soby's book *Giorgio de Chirico*, published a year or so before Plath's de Chirico poems were written. It seems reasonable to suppose that Plath got her material from this book.[2] She obviously did not merely see an isolated reproduction of a de Chirico painting, but was for a time absorbed in his work. These two poems are direct evidence of the pervasive and strong effect of de Chirico's influence.

The terms in which Ted Hughes describes the landscape of Plath's late poems apply to the work not only of "Primitive" painters but of de Chirico:

And there is a *strange* muse, bald, white and wild, in her 'hood of bone, floating over . . . a burningly *luminous* vision of a Paradise . . . which is at the same time *eerily* frightening, . . . her poems, . . . those incredibly beautiful lines and *hallucinatory* evocations. [Italics added.]

Similarly, the dustjacket of Soby's book notes de Chirico's

. . . sense of *luminism,* creating paintings whose *eerie* glow is part of their hypnotic spell. . . . *strange, hallucinatory* images . . . [Italics added.]

It was the vision of de Chirico's "metaphysical" period that influenced Plath. His "metaphysical" landscapes, meant to evoke and to embody certain profoundly moving and universally felt emotions, conveyed a

. . . sense of vastness, solitude, immobility and ecstasy which sometimes is produced in our souls by certain spectacles of memory when we are asleep.[3]

Also characteristic of these early paintings is the evocation of intense nostalgia, melancholy, and a sense of timelessness.

De Chirico acknowledged as one source of his inspiration the

. . . strange and profound poetry, infinitely mysterious and solitary, based on . . . the *Stimmung* of an autumn afternoon when the weather is clear and the shadows are longer than in summer, . . .[4]

The feelings evoked by such afternoons were like epiphanies, and similar in many ways to "the feeling of prehistory." In the essay of this title, de Chirico attempted to evoke poetically the phenomenology of "prehistory," with which he associated mystery and myth.

The characteristic landscape and visual devices which have been called "Chirico City" were designed to intensify or awaken these emotions, and both the visual images and the underlying meanings of this landscape deeply affected Plath.

"Chirico City" is

. . . a vista of silent squares, peopled by shadows and statues, bounded by distant horizons and marked by an elegiac beauty and vast dignity . . . , the world . . . is a dream world . . . a romantic territory . . . , [de Chirico] had . . . found a personal way to describe this territory in terms of a strange and memorable foreboding, to portray it as alive but haunted, . . . [there were] dramatic properties—old architecture, curtained doorways, distant horizons, mourning figures in a failing light . . . [transposed] evocatively from everyday reality to dream, to create [a] striking . . . imagery of counterlogic. [Soby, p. 34]

The "metaphysical" landscapes produced an

. . . illusory atmosphere of infinity, wherein architecture, figures, objects and statuary would appear utterly detached from a near and present reality. [P. 41]

Deep perspective, along with the "illusion of endless distance" was also a major effect, achieved by a variety of means: by architectural structures diminishing to a distant point; "by the abrupt scaling-down of . . . figures"; by a "system of projecting objects against an infinity of space"; and by the long autumnal shadows cast by objects, figures, and architecture. All of these perspectival devices contribute in turn to the illusion of endless time—to the atmosphere of infinitude.

De Chirico's idiosyncratic titling of these paintings emphasizes their "metaphysical" meanings. For example: *The Nostalgia of the Infinite, The Mystery and Melancholy of a Street, The Anguish of Departure, The Uncertainty of the Poet, The Lassitude of the Infinite, The Joys and Enigmas of a Strange Hour.*

A few years after de Chirico initiated his "metaphysical" landscapes, he began populating them with the strange figures of mannequins, or tailors' dummies. The heads of the dummies were generally featureless and bald; sometimes their bodies were portrayed as stone columns. Many of the heads resemble moons; of the mannequin in *The Seer*, Soby writes, "Its white head is astonishingly luminous, . . ." (p. 105). This may have been a source of Plath's later identification of the moon as the head of her muse.

The setting of mannequin figures in a "metaphysical" landscape created the effect of placing motionless protagonists on a haunting and timeless stage:

> . . . the [*Disquieting*] *Muses* . . . attracts and repels, beguiles and frightens, conveys a warm nostalgic aura but at the same time suggests an impending catastrophe. There is no action; the piazza is still; the figures wait. What will happen? There is no answer, for this picture is the exact opposite of those seventeenth-century paintings of *banditti* in which a specific, disastrous outcome is foretold. De Chirico's image—his early art as a whole—appeals directly to the counter-logic of the subconscious, to those swamp-like regions at the edge of the mind where ecstasies bloom white and the roots of fear are cypress-black and deep. [Soby, p. 136]

For Sylvia Plath, the typical "metaphysical" landscape provided a visual setting for the fixed, super-real, ominous, inaccessible drama of the psyche. The mannequins—especially the "disquieting muses"—became the presiding spirits of the drama. Onto such a stage she could easily project her autobiographical and psychological concerns.

De Chirico's setting is not only appropriate for the enactment of symbolic psychological dramas, but was explicitly used by him for this purpose. Paintings such as *The Child's Brain* and *The Mystery and Melancholy of a Street* offer images of childhood as a source of certain "metaphysical" feelings. *The Child's Brain* re-creates the child's perception of an authoritarian father as a Victorian-Freudian nightmare figure. In the second picture, the adult mind watches as a little girl rolls a hoop down one of the vast diminishing spaces of "Chirico City." The viewer feels uneasy on her behalf—for the painting has that typical quality of unexplained omen—and also feels an intense nostalgia for the distant innocence and mystery of childhood.

A passage from Plath's novel, *The Bell Jar*, suggests the appeal and the relevance of such imagery to her imagination. Her heroine Esther Greenwood says, on revisiting Boston Common:

> Everything I looked at seemed bright and extremely tiny.
> I saw, as if through the keyhole of a door I couldn't open, myself and my younger brother, knee-high and holding rabbit-eared balloons, . . .[5]

Through the use of Chiricoesque qualities, she displays the link between her present state of being and the mourned-for, irrecoverable past.

De Chirico's essay on "prehistory" describes a world in which myths appear as literal truths, and where a sense of mystery characterizes an eternal present. It is a world of omens and foreboding. Similarly, in Plath's late poems, objects frequently appear with heightened significance and carry a suggestion of doom, because everything in some way echoes the underlying structure of a timeless mythology. As in a primitive world, things are omens (poppies are "bloody skirts"; a bee box is a "coffin"; smiles are "hooks"). The entire poem "The Couriers" is a series of omens which the poem first identifies and then divines.

The way in which Plath's later poetry qualifies 'reality,' suggesting that for her the 'real' is not identical with the mundane, is similar to de Chirico's technique of making an otherwise familiar scene seem hallucinatory. In his landscapes the hallucinatory effects never eclipse familiar reality, so that the viewer is not alienated:

. . . he has been the painter of what might be called a "jarred" reality in which chimerical allusions are restrained and held in careful, and therefore all the more disturbing, relationship to the plausible and the known. Even the powerfully fantastic *Disquieting Muses* of 1917 . . . uses as a setting a fairly exact replica of the Castello Estense . . . so that our credulity is not destroyed but upset. De Chirico seems to have avoided total fantasy for the simple reason that it could be too quickly rejected as such. [Soby, p. 30]

In Plath's late poems, hallucinatory or surreal elements qualify the psychological drama, but the poems never descend into the merely fantastic. "The Bee Meeting," for example, begins with a 'realistic' landscape:

> Who are these people at the bridge to meet me? They are
> the villagers—
> The rector, the midwife, the sexton, the agent for bees.

The landscape becomes increasingly surrealistic; the 'reality' is jarred:

Which is the rector now, is it that man in black?
Which is the midwife, is that her blue coat?
. . .
Their smiles and their voices are changing. I am led through
    a beanfield,
. . .
Creamy bean flowers with black eyes and leaves like bored
    hearts.
Is it blood clots the tendrils are dragging up that string?
No, no, it is scarlet flowers that will one day be edible.

The poem concludes with a moment of prophetic vision which has
the force of hallucination:

I am exhausted, I am exhausted—
Pillar of white in a blackout of knives.
I am the magician's girl who does not flinch.
The villagers are untying their disguises, they are shaking
    hands.
Whose is that long white box in the grove, what have they
    accomplished, why am I cold.

Because, in "The Disquieting Muses" as in the late poems, all of
the important motifs converge in the image of the muses (or muse),
the muses in the early poem hold special interest, for the evolution
of this image is bound up with that of the later total vision.

THE DISQUIETING MUSES

Mother, mother, what illbred aunt
Or what disfigured and unsightly
Cousin did you so unwisely keep
Unasked to my christening, that she
Sent these ladies in her stead
With heads like darning-eggs to nod
And nod and nod at foot and head
And at the left side of my crib?

Mother, who made to order stories
Of Mixie Blackshort the heroic bear,
Mother, whose witches always, always

Got baked into gingerbread, I wonder
Whether you saw them, whether you said
Words to rid me of those three ladies
Nodding by night around my bed,
Mouthless, eyeless, with stitched bald head.

In the hurricane, when father's twelve
Study windows bellied in
Like bubbles about to break, you fed
My brother and me cookies and Ovaltine
And helped the two of us to choir:
"Thor is angry: boom boom boom!
Thor is angry: we don't care!"
But those ladies broke the panes.

When on tiptoe the schoolgirls danced,
Blinking flashlights like fireflies
And singing the glowworm song, I could
Not lift a foot in the twinkle-dress
But, heavy-footed, stood aside
In the shadow cast by my dismal-headed
Godmothers, and you cried and cried:
And the shadow stretched, the lights went out.

Mother, you sent me to piano lessons
And praised my arabesques and trills
Although each teacher found my touch
Oddly wooden in spite of scales
And the hours of practicing, my ear
Tone-deaf and yes, unteachable.
I learned, I learned, I learned elsewhere,
From muses unhired by you, dear mother,

I woke one day to see you, mother,
Floating above me in bluest air
On a green balloon bright with a million
Flowers and bluebirds that never were
Never, never, found anywhere.
But the little planet bobbed away
Like a soap-bubble as you called: Come here!
And I faced my traveling companions.

Day now, night now, at head, side, feet,
They stand their vigil in gowns of stone,
Faces blank as the day I was born,
Their shadows long in the setting sun
That never brightens or goes down.
And this is the kingdom you bore me to,
Mother, mother. But no frown of mine
Will betray the company I keep.

With their featureless, bald heads, and "gowns of stone," these "disquieting muses" are clearly de Chirico's. Their presence at the left side of the crib indicates the 'sinister' fate of the godchild. But in this tale—unlike the "Sleeping Beauty" to which it also refers —no kindly godmother mitigates the spell. Other details in the poem confirm that the speaker recognizes and accepts the Muses' prophecy with a clear sense of her own past, present, and future— even the last of which has in some sense already happened, just as the future has happened to Oedipus even before he enacts it. The absoluteness with which the speaker announces and accepts the prophecy implies that her muses are the muses of tragic poetry, and they obliterate all others. Her special poetic vision, a result of the wound prophesied at birth and received in childhood, is connected with her destiny as poet. On the level of autobiography, the muses refer to her father's death, which she presents in her writing as a disaster after which (as she says in *The Bell Jar*):

. . . in spite of the . . . piano lessons and the water-color lessons and the dancing lessons . . . —I had never been really happy again. [P. 82]

Through de Chirico's images, she envisions autobiography as a drama enacted on a timeless stage dominated by a "muse" who is the *genius loci* of that drama. The nostalgic, melancholy "Stimmung" of autumn afternoons described and illustrated by de Chirico, appears in the long shadows of the speaker's childhood (both Plath's birthday, October 27, and the day of her father's death, November 5, occurred in autumn):

They stand their vigil in gowns of stone,
Faces blank as the day I was born,

Their shadows long in the setting sun
That never brightens or goes down.

The meaning of the fixed failing light is expressly attached to the muses who rule the life of the poem's protagonist. In a number of Plath's poems of this period, a Chiricoesque landscape can be said to imply the ruling muses, because both belong to a single vision which is intimated by its parts (by the psychological landscape or by the spirit of the vision personified as a muse). In the late poems a characteristic landscape and its muse re-emerge, and a similar relation of mutual implication holds there, too.

De Chirico's vision, his landscape, muses, and strong unchanging lights and shadows appear recognizably in other of Plath's early poems, testifying to the pressure she felt to integrate certain concerns, and to the fact that she had not yet evolved her own language for doing so. "Electra on Azalea Path" attempts to present autobiography as drama by staging an "Electra complex" in a Chiricoesque setting. (It should be compared with "Daddy," in which the protagonist speaks as if she really were a character such as Electra.) "Electra on Azalea Path," addressed to the speaker's father, might be considered a companion-piece to "The Disquieting Muses," addressed to the speaker's mother. In both poems aspects of the "Sleeping Beauty" story are combined with borrowings from de Chirico. Electra's "stony actors," obviously ruled by and kin to de Chirico's stone-gowned muses, are placed on a Chiricoesque stage.

In "The Colossus," "The Eye-Mote," "Barren Woman" ("Small Hours"), "On the Decline of Oracles," and "Insomniac," aspects of a Chiricoesque landscape also appear without a muse, while still belonging to that context. The Chiricoesque details and various other devices create a striking atmosphere, but such poems do not yet have a unified vision.

It is, however, in her poem "A Life," written several years after "Electra on Azalea Path" and just months before most of the late poems, that the landscape finally seems to be a coherent whole, characterizing a vision broad enough to unify Plath's primary concerns in terms which seem very much her own. The "life" is fixed and unalterable, a scene in a glass paperweight in which everything 'looks real' but lies beyond the possibility of change. Perhaps this image was inspired by the symbol of the glass paperweight representing Kane's inaccessible childhood in Orson Welles's film *Citizen Kane*. In Plath's poem, the past is similarly frozen:

> Here's yesterday, last year—
> Palm-spear and lily distinct as flora in the vast
> Windless threadwork of a tapestry.
>
> . . .
>
> The inhabitants are light as cork,
> Every one of them permanently busy.
>
> . . .
>
> . . . the neat waves bow in single file,
>
> . . .
>
> Stalling in midair, . . .

Although there is movement in the present tense of the "life," this too, with its quality of mechanical repetition, also seems frozen, eternal, and fixed:

> Elsewhere the landscape is more frank.
> The light falls without letup, blindingly.
> A woman is dragging her shadow in a circle
> About a bald hospital saucer.
> It resembles the moon, or a sheet of blank paper
> And appears to have suffered a sort of private blitzkrieg.
> She lives quietly
>
> With no attachments, like a foetus in a bottle, . . .

The inaccessibility of the past, the inability of the present to affect it, is emphasized by portraying it as an order of reality which is logically impossible to invade:

> The obsolete house, the sea, flattened to a picture
> She has one too many dimensions to enter.

She does not use de Chirico's muses or title, but the poem is related to him through the familiar-yet-surreal landscape in which the meanings embodied by unchanging light are permanently fixed. This, together with the elements of baldness, ominousness, and suspended time, echoes de Chirico; yet these features have now been detached from their derivative context and reassigned in a landscape that seems to be Plath's own.

In the late poems, although aspects of de Chirico's landscape survive in the surreal and ominous atmosphere, Plath no longer "borrow[s] the stilts of an old tragedy," or introduces external details as a scaffolding for her themes. The moon (in "The Detective," "The Moon and the Yew Tree," "Lesbos," "Edge") illuminates a wounded landscape of harsh contrasts—of light and shadow, often unnaturally brilliant, and with a suggestion of the violent, the uncontrollable, or the supernatural. Even her domestic interiors have this severity, and also convey the sense of threat ("A Birthday Present," "Wintering"). But Plath has abandoned the clumsy technique of trying literally to stage the drama. The scaffolding is internalized, and the stage is wherever the protagonist happens to be.

Although the "disquieting muses" and their landscape (as well as borrowings from other mythologies) do not appear in the late poems in literal and awkward form, the function of the "muses," their landscape, and some of their physical qualities survive and are amplified in the more powerful image of the Moon-as-muse. The moon is a muse's 'head': featureless, bald, purified, and luminous.

The disquieting muses were severely limited by the specificity of their source, and because they were so patently artificial they were limited too in the context in which they could appear. To evoke them was self-consciously to call attention to the poet in the act of metaphor-making.

The moon, as a feature of the natural world, is free from such limitations. It does not have to be excused or explained. While the "disquieting muses" could only be fantastical and surreal, the Moon-muse can appear in either a real or a surreal landscape and can simultaneously suggest both. It avoids the need for external scaffolding, for the Moon-muse supports an almost limitless multiplicity of connotations. Many of these connotations—and this is true of other images in Plath's late poetry—are descended from prior mythologies, although the degree to which Plath appropriates other sources has not been recognized. This is probably in part because the details she adapts are fully at home in the mythic world of her vision.

The opposite is true of a poet such as Eliot, whose effect frequently depends either on the reader's recognition of his sources and allusions, or at least the recognition that some allusion or other is being made. *The Waste Land* and "Sweeney Among the Nightingales," for example, make a point about mythology from the outside, requiring the reader to know what myths are being alluded to. Had Eliot attempted there to present a myth of his own, however, an awareness of his sources would have been a distraction.

The Moon-muse of the late poetry is so central and powerful a symbol, that many other images, particularly those which partially resemble the moon, come to share in its symbolism. There is, for example, a natural affinity between the moon and an ovum. Like the moon, an ovum is white, blank, and spherical, and the moon's monthly cycle 'rules' the cycle of ovulation and menstruation ("the Moon, being a woman, has a woman's normal menstrual period . . . of twenty-eight days").[6] Each turn of the moon-ruled cycle insures barrenness. These connections are made in "The Munich Mannequins," in which ova are seen as barren "moons" within the moon-ruled bodies of women:

> Perfection is terrible, it cannot have children.
> Cold as snow breath, it tamps the womb
>
> Where the yew trees blow like hydras,
> The tree of life and the tree of life
>
> Unloosing their moons, month after month, to no purpose.

The Moon is an organizing principle of this poem; it is evoked first by the mention of the ova, the female "moons" for whose infertility–or fertility–the Moon-muse is, in a sense, responsible. The "naked and bald" mannequins which, like the Moon and the unfertilized ova, are perfected—completed—and therefore incapable of reproduction, also bespeak female sterility. And there may be an analogue implied between the self-sufficient purposelessness of the menstrual cycle and the self-sufficiency and perfection of the cycle which brings to completion a work of art; for art itself is barren, even if the artist is 'productive.' Unlike one whose child becomes a link in an ongoing chain, involving her in a kind of immortality, the poet must begin each poem anew. She has to keep on going—she can never rest content with any one poem. So the finished work is unloosed just as the ovaries unloose an individual egg, and she then begins producing a new work.[7] No endless chain or natural process carries on outside of her. The poet gives birth to "children" who do not resemble her humanity and who themselves "cannot have children." As a biological female, then, one would not want to *be* like the Munich Mannequins—perfect, but unable to bear children; as an artist, however, one would want one's poems to achieve their terrible perfection and self-containment.

These mannequins are handmaidens of the Moon-muse, which they resemble in being bald, featureless, cold, sterile, and perfect. They are virginal "madonnas," figures related to the disquieting muses, as a number of cross-references make plain. "The Bald Madonnas," for example, is an early title of the poem. This in turn echoes the description of the moon as a "stone madonna" in "The Net Menders." The disquieting muses, the Moon, the madonnas, the mannequins, are all bald—and all related—and the interconnections suggest that the poem might easily have been called "The Munich Muses."

These are a few examples of the way in which, in the late poems, the symbol of the Moon-muse underlies all aspects of female identity, in particular that of the protagonist. Just as the ova are seen to resemble moons, the visual appearance of the Moon itself is often invested with female attributes:

> The moon . . . is a face in its own right,
> White as a knuckle and terribly upset.
> . . .
> . . . She is bald and wild.
> > ["The Moon and the Yew Tree"]
>
> Her O-mouth grieves at the world; . . .
> > ["The Rival"]
>
> Grieving & flat, like a childless woman.
> > [draft of "Elm"]
>
> Diminished and flat, as after radical surgery.
> > ["Elm"]

The Moon's flatness means it is barren. Because it can exercise a sympathetic influence on women, both inducing and symbolizing this affliction, it is a threat to them.

"The Munich Mannequins" implies that the quality of "perfection" is not only a characteristic of the Moon but also a power or emanation of it. In her radio play *Three Women*, written just before the bulk of the late poems, a woman who has miscarried looks from her hospital bed at the Moon's cold light:

> I feel it enter me, cold, alien, like an instrument.
> And that mad, hard face at the end of it, that O-mouth
> Open in its gape of perpetual grieving.
> It is she that drags the blood-black sea around
> Month after month, with its voices of failure.
> I am helpless as the sea at the end of her string.
> I am restless. Restless and useless. I, too, create corpses.

The Moon's flatness might have had a private meaning for Plath. In German, the word "flat" is *platt*, which is similar in appearance and nearly identical in sound to the name Plath.[8] Perhaps because of this Plath felt yet another link between the Moon and herself.

Plath's protagonist actually claims the Moon-muse as her "mother" in the fully developed mythology, just as she claims as her true kingdom a landscape consistent with a vision of her life as tragic drama. This is prefigured by the rejection of her natural mother's muses and landscape in "The Disquieting Muses." Here, the mother's "muses" give the daughter piano lessons—unsuccessfully, because:

> I learned, I learned, I learned elsewhere,
> From muses unhired by you, dear mother, . . .

The speaker's unbidden muses, the "dismal-headed godmothers," overshadow her mother's well-meaning muses, who inhabit a world where evil has no place, where witches always get "baked into gingerbread." Such a world cannot admit tragedy (the mother, obviously, could not even 'see' the dismal godmothers who attended the christening). Her world is too childlike, too saccharine; it is as unreal and benign as a cartoon-world, and as easy to reject:

I woke one day to see you, mother,
Floating above me in bluest air
On a green balloon bright with a million
Flowers and bluebirds that never were
Never, never, found anywhere.
But the little planet bobbed away
Like a soap-bubble as you called: Come here!

The mother's Never-Never Land floats off, and the poem ends with the speaker's affirming the Chiricoesque muses and their kingdom as her fated lot:

And I faced my traveling companions.

Day now, night now, at head, side, feet,
They stand their vigil in gowns of stone,
Faces blank as the day I was born,
Their shadows long in the setting sun
That never brightens or goes down.
And this is the kingdom you bore me to,
Mother, mother. But no frown of mine
Will betray the company I keep.

The daughter has actually defined her own landscape and muses partly by rejecting those of her mother, a device which appears as a general stance of the late poetry, in which the heroine, sometimes through explicit statement, usually by implication, contrasts a benign vision with her own tragic one. Both "moon" and "muse" have rich enough connotations in myth, religion, and literature to supply a wide range of such rejected meanings.

These sets of opposing landscapes and muses are bound up with the conflicts between false and true selves, and between death and rebirth. The impulse to reject an inauthentic self or life and to claim a true one is expressed through images of muse and landscape in "The Moon and the Yew Tree":

The moon is my mother. She is not sweet like Mary.
Her blue garments unloose small bats and owls.
How I would like to believe in tenderness—
The face of the effigy, gentled by candles,
Bending, on me in particular, its mild eyes.

. . .

Inside the church, the saints will be all blue,
Floating on their delicate feet over the cold pews,
Their hands and faces stiff with holiness.
The moon sees nothing of this. She is bald and wild.
And the message of the yew tree is blackness—blackness
    and silence.

The speaker's true element is not the mausoleum of a familiar
and debased Christianity, but the outdoor panorama of yew tree
and sky, ruled by the Moon, her true "mother." The Moon, because
a tragic Muse, is not "sweet like Mary": she is "bald and wild,"
the emblem of a stark, unromanticized world, and sees nothing of
the mild comforts (and stiff holiness) of Christianity.[9] The true religion is a pagan one of ecstasies, oracles, prophecies, and omens: the
initiate divines the "message of the yew tree."[10] De Chirico's "Feeling of Prehistory" comes to mind:

The first man must have seen auguries everywhere, he must have
trembled at each step he took.
    The wind rustles the oak leaves: it is the voice of a god which speaks,
and the trembling prophet listens, . . .
    What is the trembling that the mystic priest feels as on a stormy night
he draws close to the sacred oak? [Soby, p. 248]

In most of the late poems, an alien muse or landscape is not
generally rejected as explicitly as in "The Moon and the Yew Tree,"
though a poem such as "Kindness" makes the contrast plain enough:

Kindness glides about my house.
Dame Kindness, she is so nice!
The blue and red jewels of her rings smoke
In the windows, the mirrors
Are filling with smiles.
        . . .
Sugar can cure everything, so Kindness says.
Sugar is a necessary fluid, . . .
        . . .
O kindness, kindness
Sweetly picking up pieces!
My Japanese silks, desperate butterflies,
May be pinned any minute, anesthetized.

And here you come, with a cup of tea
Wreathed in steam.
The blood jet is poetry,
There is no stopping it.
You hand me two children, two roses.

"Dame Kindness" was "Godmother Kindness" in the first draft of the poem, suggesting that she was conceived in opposition to a "dismal-headed" godmother. Dame Kindness personifies friendly concern and well-meant words of comfort. She probably also personifies the natural order itself, for this is what "kynd" means. (Plath would have had a model for "Dame Kind" in Auden's poem of that title.)[11] The natural order, which includes childbearing, is not so readily dismissible an alternative as the mother's world in "The Disquieting Muses," for it is not mere sentimentalism. (The figure of kindness is also, through her "blue and red jewels," associated with Christian iconography and the figure of Mary, rejected elsewhere.)

The speaker's state of being, however, precludes any way in which the natural order, or the comforts of ordinary Christianity, can make a difference. The ministrations of Dame Kindness only intensify the speaker's sense of isolation and her conviction of doom. Homely platitudes ("Sugar can cure everything, so Kindness says") do not cure anything. The implied presence of a dismal-headed godmother explains why this is so. Some Muse other than Kindness must rule the reality that dictates:

The blood jet is poetry,
There is no stopping it.

This process is illustrated in the final line of the poem, "You hand me two children, two roses." As Kindness hands the two children to the speaker, they are mythically transformed.

A further dimension is added by a reading of Ted Hughes's radio play "Difficulties of a Bridegroom" (transmitted on the BBC Third Programme on January 21, 1963, about two weeks before "Kindness" was written), in which the "bridegroom" runs over a hare, which he then sells. With the "blood money" ("converted in heaven") he buys two roses for a woman called his "bride." Although horrified by the incident, she accepts them.[12] Quite possibly the unnamed antagonist to Dame Kindness in Plath's poem—her deathly, disquieting Muse—is implicitly identified or allied with the father of the children, for both have in different ways transformed them into roses in exacting the tribute of "the blood jet."

In "Edge," the transformation of the two children into roses is a completed event:

> She has folded
>
> Them back into her body as petals
> Of a rose close . . .

In both cases, life—the natural order or "kynd"—is finally devoured by, perhaps sacrificed to, an art and a muse which demand perfection.

THE MOON-MUSE: THE WHITE GODDESS
OF LIFE-IN-DEATH AND
DEATH-IN-LIFE

'It is death to mock a poet, to love a poet, to be a poet.'
ancient Irish *Triad*, quoted by
Robert Graves in *The White Goddess*

The Moon-muse of the late poems is a kind of witch, resembling the witch-goddess Hecate. Like other goddesses in a wide range of related mythologies, she is muse, prophetess, and hag, portending death or doom. The witch or hag is a single aspect of a more inclusive traditional moon-goddess whose full symbolism includes the cycles of birth, life, death and rebirth; and the female functions of menstruation, and fertility or barrenness. And she is symbol of the origins of poetic inspiration. The 'life' of a moon-goddess typically includes the death of a male god, whose loss she either mourns or celebrates, depending on the story. And in this and several other notable particulars, the 'life' of the goddess parallels that of Sylvia Plath and her mythic protagonist.

Plath's chief source for this and related material was Robert

Graves's *The White Goddess: A historical grammar of poetic myth*, a book which was of crucial importance for her life and her work. She had encountered many of these myths elsewhere, but the manner in which they are organized and analyzed by Graves invested them with unique relevance to her life as a woman and as a poet. As did the circumstances under which she was first introduced to, or, rather, initiated into, the realm of the White Goddess.

Ted Hughes, whom she met at Cambridge in February 1956—during her initial year as a Fulbright scholar—has confirmed her familiarity with the book (and he has indicated that he was the person who introduced her to it, shortly after they first met).[13] He and a friend had a "cult" of the White Goddess, which Sylvia Plath "immediately took up."[14] In June 1956, less than four months after their first meeting, she and Ted Hughes were married. Later in their marriage, they had as a wall decoration in their flat a poster enlarged from an astrology book depicting the great Moon-goddess, "Isidis"—"Magnae Deorum Matris"—and listing various of her epithets, including "Hecate," "Proserpina," "Diana," and "Luna."

As an initiate in the White Goddess "cult," Plath undoubtedly knew more about the long association between Robert Graves and Laura Riding than is mentioned in *The White Goddess.* "His response to the poetry and personality of Laura Riding," and to her "remarkably complicated view of life," has been described as one of the "two main events in his poetic life" (the other being his experience of trench warfare in World War I). They had made an "attempt to achieve an existence that accorded with the goodness that Graves and (at that time) Laura Riding saw as residing in poetry above every other human activity," and had undertaken the "prodigious enterprise of creating . . . an existence in which poetry and what it represents would be a natural way of life."[15] For Sylvia Plath and Ted Hughes the White Goddess of poetic inspiration, their common Muse, may have symbolized their marriage as a similar cooperative heroic venture.

But the importance to Plath of the White Goddess was far more than as the symbol of poetic inspiration which she and her husband shared in their capacity as poets. Not only was the White Goddess her Muse, but the myth of the White Goddess seemed to be her myth. Of their common features no doubt the parallel between the goddess mourning her god, and the poet her father, was the most important. But the confirmations of a great variety of details, including histories, dates, and names, especially to a mind attuned as hers was to coincidences and symmetries, must have seemed uncanny. The significance of coincidences would have become increasingly meaningful—but she had long been so attuned. Ted Hughes was interested in astrology and the Tarot, and she took these and related bodies of symbolism very seriously—she wrote to her mother of planning to become a "seeress," of getting a Tarot deck, and of learning to read horoscopes, and mentioned telling her publisher "how superstitious I was."[16] It may be assumed that not only was she aware of all the coincidences that can be discovered, but also that she considered them important.

The earliest reference in her poetry to themes from *The White Goddess* may be in "Faun" (also called "Metamorphosis"), a poem written in the same year that she became immersed in the book. She said in a letter to her mother that the poem is about Ted Hughes,[17] and although this is a purely private reference, it is important in indicating that she began by incorporating him into this mythology. The effect of *The White Goddess* seems plain not only in other poems of that period such as "Mad Maudlin" (later called "Maudlin"), but also in slightly later ones such as "The Death of Mythmaking" and "Ouija." Although these poems display some of the impressive technical effects that characterize even her early work, the mythological and stylistic elements appear overwilled and often unconvincing. "Moonrise," probably written in 1959, reveals the materials of *The White Goddess* considerably further appropriated, without the overenthusiasm of the novitiate. The poem is, quite simply, built on a bit of information given by Graves: that the mulberry, which ripens from white to red to black, is sacred to the White Goddess, whose emblematic colors these are.[18] "Moonrise" follows ripening mulberries through these changes of color—also undergone by the Moon—and ends with an apostrophe to the Moon, addressed as "Lucina, bony mother." Lucina is a goddess associated with childbirth. And the ending of the poem, "The berries purple/And bleed. The white stomach may ripen yet," clearly connects the Moon and, through the mulberry imagery, the White Goddess, with the process of pregnancy. (Plath probably wrote this poem while pregnant with her first child.)

The White Goddess myth, when Plath first encountered it, seemed to her to order her experience;[19] and it continued to do so, and was more and more completely appropriated by her, so that she increasingly saw her life as defined by it. Her further experiences, particularly of pregnancy and motherhood, were very readily absorbed into this framework. The culminating confirmation of her identification with the White Goddess would come a few years later, through her separation from her husband—an event that she saw as a repetition of abandonment and bereavement. By this time her sense must have been that the White Goddess mythology had appropriated *her*, as her fate—that her life was magically entwined with the myth.

On April 1, 1960, she gave birth to her first child, a daughter; and in February 1961 had a miscarriage and soon after again became pregnant, events of a sort that she related to the Moon. In mid-1961, she wrote "The Rival," a poem "leftover from a series specifically about that woman in the moon, the disquieting muse."[20] Here, and in the series as a whole, she creates an extended portrait of her Muse personified as an implacable, threatening woman, demanding of self-sacrifice. But her identification with the White Goddess mythology had not yet taken its final form.

In the late summer of that year Plath and her husband moved to an old manor house they had bought in Devon—a location propitious in relation to the White Goddess: Graves mentions in a postscript to *The White Goddess*, dated 1960, that he received the sudden inspiration for it, and began it, in Devon. Graves himself was, in fact, in England at that time (in November 1961, Plath fortuitously appeared in a reading with him),[21] gi ing a number of public lectures, including the three he delivered as Professor of Poetry at Oxford. These talks, incorporating material stated earlier in *The White Goddess*, mention the idea of a Muse and that of a Muse-poet.[22]

Although Graves's Muse-poet lectures were not published until the next year, it seems that "The Moon and the Yew Tree," written around October 1961,[23] was influenced not only by *The White Goddess* but also (at least indirectly) by these lectures. Ted Hughes recalls his suggesting to her as an exercise that she write a poem about "the full moon setting onto a large yew that grows in the churchyard." He says of the resulting poem that "She insisted that it was an exercise on the theme," whereas it struck him as "a statement from the powers in control of our life."[24]

If the poem began as an exercise, it was ultimately an instrument of discovery and commitment, providing a channel for those "powers." In the poem she declares herself a "Muse-poet" in Graves's sense,[25] implying a personal mythology allied with the moon, and identifying herself with the White Goddess myth through the witch-goddess aspect of her Muse. The claim that "The moon ["bald and wild"] is my mother," and that "She is not sweet [and "mild"] like Mary," presents precisely the distinction made by Graves between the "cruel, capricious, incontinent White Goddess and the mild, steadfast, chaste Virgin" (p. 423).

The identification of her muse as a kind of witch—in particular, a prophetic witch of death—which is an underlying assumption of the late poetry, was prefigured though not fully developed in "The Disquieting Muses":

> Mother, whose witches always, always
> Got baked into gingerbread, I wonder
> Whether you saw them, whether you said
> Words to rid me of those three ladies
> Nodding by night around my bed,
> Mouthless, eyeless, with stitched bald head.

Graves, in discussing Hecate, gives an example of a muse-as-witch:

Spenser addresses the Muses as 'Virgins of Helicon'; he might equally have called them 'witches,' for the witches of his day worshipped the same White Goddess—in *Macbeth* called Hecate— . . . and were similarly gifted in incantatory magic . . . [P. 384]

Hecate is also "mother of witches," "supreme source of prophecy," "Goddess of Destiny"; she, and such others as Circe, Hera, and

Persephone, are all "Death aspects of the Triple Moon-goddess," "the White Goddess of Life-in-Death and Death-in-Life."[26]

The Moon-muse in "Edge" is of a similar nature; she presides over the dead woman:

> Staring from her hood of bone.
> . . .
> Her blacks crackle and drag.

Many other details in the late poems reinforce the implicit characterization of the Moon-muse as witch. That she is chilly, bald, merciless, barren, and ominous (though she may also appear as a "beautiful, but annihilating" ["The Rival"] type of witch), are all consistent with such a characterization. If "The Moon and the Yew Tree" were taken to be the first of the late poems, they could be said to begin and end with this relation to the Moon. Around October 1961 Plath wrote that "The Moon is my mother"; in February 1963 she wrote in "Edge" (probably her last poem) of the Moon looking down from her "hood of bone" on the completed drama.

But because of its somewhat programmatic nature, "The Moon and the Yew Tree" should not be regarded as the first of the poems in which Plath has completely appropriated her myth, but as the announcement of that act. One might, for different reasons, regard "Tulips," written a few months earlier, as the first of the late poems, this being, according to Ted Hughes, the first poem written "at top speed, as one might write an urgent letter. From then on, all her poems were written in this way."[27] Although she had found her voice, she had not yet consolidated her vision. In the five months between November 1961 and April 1962, she apparently wrote no new poem that satisfied her.[28]

A partial explanation is that she was pregnant with the son she gave birth to on January 17, 1962, and that she characteristically felt "lazy" in the weeks before giving birth; though she expected that after the birth she would have a burst of creative activity, as had been the case after the birth of her first child.[29] Despite the demands on her time in caring for one and then two young children, and although she had been working satisfactorily on *The*

Bell Jar, she felt she was doing little work[30]—by which she obviously meant, work on poems. She wrote around that time to a former teacher at Smith, complaining that she had a "writing block," and asked him to airmail to her some "pink Smith College memorandum paper," about which she had a "fetish" and which she thought might help.[31]

There is a clear record of her poetic activity during this time in a long, rambling series of closely-connected, unfinished poems, consisting of false starts for a number of poems, most of which modulate into or give rise to another. Certain recurring themes, images, and phrases, in a wide variety of contexts, seem desperately to be seeking a home—which nearly all of them do find, but only in various of her later poems. "The Ninth Month" (one of several titles for an early unfinished attempt) would seem to date from just before the birth of her son, and it is linked by several images to "Fever," which refers to the birth. "The Ninth Month" (also at one point called "Woman as Landscape") and "Fever," as well as another unfinished poem called "Fever in Winter," contain images which anticipate the *Ariel* version of "Elm." Compare "The trees stiffen . . . like burnt nerves" ("The Ninth Month"); "The nerves sizzle in my hands—little red, burnt trees" ("Fever"); and "The elm is a clot of burnt nerves" ("Fever in Winter") with "My red filaments burn and stand, a hand of wires" ("Elm"). But she does not actually begin a poem about a 'female' tree ("she is huge, like a laboring woman") in relation to the moon ("She has eaten its color") until early spring; and only in April does a poem appear that satisfies her—the "Elm" familiar from *Ariel,* and quite different from her first attempts at the subject.

ELM

I know the bottom, she says. I know it with my great tap root:
It is what you fear.
I do not fear it: I have been there.

Is it the sea you hear in me,
Its dissatisfactions?
Or the voice of nothing, that was your madness?

Love is a shadow.
How you lie and cry after it.
Listen: these are its hooves: it has gone off, like a horse.

All night I shall gallop thus, impetuously,
Till your head is a stone, your pillow a little turf,
Echoing, echoing.

Or shall I bring you the sound of poisons?
This is rain now, this big hush.
And this is the fruit of it: tin-white, like arsenic.

I have suffered the atrocity of sunsets.
Scorched to the root
My red filaments burn and stand, a hand of wires.

Now I break up in pieces that fly about like clubs.
A wind of such violence
Will tolerate no bystanding: I must shriek.

The moon, also, is merciless: she would drag me
Cruelly, being barren.
Her radiance scathes me. Or perhaps I have caught her.

I let her go. I let her go
Diminished and flat, as after radical surgery.
How your bad dreams possess and endow me.

I am inhabited by a cry.
Nightly it flaps out
Looking, with its hooks, for something to love.

I am terrified by this dark thing
That sleeps in me;
All day I feel its soft, feathery turnings, its malignity.

Clouds pass and disperse.
Are those the faces of love, those pale irretrievables?
Is it for such I agitate my heart?

I am incapable of more knowledge.
What is this, this face
So murderous in its strangle of branches?—

Its snaky acids hiss.
It petrifies the will. These are the isolate, slow faults
That kill, that kill, that kill.

A great many of the images from these tentative poems appear
also in *Three Women*, particularly those connected with the themes
of women, childbirth, and the Moon. But this radio play is essentially plotless. What structure it has it gets from working variations
on the themes of fertility and barrenness, without the sudden
insight or resolving image which motivates so many of her late
poems.

In retrospect it is clear that during this relatively fallow period
Plath's mythic vision was being, no doubt partly unconsciously,
gestated and elaborated. Around the time of the first draft of
"Elm," in a period when she was preoccupied with images relating
women (and a speaking female tree) to the Moon, the rush of late
poems began. On April 1, 1962, when at least sixty of her poems,
including almost all the ones in *Ariel*, were yet to be written, she
heard a BBC radio broadcast of introductory remarks and poems
by Laura Riding. The manuscript of "Little Fugue," dated April
2, bears the notation "on listening to Laura Riding." Perhaps it was
nothing more than Plath's knowledge of the important poetic,
intellectual, and personal influence which Laura Riding had exer-
cised on Robert Graves; perhaps it was the example Laura Riding
had offered, as one who had single-mindedly pursued the Muse;
perhaps it was the content of the remarks by Laura Riding, the first
public expression of her revised view suspecting the values of
poetry "of being linguistically unsound, and spiritually defective";
or perhaps it was her (old) poems, which were nevertheless read.[32]
Whatever it was, it crystallized in Plath's mind critical associations
of the themes of *The White Goddess* with those of her own life:
the subject-matter of "Little Fugue"—the mourning of the heroine
for her dead father—is expressed through the material of *The White
Goddess*.

The poem begins with the line "The yew's black fingers wag,"
and proceeds to play upon various meanings of the yew discussed
by Graves (particularly the yew as the "death-tree" sacred to

Hecate and to witches, and as an element of the "finger alphabet" of ancient Druids). The first draft of the poem echoes Graves's wording—perhaps Plath had even recently reread the book (several editions of it were published during her lifetime), although she did know it extremely well. Graves had written of a belief that

> . . . church-yard yews will spread a root to
> the mouth of each corpse. [P. 192]

Plath, in the draft of "Little Fugue," says:

> The yew is many-footed.
> Each foot stops a mouth.

And:

> A cartoon balloon rooted in the mouths of the dead.

During this period she began to sense that all was not well with her marriage. (By May she had written several poems which deal with themes of marital distress.) In July "her personal world fell apart"[33] when she learned with certainty that her husband was involved with another woman, Assia Gutman. (It is apparently the sense of this trauma that is conveyed in "Words heard, by accident, over the phone.") By early October 1962, Sylvia Plath and Ted Hughes had separated; she remained for several months in Devon before moving to a flat in London.

Robert Graves has a dictum that the Muse must never become ordinary and must resist "the temptation to commit suicide in simple domesticity [which] lurks in every maenad's and muse's heart" (p. 447).[34] For Plath this would mean that through domesticity she risked both relinquishing her role as her husband's Muse and smothering the Muse in herself. Yet she had evidently been willing to take these risks, even glorifying her role. When her marriage collapsed, the sacrificing and submission it had incurred no doubt seemed betrayed,[35] but more importantly aspects of the role she had accepted seemed in retrospect a self-betrayal, a false self.

This theme, which is the subject-matter of the most powerful poems of her most prolific period ("Lady Lazarus," "Stings," and

"Purdah" were among the twenty-six poems, most of them included in *Ariel,* that she wrote in October), finds almost automatic
expression through the White Goddess mythologies, in particular
through the two motifs of these mythologies which are now fused
in Plath's myth: the killing of the male god (reidentified as a devil
or oppressor, whose death, or absence converted into death, is no
longer mourned but celebrated) and the associated rebirth of the
goddess. The self liberated through its triumph over an expend-
able male now sees its reflection in such emblems of the White
Goddess as the queen bee and the lioness.

While knowing the correspondences of Plath's biography to
the life of her heroine in the poems—for example, that her father
died prematurely—allows the reader to confirm what the poems
mean as literary creations, knowing of such correspondences does
not explain the power of her poetry. (The question of knowing
biographical or other detail without which a poem remains obscure—though extraneous details may find their way into an enrichment of an already satisfactory poem—is another issue: such
instances are rare in Plath, but when they do occur the poem to that
extent is weakened.) It is important to separate the aesthetic success of her poems from the biography, on which it does not depend.
One can certainly read the poems just for biography or 'confes-
sion,' simply to 'get the story' and 'find out what happened to her';
but if one does this—as is fairly common among her readers—one
has in a sense predetermined the scope of one's reading, prejudged
what one is reading for ('the life of a suicidal, male-exploited
genius'—the source and nature of whose genius is, however, oddly
taken for granted; or not inquired into; or by some peculiar logic
ascribed to her suffering). One therefore misses *other* meanings,
not relevant to a focus on sensationalistic confessional aspects, by
a priori screening them out.

Biographical detail, then, does not explain the impact of her
poems as works of art (in reading a really *bad* sensationalistic
confessional poem, we can readily perceive that the subject-matter
shocks, fascinates, and moves us, while on the other hand, we
see quite clearly that the poem has no value as art). Knowledge
of a major source of meaning of the poetry, such as the White

Goddess mythologies, is, however, relevant to the poems as such, and does explain one aspect of their power—the magic that accrues to events absorbed into and transfigured by the universalizing function of myth, in a poet whose imagination, intelligence, language, craft, and openness to contact with the unconscious are developed to an extraordinary degree.

Since what appealed to Plath in the White Goddess myths was not merely the single image of a muse-as-witch, but the entire structure of the mythology, with a Moon-goddess Muse as emblem of it, a discussion of the White Goddess material will shed light on the structure of the mythicized biography as a whole, as well as on the nature and evolution of the Moon-muse. The accuracy of Graves's scholarship and the soundness of his theories are of no account here. Plath embraced the poetic vision of *The White Goddess* (which T. S. Eliot in a note for the publisher described as "A prodigious, monstrous, stupefying, indescribable book"),[36] and its compellingness for her as vision in no way depends on its scholarly soundness.

The myth essentially concerns a Triple Moon-goddess—associated with poetic inspiration—each individual manifestation of whom (Hecate, Juno, Diana) encodes some phase in the life, death, and rebirth cycle of which the Goddess is the cumulative concrete symbol. In a number of her incarnations, the Goddess has a consort: a Sun-god, king, or hero, who dies—and is mourned by the Goddess (although sometimes the god is killed, and a substitute takes his place). This is the motif of 'the dying god and the mourning goddess,' of which Graves considers the Virgin mourning Christ to be a variation.

The note on the cover of a recent edition of Graves's book summarizes its content in this way:

The earliest European deity was the White Goddess of Birth, Love and Death, visibly appearing as the New, Full and Old Moon, and worshipped under countless titles. . . . she continues as the Ninefold Muse, patroness of the white magic of poetry.

Mr. Graves' proposition is that "true poetry" or "pure poetry" . . . has only a single language and a single infinitely variable theme. . . .

this theme is inseparably connected with the ancient cult-ritual of the White Goddess and her Son. The language is called myth and is based on a few simple magical formulas, . . . Poetry is "true" or "pure" to the degree that the poet makes intuitive use of the formulas.[37]

According to Graves, "the capricious and all-powerful Threefold Goddess" is 'mother, bride and layer-out" of the "God of the Waxing Year" (p. 24), the Sun-god, whose 'death' and 'rebirth' are entailed in the cycle of seasons:

The Triple Muse, or the Three Muses, or the Ninefold Muse . . . or whatever else one may care to call her, is originally the Great Goddess in her poetic or incantatory character. She has a son who is also her lover and her victim, the . . . Demon of the Waxing Year. He alternates in her favour with . . . the Demon of the Waning Year, his darker self. [Pp. 390–91]

. . . one succeeds the other in the Moon-woman's favour, as summer succeeds winter, and winter succeeds summer; as death succeeds birth and birth succeeds death. The Sun grows weaker or stronger . . . but the light of the Moon is invariable. She is impartial: she destroys or creates with equal passion. [P. 386]

All true poetry— . . . celebrates some incident or scene in this very ancient story, and the three main characters are so much a part of our racial inheritance that they not only assert themselves in poetry but . . . in the form of dreams, paranoiac visions and delusions. . . . a true poem is necessarily an invocation of the White Goddess, or Muse, the Mother of All Living, the ancient power of fright and lust—the female spider or the queen bee whose embrace is death. [P. 24]

[the Triple Goddess] was a personification of primitive woman—woman the creatress and destructress. As the New Moon or Spring she was girl; as the Full Moon or Summer she was woman; as the Old Moon or Winter she was hag. [P. 384]

The "White Lady of Death and Inspiration" (p. 67) is also a goddess of destiny:

The Three Fates are a divided form of the Triple Goddess, and in Greek legend appear also as the Three Grey Ones and the Three Muses. [P. 224]

Many aspects of Graves's historical analysis of the White Goddess, and his view of the evolution of poetry and its relation to the poet, would also have appealed to Plath:

Poetry began in the matriarchal age, and derives its magic from the moon, . . . 'to woo the Muse' . . . [refers to] the poet's inner communion with the White Goddess, regarded as the source of truth. . . . The poet is in love with the White Goddess, with Truth . . . [P. 446]

Dionysian or Muse-inspired poetry, and not Apollonian poetry is true poetry; and this opposition gives yet another level to the male/female, Sun/Moon oppositions of the White Goddess myths:

Must poetry necessarily be original? According to the Apollonian, or Classical, theory it need not be, . . . [P. 440]

The true poet must always be original, . . . he must address only the Muse . . . and tell her the truth about himself and her in his own passionate and peculiar words. [P. 442]

. . . a cleavage . . . apparent between the devotees of Apollo and those of the White Goddess . . . [P. 449]

. . . as soon as Apollo the Organizer, God of Science, usurps the power of his Mother the Goddess of inspired truth, wisdom and poetry, . . . inspired magic goes, . . . [P. 471]

I cannot think of any true poet from Homer onwards who has not independently recorded his experience of her. The test of a poet's vision, one might say, is the accuracy of his portrayal of the White Goddess . . . [P. 24]

Clearly, the fundamental White Goddess myth embraces virtually all of the major motifs of Plath's mythicized biography, and organizes them in a similar drama, thus providing a narrative model for her myth complete with a fully developed network of interrelated meanings and images, countless examples of which are to be found in a wide range of subsidiary mythologies. The White Goddess material demonstrated to Plath how a myth engenders and becomes embodied in its own particulars—that is, in its narrative forms, its personae, its incidental details. In doing so, it provided an example of how her own myth could be given legitimate and compelling form. As a source of poetic inspiration this was clearly superior to the ready-made vision of de Chirico, which provided images but not narrative meanings. Although Plath could project her psychological drama onto de Chirico's stage, he did not provide her a complete mythological model.

Plath would have found especially significant the parallel between the 'dying god and mourning goddess' motif and her mourning for her father. This parallel would have been reinforced by the fact that both Plath's birthday, October 27, and the day of her father's death, November 5, just after All Souls' Day (November 2), when the dead revisit the living and must be appeased (though it seems that Plath may mistakenly have believed that her father died on All Souls' Day) occur at a time which figures significantly in these myths: October was the season of the Bassarids, the maenads who worshipped Dionysus (a Son of the White Goddess), and

. . . the Goddess of . . . Life-in-Death and Death-in-Life . . . early in November, when the Pleiads set, sent the sacred king his summons to death . . . [P. 186]

This motif of 'dying god' is in Plath's myth amplified to include the loss of her husband, also in the season of the Bassarids.

The Moon-muse of the mythicized biography remains "embalmed" in her aspect of Hecate, surveying a characteristic type of dying god and mourning goddess story: "She is used to this sort of thing":

It is a case of vaporization.
. . .
. . . , there were two children
But their bones showed, and the moon smiled.
. . .
There is only the moon, embalmed in phosphorus.
["The Detective"]

Both in "The Detective" and "Edge," there is a tableau of the final scene of a tragedy: a dead woman, her two dead children, the husband absent, and a Hecate-like, cold, deathly Moon-muse, presiding over and emblemizing the drama.

Graves's view that all aspects of the White Goddess myth ultimately reveal a connection with poetry, and that poetry originally
was and ideally ought to be a way of worshipping the Goddess in
one or another of her forms, probably also held great significance
for Plath. That the very act of creating poetry was closely associated with a Moon-goddess meant that the White Goddess myth
claimed parallels with her life not only in terms of her family history but also asserted a connection with her vocation as poet. If
on one level the 'dying god and mourning goddess' icon represents a critical trauma in both lives, then on another level the connection with poetry can be said to represent the outcome of that
trauma: the White Goddess myth contains ways of referring both
to the historical 'cause' of the sublimating into poetry and to the
'sublimation' itself—the actual poetry. *The White Goddess* confirmed for Plath that her life already had the contours of myth.

Plath's mythology may be seen as a self-contained mythological
story belonging to a large class of Moon-goddess mythologies. The
family resemblances are manifold. "The Bee Meeting," for example, enacts a sacred grove ritual, and "Purdah" the ritual murder of a Sun-king by his Moon-queen consort. The relevance of
both these themes to Moon-goddess myth is generously illustrated
by Graves.[38] Yet because of rather than despite their enactment
of these ancient rituals, "Purdah" and "The Bee Meeting" express
a unified poetic vision and stand utterly on their own. The old
rituals have been taken over in the service of a new religion.
(Graves's word for this is "iconotropy.")

When Plath employed the motif of a dying god and mourning
goddess in her earlier work, her intention was clear, but either
her poems seemed flatly autobiographical or the sources of the
motif in some way obtruded. In "The Colossus," for example,
the reader is deliberately made aware that the speaker is comparing herself to a Greek heroine tending an idol, like Iphigenia
in Tauris. "Full Fathom Five" refers to the retelling of the speaker's life in obviously Shakespearean terms: her father, by dying,
has undergone a "sea-change," becoming a sort of underworld
king whose daughter, exiled from his kingdom, is condemned to
life. The allusion both states that her father is dead and intimates

that, like Ferdinand's father, he still lives. In "Electra on Azalea Path," the speaker makes a point of admitting that she uses "the stilts of an old tragedy."

The dying god motif in the late poems is an integral part of the mythology. (In "Daddy," for example, the identification of father-as-colossus—"Ghastly statue with one grey toe/Big as a frisco seal"—enters the poem as a fully integrated detail of Plath's myth.) Both in "Daddy" and in "Little Fugue," the protagonist's deepest self is, through her unresolved mourning, in effect a sacrifice to the god, and what remains of her, the self that goes through the motions of living, feels false, unreal, incomplete. The cycle of mourning must be broken and the false self supplanted by the true one.

The poems just mentioned, and many other of the late poems, include both false and true faces—the 'before' and 'after' of the protagonist. In a sense, the heroine may be said to undergo phasal changes, like the Moon whose old self inevitably gives birth to the new. The rebirth artist Lady Lazarus and the speaker of "Fever 103°" who ascends from Hell to Paradise are examples of the reborn or true self appearing as a literally resurrecting heroine. Elsewhere, the poems focus not on rebirth, but on some form of death, the phase which necessarily precedes rebirth. In "Getting There," as in "A Birthday Present," most of the poem details the torture of death-in-life, and the connection with rebirth becomes clear only in the final lines.

The motifs of the Moon-goddess drama are often implicit in much of Plath's imagery. A red figure against a pale background, as in "Poppies in October," is one such case. Another, one of Plath's most persistent images, is that of being enclosed or cut off by glass, a detail which is also an element in some White Goddess myths:

. . . Snow White is laid as if dead in a glass coffin on top of a wooded hill; . . . The glass coffin is the familiar glass-castle where heroes go to be entertained by the Goddess of Life-in-Death, . . . These deaths are therefore mock-deaths only—for the Goddess is plainly immortal— . . . [P. 419]

Plath referred to the "Sleeping Beauty" story in "The Disquieting Muses," in which the speaker, like the sleeping beauty, is cursed at her christening by a type of witch and sentenced to a death-in-life resembling the mock-death mentioned by Graves. That Plath also thought of glass as some sort of mythological element is obvious in these lines from an unfinished poem about "Frost on Dartmoor":

> This is newness   no snow, only a huge
> Condensing of vacancies
> . . .
> It is the fabulous, ice-sided hill—
> Rocks & grass clubs glittering chain-mail

The death-in-life of Plath's protagonist (in a sense, her mock-death) either seals off the self from the rest of the world or divides one part of the self from another. In permitting the illusion of unity with the world while preventing that unity, the image of glass perfectly expresses such mock-death. The "glass coffin" mentioned by Graves allows rebirth and is therefore a 'cradle' even while it is a coffin. Many images of encapsulation in Plath's late poems possess a similar duality:

> If my mouth could marry a hurt like that!
>
> Or your liquors seep to me, in this glass capsule, . . .
>
> ["Poppies in July"]

> The still waters
> Wrap my lips,
>
> Eyes, nose and ears,
> A clear
> Cellophane I cannot crack.
>
> ["Paralytic"]

> I shall take no bite of your body,
> Bottle in which I live, . . .
>
> ["Medusa"]

> That . . . is the impossibility!

That being free
Of the bell jar in which I am the dead white heron[39]

[draft of "The Jailor"]

Elsewhere, death-in-life is expressed not by encapsulation in glass, but by glass as a barrier dividing what ought to be whole:[40]

Cold glass, how you insert yourself

Between myself and myself.

["The Other"]

From an early version of "Elm":

In pools, I am beautiful.
I scratch on the glass: the eyes within avert themselves.
Is the soul of oneself so inaccessible?

From a draft of "Burning the Letters":

This is what it is to be loveless!
It is a glass case
How it flickers
between me and everything I look at.
Do not touch.

The colors of the Triple Moon-goddess—white, red, and black—are the dominant and emblematic colors of Plath's late poems, constituting a system of images which refers to the whole mythology. Graves says:

I write of her as the White Goddess because white is her principal colour, the colour of the first member of her moon-trinity, but when Suidas the Byzantine records that Io was a cow that changed her colour from white to rose and then to black he means that *the New Moon is the white goddess of birth and growth; the Full Moon, the red goddess of love and battle; the Old Moon, the black goddess of death and divination.* [P. 69; italics added.]

In the White Goddess myths and in Plath, the meanings of these three colors are roughly parallel. (In both, too, colors such as purple or blue sometimes have the same function as black.) Of the forty-three poems in *Ariel* (U.S. edition), all but four directly mention one or more of these colors, which are also widely evoked indirectly (other colors are only sporadically mentioned). White, for example, is implicit in "clouds," "snow," "pallor"; and, of course, in images of the moon.

It seems evident that *Three Women*, which Plath said was inspired by an Ingmar Bergman film, has a connection with the White Goddess myth as well:

The *three standing stones* . . . from Moeltre Hill . . . in Wales . . . may well have represented the Io trinity. *One was white, one red, one dark blue, and they were known as the three women.* [Graves, p. 69; italics added.]

Each of these "three women" represents one of the Triple Goddess' principal phases; and each of the women in Plath's radio play represents one of the same three phases.

White, the New Moon color of "birth and growth" (though Graves discusses the common variant, the negative aspect of whiteness, as in leprosy or corpses),[41] expresses the fate of the "Wife"[42] who gives birth to a son. Red, the Full Moon color of "love and battle," expresses the fate of the unmarried "Girl" who gives up her newborn daughter. Black, the Old Moon color of "death and divination," expresses that of the "Secretary" who has miscarried. (The lines spoken by each of the women refer to all three colors and not just to that color which symbolizes her fate—as is consistent with a general linking of female destiny with the moon.) Of the thirty speeches in *Three Women*, twenty-seven directly name one or more of the Moon's three colors. These recur so insistently that the play has the quality of a hymn chanted by the three women to the Moon which, consciously or not, they acknowledge as their ruling planet.

The first speech of the Secretary contains these lines:

When I first saw it, the small red seep, I did not believe it.
. . .
The letters proceed from these black keys, and these black
    keys proceed . . .
. . .
The white sky empties of its promise, like a cup.

And later:

> There is the moon in the high window. . . .
> How winter fills my soul! And that chalk light
> Laying its scales on the windows, . . .
>
> . . .
> . . . I feel a lack.
> I hold my fingers up, ten white pickets.
> See, the darkness is leaking from the cracks.
> I cannot contain it. I cannot contain my life.

Here is the Wife in labor:

> The sheets, the faces, are white and stopped, like clocks.
>
> . . .
> And I, a shell, echoing on this white beach . . .
>
> . . .
> . . . There is this blackness, . . .
> This ram of blackness.

The Girl says:

> I have seen the white clean chamber with its instruments.
>
> . . .
> The night lights are flat red moons. . . .
>
> . . .
> The flowers in this room are red and tropical.
>
> . . .
> Now they face a winter of white sheets, white faces.

These colors pay tribute to the White Goddess myth and at the same time express Plath's central concerns. The contrast of red with a white background, for example—mentioned earlier as encoding the death/rebirth motif—is a common aspect of this color system (the red of "love and battle"—of vitality—opposing the white of falseness or death-in-life).

"Little Fugue" interweaves the whiteness of death-in-life ("Now similar clouds/Are spreading their vacuous sheets"; "The clouds are a marriage dress, of that pallor") with the blackness of the yew, Hecate's death-tree (the whiteness has been caused by the blackness). The father's ghost has made his daughter "lame in the memory":

Such a dark funnel, my father!
I see your voice
Black and leafy, as in my childhood,

A yew hedge of orders, . . .

. . .

Death opened, like a black tree, blackly.

There is a kinship or identity between the White Goddess and all of the subsidiary heroines and goddesses who enact aspects of her myth, for these are all facets or versions of the same White Goddess. Graves writes, "The daughters were really limited versions of herself—herself in various young-moon and full-moon aspects" (p. 387). Plath's protagonist (in all her guises) is in a similar sense a facet or version of the Moon-muse. And just as various qualities of the Triple Moon-goddess (such as fertility, barrenness, prophecy, poetic inspiration, youth, old age) are bestowed upon her various "daughters," so Plath's heroine and her Moon-muse frequently resemble one another, and have in some respects similar 'personalities.' In this connection, it is worth recalling the relation between the name "Plath" and the characteristic flatness of the Moon-muse.[43] In a sense the Moon-muse and the heroine are magically identified, partaking of the same soul or essential being—perhaps as the familiar of a witch shares her soul, what befalls one befalling the other.[44]

"Edge" (in which the dead heroine and the Moon-muse are in phase) exemplifies this connection. Both the Moon, which surveys the death-scene, and the heroine are dead, cold, "perfected." This scene, and the speaker's tone of resignation, imply that the Moon and the dead woman have achieved their final relation. Just as the dead mother "has folded" her two children "back into her body," so the Moon—the mother of the woman—has in some sense folded her daughter back into herself, reclaiming and reabsorbing her.

In her honors thesis, "The Magic Mirror: A Study of the Double in Two of Dostoevsky's Novels," Plath refers to the idea of magical identification. What she calls Golyadkin's "ambiguous proverb" (and which she used as the title for one of her chapters)

—"the bird flies itself to the hunter"[45]—is an image of magnetism between an individual and a certain fate, and a comparable magical affinity seems to link Moon-muse and heroine. Such an affinity may entail that the Muse governs and reflects the speaker's state of mind, or it may represent a desired state of being, as in "Lesbos." Here the drama involves the speaker and a woman who is entrapped in a web of squalid domestic relationships:

> His Jew-mama guards his sweet sex like a pearl.
> . . .
> He is hugging his ball and chain down by the gate . . .

Because of her own domestic problems, the speaker is particularly vulnerable to and threatened by her sympathy for the woman, whom she resents for exploiting her sympathy:

> Your voice my ear-ring,
> Flapping and sucking, blood-loving bat.

The woman's advice to the speaker, to "wear tiger pants" and to "have an affair," seems painfully irrelevant. The woman is, in a sense, asserting her kinship with the speaker, and offering herself as a model of a life they can share.

As the speaker recollects an unpleasant incident between the woman and her husband, she also recollects the moon rising over that scene, and the memory of the moon appears as a portent—*another* female offering herself as a model:

> That night the moon
> Dragged its blood bag, sick
> Animal
> Up over the harbor lights.
> And then grew normal,
> Hard and apart and white.

What the speaker suffers and desires, the moon sympathetically undergoes and achieves. When still mingled with the scenery of earth, the moon first rises blurred and reddish, tainted with blood, and "sick." Then, rising above the earth and the scene of the drama, it becomes increasingly "normal, / Hard and apart and white." It comes clear of its earthbound identity (as a "sick animal") and achieves the detachment and self-sufficiency that the speaker would like to have, and toward which, by the end of the poem, she is moving.

If this kinship between Moon-muse and heroine is understood as a basic assumption of Plath's mythology, then personae such as Lady Lazarus, the woman in "Purdah," and the victims in "The Jailor" and "The Detective" can be seen as particular incarnations of an underlying identity. Their true selves share a characteristic voice: prophetic, heroic, fearless, and of mythic dimension.

To put Plath's protagonist in proper perspective, one might imagine one of the heroines or goddesses described by Graves, aware of the workings of that myth which is her 'life,' suddenly speaking out in verse. If the scene were that of a Moon-goddess about to ritually murder her Sun-god consort, the result might be lines such as these from "Purdah":

> . . . at his next step
> I shall unloose
>
> I shall unloose—
> From the small jeweled
> Doll he guards like a heart—
>
> The lioness,
> The shriek in the bath,
> The cloak of holes.

Although the affinity between protagonist and Moon-muse clearly derives its major inspiration from *The White Goddess*, there were many other sources which contributed to Plath's delineation of her Muse. In astrology, for example, one's "Moon sign" represents a primary astrological influence, the unconscious or subjective aspect of personality, "the intuition which is beyond" either body or mind.[46] In other contexts, too, the moon represents a female principle or a principle of subjectivity. One might say that certain meanings of the moon in Plath's mythology would have received a wide confirmation: as the ruler of her biology, of her fate as woman, as poet, and as tragic heroine. Related meanings and images seem, in fact, to cling to her Moon-symbol by a natural sympathy. Her motifs and images harmonize so well because in other Moon-mythologies similar motifs and images are themselves similarly interrelated.

The Moon-muse of Plath's mythology, especially in that she represents the tragic fate of the heroine, is a sort of "rival" (merging her roles as inspirational mother and evil godmother). This function is not merely abstract or symbolic. The Moon-muse also has proxies, primary among whom is a human rival who incarnates the aspect of death-witch. The Moon-muse is the comprehensive symbol for the whole drama, including the actions of the three main characters: heroine, rival, and dead and resurrected 'gods.' It is in terms of this symbolic system that Plath's real-life rival becomes mythologized.

The proxies of the Muse evolve from the disquieting muses to the cold beauties—human, but with certain inhuman qualities—depicted in "The Rival," "An Appearance," "Childless Woman," and in "The Other" (where the rival has the character of 'the other woman' by explicit virtue of being, if not an incarnation, an emanation of the Moon—a "moon-glow"). If the disquieting muses of 1958 were rivals or adversaries, as representatives of the heroine's shadowed, intractable destiny (Fate itself as the "rival"), then their meaning and presentation become amplified subsequently: there is both a "woman in the moon" and one out of it. Incarnated, she is typically cold, barren, powerful, merciless, and beautiful. While the Moon in "The Detective" symbolizes the drama, which she distantly surveys, of losing and mourning the god, the rival in "The Other" is an agent of the loss, a mythic enemy—a beautiful death-witch—who can draw blood while remaining invulnerable, as if she herself (like the Moon) had no blood to be spilled (in the poem, her blood is "a cosmetic"). The incarnated rival does not stand outside the parallel between *The White Goddess* and Plath's myth; the relation of the rival (meaning, unless otherwise indicated, the incarnated rival) to heroine and god, with a simple inversion of gender, is mirrored in the mythic prototypes of *The*

White Goddess. In connection with his remark that "All true poetry . . . celebrates some incident or scene" in the "ancient story" of the White Goddess and her Son, Graves repeatedly uses the term "rival." And just as Plath's rival has more than one form, so the rival in the White Goddess myths may be in nightmare a "bed-side spectre," but also take "countless other malevolent or diabolic or serpent-like forms" (p. 24).

The poet participates by proxy in the ancient story celebrated in poetry, the story also being in some sense that of the poet's relationship with the Muse:

The Theme . . . is the antique story . . . of the birth, life, death and resurrection of the God of the Waxing Year; the central chapters concern the God's losing battle with the God of the Waning Year for love of the . . . Threefold Goddess, their mother, bride and layer-out. *The poet identifies himself with the God of the Waxing Year and his Muse with the Goddess; the rival is his blood-brother, his other self, his weird.* [P. 24; italics added.]

The poet identifies himself with the Star-son, his hated rival is the Serpent; . . . [P. 386]

. . . the Serpent . . . the Demon of the Waning Year, his darker self. [P. 391]

The poet is in love with the White Goddess, with Truth: his heart breaks with longing and love for her. [P. 446]

. . . the Sacred King as the Moon-goddess's divine victim; . . . every Muse-poet must, in a sense, die for the Goddess whom he adores, just as the King died.[47] [P. 489]

If the poet is a woman (and Graves usually takes it for granted that the poet is male),[48] a simple and obvious inversion might present itself. Instead of two male rivals contending for the favor of a Muse-goddess, two female rivals might contend for the favor of a god. (This might be cosmologically insupportable to Graves, but it makes a good story.)

Not one, but two structures in Plath's myth are, then, connected with the White Goddess myths, representing two related perspectives on the same pattern of fate. In the first, a heroine,

like a form of the White Goddess, successively marries and mourns
her god:

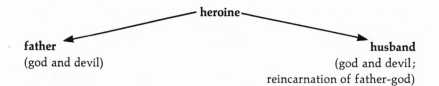

father   husband
(god and devil)   (god and devil;
                                              reincarnation of father-god)

In the second, the gender is inverted and reveals *how* the god
is lost (to a rival):

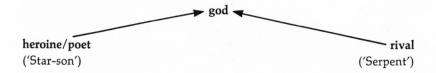

heroine/poet   rival
('Star-son')   ('Serpent')

If a woman poet identified herself with a female Spirit of the Waxing Year, she would fight with a female rival or Serpent the losing
battle that nevertheless culminates in her rebirth. The prize would
be the male god (perhaps magically associated with the perpetua-
tion of the Muse in herself). Within the structure of the same type
of myth, then, either or both the god and the heroine can die
and be reborn.[49]

The 'Freudian' nature of the two patterns is obvious. If, when
the heroine successively marries and mourns each of the two
gods, her character as daughter is emphasized, then the gods—
father and husband—obviously become rivals (particularly in
that the husband inevitably usurps the father's role). If, when
two female rivals fight for the one male god, the god's character
as father is emphasized, then the women rivals are clearly mother
and daughter.[50] These two patterns and the other variations do
not exclude one another but coexist, and in any case the same
underlying problem remains: the false self or death-in-life due to
the absence of the 'god,' and the wish of the true self to be reborn.

In the myths and rituals discussed by Graves, the death of the
god or his representative frequently occurs at the end of a fixed

term, often after seven or eight years.[51] The length of the term has significance both for Plath's life and for her myth. Her father, having died a few days after her eighth birthday, had served as her 'god' for eight years; her husband, from whom she separated in the seventh year of marriage, had been 'god' for seven years. Inversely, if the heroine identifies with the Waxing aspect, it is *she* who has lived a term of eight or seven years (until her father's death, or the absence of her husband, causes her death-in-life; in the latter case, the heroine's 'death' after a set term is linked with a female rival).

In notes jotted down for an outline of the novel which she was working on at the end of her life, she refers to the principals as "heroine," "rival," "husband," and "rival's husband." Although this must have been partly because she had not yet settled on definite names for her characters, it also indicates a mythic view of these roles.[52]

Early in July 1962, before she wrote most of the late poems, she learned her husband was involved with Assia Gutman, a rival for whom, in her poetry, a mythic context had long existed. The Moon had already appeared as a sort of muse-rival in "The Moon and the Yew Tree," and in "The Rival" the rival as a "woman in the moon." Any flesh-and-blood rival, merely by being such, would automatically qualify for a place in the mythic structure. Assia Gutman was particularly well qualified because she not only had no children, but was, apparently, willfully childless, having had several abortions—such a 'sterile beauty' (who had the looks of a model) would be a natural ally of the barren and barrenness-inflicting Moon-muse, already evident in the poetry.

Fertility and barrenness, whose opposition is encompassed by the Moon, are pivotal in defining the relationship between heroine and rival and between heroine, rival, and Moon. Early in 1961, and before Plath had even met Assia Gutman, a model for the rival appeared in "Barren Woman," published originally as "Small Hours." (The poem might have been occasioned by Plath's own recent miscarriage.) However, for the character in "Barren Woman" her lack of fertility does not signify, as it does for the rival, an alliance with the Moon, but a victimization by it.

The description of the "Barren Woman," as a "museum without statues," having "pillars, porticoes, rotundas," suggests that her body (like that of a "Munich Mannequin") is merely decorative, functionless architecture. A marble building empty of statues is not a museum but a mausoleum, and other details of the poem confirm this: "Marble lilies/Exhale their pallor like scent." Were she not barren, the woman/museum imagines she might be "Mother of a white Nike"—mother of a white marble statue, an ironic and ambiguous image. In the final lines of the poem, the moon, obviously connected to the woman's childlessness, makes a gesture as if to comfort her, but the gesture also marks her as the victim of this mother: "The moon lays a hand on my forehead, / Blank-faced and mum as a nurse."

"The Rival," originally a three-part poem of which Plath finally kept only one part, was probably written just before she first met the woman who would eventually precipitate the rift in her marriage. It is worth quoting the original series in its entirety because it gives an elaborate portrait of a woman who is "beautiful, but annihilating," like the moon, and baleful, stony, and omnipresent, like a disquieting muse:

1.

If the moon smiled, she would resemble you.
You leave the same impression
Of something beautiful, but annihilating.
Both of you are great light borrowers.
Her O-mouth grieves at the world; yours is unaffected,

And your first gift is making stone out of everything.
I wake to a mausoleum; you are here,
Ticking your fingers on the marble table, looking for
    cigarettes,
Spiteful as a woman, but not so nervous,
And dying to say something unanswerable.

The moon, too, abases her subjects,
But in the daytime she is ridiculous.
Your dissatisfactions, on the other hand,
Arrive through the mailslot with loving regularity,
White and blank, expansive as carbon monoxide.

No day is safe from news of you,
Walking about in Africa maybe, but thinking of me.

2.

Compared to you, I am corruptible as a loaf of bread.
While I sleep, the black spores nod
Their magnified heads and plan to kill me as soon as possible.
The wrinkles creep up like waves,
One camouflaging itself behind another.
I should have a steel complexion like yours
In which the minutes could admire their reflections and
    forget about me.

What did you have to sacrifice
To come up out of the stones, down out of the stars
And put on such a usual body?
I have a baby you like.
You sat in the next room while I crawled on all fours,
A sow or a cow, no better.
Now you must be telling lies: the baby is smiling.

3.

I try to think of a place to hide you
As a desk drawer hides a poison pen letter,
But there is no drawer to hold you.
Blue sky or black,
You preoccupy my horizon.
What good is all that space if it can't draw you off?
You are the one eye out there.

The sea, also, is ineffectual.
It keeps washing you up like an old bone.
And I, on the sky-mirroring, bland sands
Find you over and over, lipped like a skate and smiling,
With the sound of the sea in your mouth.
Angel of coldness,
Surely it is not I you want so badly.

I thought Earth might use you.
She has a terrible way with minerals.

But even her tonnage doesn't impress a diamond.
Your facets are indestructible;
Their lights whiten my heart.
Toad-stone! I see I must wear you in the center of my
    forehead
And let the dead sleep as they deserve.

Like the Moon, this rival is merciless, undecaying, and unavoidable. Although the speaker addresses her in a grimly resigned tone, there is also a note almost of affection; she cannot help admiring her, even though it is as one admires a fearful machine or a brilliant but sinister work of art. Any women who were models for this incarnation of the Moon would have inspired the poem precisely due to their possession of the qualifying characteristics through which the disquieting Moon-muse makes her presence felt and to which the various manifestations of the rival are kin. Thus the disquieting muses are stone-gowned; the "rival" has the gift of "making stone out of everything," and the "other" is a stone statue. Certain qualities are caught from the Moon,[53] not only for the obvious reason that, because the Moon with its white light looks cold, the women who represent it should be cold, but because Fate itself, like "fixed stars," is frozen, indifferent, immutable as a marble tomb. In "The Other," which Plath did write after meeting her actual rival, a marble museum has indeed given birth to its "white Nike." The "other" is clearly an agent of the Moon and descended from the long line of threatening females who had haunted Plath's poetry.[54]

The rival in Plath's poems is not merely 'the other woman' (in the sense in which adultery is betrayal, *ad + alter*, to an other), but has a more profound otherness, a mythic oppositeness embodying a rival way of being. That Plath considered the opposition of childlessness and motherhood to be of crucial significance is evident from the following passage, which she copied out from *The Golden Bough:*

The magic virtue of a pregnant woman to communicate fertility . . . On the other hand . . . a barren wife infects her husband's garden with her own sterility & prevents the trees from bearing fruit; hence a childless woman is usually divorced.[55]

The rival's artificially maintained beauty and her childlessness are a primary source of her otherness; they are a touchstone in the late poetry because the rival's choices epitomize the road not taken by the heroine, which is perhaps why a barren, beautiful female (whether the Moon or her representative) invariably conveys a sense of dangerous otherness or rivalry. Not only "The Moon and the Yew Tree," "Elm," "The Rival," *Three Women,* "An Appearance," and "The Other," but "The Fearful," "Childless Woman," and "The Munich Mannequins" (which in part is like a meditation on the barrenness of the rival) provide good examples of this. The childless woman resembles a work of art that cannot reproduce itself ("She would rather be dead than fat, / Dead and perfect, like Nefertit" ["The Fearful"]), and like a work of art she has no issue (on her "ivory" body, her "roads bunched to a knot, / The knot myself" ["Childless Woman"]). She must celebrate "no more idols but me, / Me and you" ("The Munich Mannequins"), reflecting only her mate in "The silver limbo of each eye / Where the child can never swim" ("The Fearful"). She only "spin[s] mirrors, / Loyal to my image" ("Childless Woman"). In all these the woman *is* a work of art, but produces neither art nor children. The poems view this sort of self-containment as horrifying, unlike the self-containment of the queen bee, which is, in fact, opposite to the rival's childless, male-related state.

Plath incorporated her actual rival into her mythology by making her an agent of death-in-life, a mythic opposite who continues to play a part in the pattern of the heroine's punishment by gods. Yet as with the White Goddess myths, the rival also suggests some magical relation to the heroine, some aspect of herself. Despite the damage done by the rival, the very otherness of this "darker self" attracts or fascinates the heroine. There is an element here of hating one's evil fate, or the instrument of that fate, even while loving and welcoming it, since it is so clearly one's own and a part of oneself; there may even seem to be in it some undeniable if terrible justice.

The heroine's ambiguous attitude—her fascination and repulsion —stems from this magical relation to the rival (Muse, Moon, or woman). This relation in many respects resembles that of Golyadkin to his "double." Golyadkin—meek, subservient, and unadventurous—cannot also be brash, stylish, and daring; his double —part of his self, though his dramatic opposite—is these for him. The phenomenon of the double takes many forms, and Plath, in her study, examines them from a number of perspectives, including the mythic, the psychopathological, and the literary (*The Picture of Dorian Gray*, "Strange Case of Doctor Jekyll and Mr. Hyde," *The Double*, *The Brothers Karamazov*, and others). She notes that

. . . the Double assumes the evil or repressed characteristics of its master and becomes an ape or shadow which presages destruction and death. . . . reflects, by its increasing power over the original, the growth of degradation and disintegration in its counterpart.

In such situations, where the Double symbolizes the evil or repressed elements in man's nature, the apparition of the Double "becomes a persecution by it, the repressed material returns in the form of that which represses." . . . The confrontation of the Double in these instances usually results in a duel which ends in insanity or death for the original hero.[56]

The prototypical rivals in the White Goddess myths are also doubles as well as opposites in that they are 'blood-brothers,' 'twins,' 'other selves.'[57] The relationship between the heroine and her rival has something of this quality: in "The Rival," for example: "I try to think of a place to hide you"; "You preoccupy my horizon"; "You are the one eye out there."

Successive changes in the titling of "The Other," which Plath wrote in the traumatic month of July 1962, chart a widening of its announced scope, from 'the other woman' to more evocative and profound themes. A straightforward descriptive epithet, "Mannequin," the first title, conjures up a glamorous, artificial, sterile woman. The title "The Other One" emphasizes the rival as 'the other woman.' But "The Other" encompasses the mythic opposite who is also a double, a hated yet indispensable other, like Star-son and Serpent twins; and suggests something deeper, more ambiguous, mysterious, and frightening: this is how one might refer to Death.

The degree to which this poem is organized in terms of mythic dichotomy is still more apparent when the opposites (stated and implied) are listed.[58] Material from earlier versions of the poem is useful to such a consideration, because here, as in most of the late poems, the final selection is either a choice from an over-abundance of similar examples or of the more mythic over the more literal. Thus, "womb of marble" obviates and further mythologizes the line "seven small corpses in your handbag." Plath eliminates any history or explanation of the childlessness of the rival. Similarly, she excises explicit references to the husband; and of the elaborations of sexual rivalry there remain only "sulphurous adulteries" and "The stolen horses, the fornications." Presenting childlessness as a 'given' also seems appropriate to a mythic characterization, like beginning a tale with "Once there was an evil queen who had no children" and, without further explanation, continuing with the story.

Because the heroine and the rival are mutually defined—since the "other" *is* precisely that—it is not always necessary to present both sides of the equation (which are sometimes given, such as in the contrast between the heroine's "navel cords" and the rival's marble womb). Since the rival engages in "sulphurous adulteries," the heroine need not identify herself as a chaste wife. The rival's complexion is an unearthly white, like the Moon; and her hair unnaturally glossy and uniformly dark, like "plastic" and "shoeblack." One does not need to be told that the speaker looks quite different from this.

The cumulative impression is the contrast between the rival as representative of death and invulnerability and the heroine as representative of life and vulnerability. The rival's deathliness (and barrenness) is the major characteristic of her otherness and her embodiment of the Moon. (Her "moon-glow" identifies her as an agent of the Moon, and so do other details in the draft.)

Several months before writing "The Other," Plath had completed *Three Women*, in which the Moon appears as a glaring white death-goddess.[59] At the onset of the Secretary's miscarriage, her sickliness resembles the Moon: "And the man I work for laughed: 'Have you seen something awful? / You are so white, suddenly.' " Later, contemplating the Moon, the Secretary comments "I, too, create corpses"—implicitly blaming the Moon for her miscarriage (the Moon brings on menstruation, which, in a sense, a miscarriage also is). The reference in the draft of "The Other" to the "corpses in your handbag," apparently referring to abortions and perhaps to miscarriage, also links the rival and the Moon's deathliness. Since the rival is so plainly a 'fatal woman,' the explicit references to corpses and other excised references to funerals and death ("Death is your green alcohol") may have seemed excessive, as it would if the knight in Keats's poem were to describe "La Belle Dame Sans Merci" as a fatal woman, rather than simply relating his encounter.

An odor of deathliness and danger remains in the first line of "The Other"—"You come in late, wiping your lips"—which suggests a casual voraciousness. Only a few days earlier, in a draft of "Berck-Plage," Plath had used the same image in an ironic version of the idea of spring-as-rebirth (seen instead as death masquerading as renewal). An old man had died, and

> The tulips had a part of him that spring,
>
> The green came in late, wiping its lips.

The devouring, barren, adulterous rival in Plath's myth may also have a further connection with Graves. In his novel *King Jesus* (which Plath had read and in which many of the White Goddess themes and analyses appear), he refers to the punishment of sexual sins "by barrenness"; and aso, "Is it not written: Such is the way of an adulteress: she eats, she wipes her mouth, she says: 'I have done no wickedness'?"[60]

The drafts of "The Other" include a number of apparently literal biographical details about Plath's rival. These are typically absent from the final poem. If she were writing 'confessional' poetry, there would presumably be a premium on including precisely those juicy, convincingly specific, 'real-life' details which, when they find their way into her poems, she almost invariably and routinely eliminates *if they do not also serve a more mythic and general purpose*—which, because of her extraordinary sensitivity to correspondences with myth, they often do. (Contrast this with Robert Lowell's apparent incorporation, in a recent book, of such items as lines from his wife's letters.) Characteristically, the final version of "The Other" has relinquished those overly literal or sensationalistic details, found in the drafts, which are irrelevant to the myth.

Some of the themes of *The White Goddess,* particularly those that apply to the relationships of heroine, 'god,' and rival, are also developed in certain of the writings of Jung. She was quite possibly reading or rereading him in late 1962 (she had read some of his work earlier in connection with her thesis on *The Double*); she had, at some point, transcribed passages from his volume *The Development of Personality,* a collection of essays dealing with many topics relevant to her concerns near the end of her life. Among the topics are "the development of personality," an unusual and dangerous undertaking (exemplified by the lives of Buddha and Christ) which involves allowing the "inner voice" to "lead [one] towards wholeness"; and "marriage as a psychological relationship."[61] No doubt, given her interests (and some internal evidence from her poetry suggests this), she was also familiar with Jung's work on "archetypes of the collective unconscious."[62]

The essay on "Marriage as a Psychological Relationship" (from which she transcribed several passages, under the heading "on marriage") includes an analysis, in terms of Jung's concept of the "anima," which is germane to the relationship of heroine, 'god,' and rival in Plath's myth, and which, in its characterization of the anima, is in many details in close agreement with *The White Goddess.* The anima, according to Jung, is "the eternal image of woman" which the unconscious of every man carries as a sort of genetic inheritance. It is "not the image of this or that particular woman, but a definite feminine image. . . . Since this image is unconscious, it is always unconsciously projected upon the person of the beloved, and is one of the chief reasons for passionate attraction or aversion."[63] Jung states that in marriage one of the partners, usually the husband, is the "container," and the other, the "contained." Usually, then, the wife completely projects her "animus" (the image of man projected by the unconscious of women) onto her husband, while he is only partially able to project his anima on her:

In which case, this highly fascinating image hangs as it were in mid-air, as though waiting to be filled out by a living person.[64]

If this incomplete projection *is* filled out by a living person (rather than by a dream, for example), this person would of course be 'the other woman,' the rival of the wife.

Further:

There are certain types of women who seem to be made by nature to attract anima projections; indeed one could almost speak of a definite "anima type." The so-called "sphinxlike" character is an indispensable part of their equipment, also an equivocalness, an intriguing elusiveness —not an indefinite blur that offers nothing, but an indefiniteness that seems full of promises, like the speaking silence of a Mona Lisa. A woman of this kind is both *old and young, mother and daughter, of more than doubtful chastity, childlike, and yet endowed with a naive cunning that is extremely disarming to men.*[65] [Italics added.]

Similarly, the White Goddess is " 'old and young when she pleases' " (p. 430), "her own mother" (p. 387), and "incontinent" (p. 423). The anima clearly resembles a kind of "Belle Dame Sans Merci," like the White Goddess in many of her forms.[66]

The White Goddess sometimes manifests herself as a witch, or as a lamia or serpent. Jung (in his "Archetypes of the Collective Unconscious") says of the anima:

She is the serpent in the paradise of the harmless man with good resolutions and still better intentions.

She is

. . . a lamia or succubus, who infatuates young men and sucks the life out of them. . . . To the men of antiquity the anima appeared as a goddess or a witch, . . .

The anima (like the White Goddess)

. . . likes to appear in historic dress, with a predilection for Greece and Egypt.

The White Goddess encompasses love and death. The anima

Occasionally . . . causes states of fascination that rival the best bewitch-
ment, . . . The witch has not ceased to mix her vile potions of love and
death; . . .[67]

Jung's writing offers an explanation, in terms of his concept of
archetypes, of the source of the mythic and of its pervasiveness in
everyday life; it asserts that life *is* mythic:

In dealing with the shadow or anima it is not sufficient just to know
about these concepts and to reflect on them. . . . *Archetypes are com-
plexes of experience that come upon us like fate, and their effects are
felt in our most personal life. The anima no longer crosses our path as a
goddess,* but, it may be, as an intimately personal misadventure, . . .
*When, for instance, a highly esteemed professor in his seventies aban-
dons his family and runs off with a young red-headed actress, we know
that the gods have claimed another victim. This is how demonic power
reveals itself to us. Until not so long ago it would have been an easy
matter to do away with the young woman as a witch.*[68] [Italics added.]

He also says in the essay on marriage that "a man can create for
himself a *femme inspiratrice* [in short, a Muse] by his anima projection."[69]

Jung describes in terms of the psychological relationship of marriage what Graves describes as the relationship of the (male) poet
to his Muse, incarnate in (or, speaking psychologically, projected
onto) a woman who is a threat to domesticity. Because the Muse
does not willingly remain captive, the power of inspiration will
desert the wife who has turned domestic:

By ancient tradition, the White Goddess becomes one with her human
representative—a priestess, a prophetess, a queen-mother. . . . But the
real, perpetually obsessed Muse-poet distinguishes between the Goddess
as manifest in the supreme power, glory, wisdom and love of woman,
and the individual woman whom the Goddess may make her instrument
for a month, a year, seven years, or even more. The Goddess abides; and
perhaps he will again have knowledge of her through his experience of
another woman.[70]

"Another woman" may become inevitable when

. . . the woman whom he took to be a Muse, or who was a Muse, turns into a domestic woman and would have him turn similarly into a domesticated man . . . and as the Muse fades out, so does the poet. . . . The White Goddess is anti-domestic; she is the perpetual 'other woman,' and her part is difficult indeed for a woman of sensibility to play for more than a few years, because the temptation to commit suicide in simple domesticity lurks in every maenad's and muse's heart. [P. 447]

In light of the many coincidentally parallel major themes—and there are innumerable parallel details as well[71]—it is important to keep in mind that long before she met Ted Hughes or read *The White Goddess*, Plath had already gone far toward developing intellectual and poetic interests which were entirely consistent, thematically and symbolically, with the Graves material, which is why the material seemed so apt. She had long endured the trauma of her father's death, mourning him as if he were a lost divinity ("Lament"). She had already written conventional poems to the moon. Her undergraduate thesis on the double in Dostoevsky—a study of false and true selves—had been written in her senior year at Smith College, just before she went to Cambridge, and in the course of this study (especially through Frazer's *The Golden Bough*) she became acquainted with many of the same myths she later found discussed, from a different perspective, by Robert Graves. Other works related to this theme, and familiar to her before she read Graves, include the Greek tragedies, and Eliot's *The Waste Land*. That such material had fascinated her was due at least partly to its already-perceived relevance to her life (as Ted Hughes commented, "She looked for the intellectual influences that would influence her").[72]

Before her reading of *The White Goddess*, Plath had already attempted suicide and had undergone shock treatment—both of which were, as it turned out, experiences of symbolic oblivion followed by regeneration. The psychotherapy which followed her 1953 breakdown must have encouraged her to perceive her life in terms of certain psychoanalytic myths, while familiarizing her with certain others. Her psychoanalytic experience may have made her, more than most of us, keenly aware of the extent to which life is mythic.

The mythological explanations of her private history with which the White Goddess myths provided her, and the connections between poetry and the White Goddess, must have made it irresistible to her to immerse herself in the White Goddess "cult." The myths gave her a map on which she could, consciously or unconsciously, chart and locate her past (the relationship with her dead father), her present (herself as heroine, her husband as renewed 'god,' replacing the old dead one), and, even more surprisingly, it was a map into which major future events would also fit, for the White Goddess myths would also accommodate her estrangement from her husband (a new phase of the old cycle of union and separation), and the character of the "rival" responsible for it. All this gave Plath license and encouragement to cast herself as a mythic heroine within the drama the Moon-goddess superintends and symbolizes.

Of the other symbols and images in her mythology, none is as inclusive as the Moon-muse, which draws together and provides a context within which are encompassed her major motifs and themes, generally expressed in terms of a lunar myth, a lunar landscape, a lunar heroine in sympathy with a lunar Muse. The Moon is the hub of the meanings which constitute the whole mythology, of which various meanings are activated or 'released' at different times.

It is no exaggeration to say that the symbol of the Moon is structurally indispensable to the late poems in a way that, say, the image of red poppies is not. The late poems can be imagined without the poppies because the motif embodied in them appears elsewhere and does not require embodiment in only that particular concrete image. Compared with the Moon, the poppies are merely incidental images or partial manifestations of a motif, automatically finding their place in a pre-existing mythology by 'releasing' a pre-existing motif; the motif, and not the poppies, is indispensable to Plath's myth.

The Moon-muse, whether mentioned or implied, belongs to the level on which the total myth is conceived; it is the cumulative concrete symbol of the late poetry which gives unity and coherence to a wide variety of motifs and images by organizing them in the form of myth. No other image or symbol could be substituted for the Moon without resulting in an essentially different mythology, though it might be an equally powerful and varied one. The exclusion of the image of poppies would not substantially alter the configuration of Plath's poetry, though it would reduce the number of "chapters" in her mythology.

The presence of the Moon in her poetry is like that of the sun in a landscape painting: it is an implicit presence even where it is not directly represented. One might even, in describing its function as the spirit of Plath's myth, use Graves's words to describe how the White Goddess—even when absent—makes her presence felt:

Sometimes, in reading a poem, the hairs will bristle at an apparently unpeopled and eventless scene described in it, if the elements bespeak her unseen presence clearly enough: for example, when owls hoot, the moon rides like a ship through scudding cloud, trees sway slowly together above a rushing waterfall, and a distant barking of dogs is heard; or when a peal of bells in frosty weather suddenly announces the birth of the New Year. [P. 25]

Similarly, the Moon's luminosity pervades Plath's late poetry even where its image is not present.

IV

The Dying God and the Sacred Marriage

> . . . men . . . explained the fluctuations of growth and decay, of reproduction and dissolution, by the marriage, the death, and the rebirth or revival of the gods. . . . They set forth the fruitful union of the powers of fertility, the sad death of one at least of the divine partners, and his joyful resurrection.
>
> Sir James George Frazer, *The Golden Bough*

The Golden Bough, which Plath had cited in her undergraduate thesis[1] (completed in 1955), and which she had read about a year before discovering *The White Goddess*, sheds further light on the structure and logic of her mythology, the most significant aspects of which echo both Frazer and Graves. In both these books many of the same myths and assumptions appear,[2] and both are based on major motifs shared by Plath's mythology. But while Graves focuses on the White Goddess as both "emblem" and "real agent"[3] of a characteristic drama which he regards as the one true theme of poetry, Frazer, in discussing many of the same (or same types) of myths and rituals, focuses on the death and resurrection of the god—the vegetation deities who generally have two aspects or selves: a new, resurrected form and an old, dead form. In other words, where for Graves the Triple White Goddess is always central, for Frazer it is the Gods of the Waxing and Waning Year.

A clear reference to Frazer occurs in "Last Words," written shortly before the *Ariel* poems began:

> I do not trust the spirit. It escapes like steam
> In dreams, through mouth-hole or eye-hole.

In his chapter "The Perils of the Soul," Frazer wrote:

[sleep is the] temporary . . . absence of the soul. . . . [which] is commonly supposed to escape by the natural openings of the body, especially the mouth and nostrils.[4]

As previously mentioned, Plath had transcribed from *The Golden Bough* a remark about a barren wife infecting her husband's garden; and a line excised from the final version of "The Other"—"There are no windows or doors open for your progeny"—apparently refers to Frazer's mention of numerous practices intended to facilitate childbirth, such as "[throwing] all doors and windows wide open" (p. 279).

The starting point of Frazer's inquiry is the attempt

. . . to explain the remarkable rule which regulated the succession to the priesthood of Diana at Aricia [or Nemi]. [P. v]

A semi-divine priest served in the sacred grove of Diana (who was "conceived as the moon"). Consort as well as priest, he "bore the title of King of the Wood"; "one of [his] titles to office was the plucking of a bough—the Golden Bough—from a tree in the sacred grove." Once he possessed the Golden Bough, he could succeed the former priest by slaying him. Frazer argues that the Golden Bough contained the "life" or "soul" of the priest, who also represented a vegetation god, and who was as well "one of those sacred kings or human divinities on whose life the welfare of the community and even the course of nature in general are believed to be intimately dependent."[5] According to Frazer this slaying and many similar customs and rituals originate in the universal desire to insure the rebirth of crops each spring. Since the vigor of the vegetation is intimately connected with the well-being of the King of the Wood, the ritual slaying of the priest is a process of selection. A King of the Wood who lacks strength and alertness is soon slain by a more vigorous, and therefore more worthy, contender. Yet the priest's "life" or "spirit" is preserved intact because his individual body is only a temporary receptacle for it: the "soul" or "life" really resides in the Golden Bough, which represents the fact that the soul (the power of vegetation) is cyclically renewed, and passed on.

To support the claim that this ritual "exemplifies a widespread institution" Frazer shows that numerous myths share with it such items as "killing of the divine king" and belief in an "external soul." Frazer's outline of these rituals in terms of their constituent motifs (a good grasp of which can be had immediately merely by glancing at his table of contents) also fits Sylvia Plath's mythology. Her poetry, too, comprises "The Ritual of Death and Resurrection," "Human Scapegoats," "Incarnate Human Gods," and "The External Soul."

In a number of earlier poems, she expresses her relationship with her dead father as a 'marriage' (the dying god is often a consort; and the marriage theme naturally reinforces the identification of the female partner as a White Goddess type who mourns her absent god). Later, she either takes this marriage more or less for granted, or she tries to cancel it. Plath's relationship to her dead father obviously found confirmation in the "sacred marriage" which is an indispensable element of many of the myths and rituals discussed by Frazer and Graves, and which precedes the death (and often the resurrection) of the "dying god."

Early poems about her relationship with her father reveal her instinct to make of it something far greater than an ordinary personal event. To have portrayed it otherwise would have violated her sense of his overwhelming importance. These poems contain embellishments of her father's figure with allusions to Greek tragedy, or suggestions that he is a heroic figure. Poems in which the marriage theme is central include "Full Fathom Five," "The Colossus," "Electra on Azalea Path," "The Eye-Mote," "On the Decline of Oracles," "The Beekeeper's Daughter," and sections of "Poem for a Birthday." In these poems, the marriage (which represents an elemental psychological truth) is sometimes dramatically enacted and sometimes only alluded to, but in any case the speaker's identity is defined primarily in relation to her father. She is not a heroine in her own right, as in later poems.

In "Electra on Azalea Path," she survives and mourns her father (as Electra survived and mourned Agamemnon):

I lay dreaming your epic, image by image.

"The Colossus" more explicitly identifies her father as a Greek god to whom she has an Electra-like attachment:

> I crawl . . .
> Over the weedy acres of your brow
> . . .
> A blue sky out of the Oresteia
> Arches above us.

"The Beekeeper's Daughter" presents him as a priestly king:

> Hieratical in your frock coat, . . .
> You move among the many-breasted hives,
> . . .
> Here is a queenship no mother can contest—

In the "Poem for a Birthday" series, her father is a god manifested in animal form:

> He was bullman earlier,
> King of the dish, my lucky animal.
>
> ["The Beast"]

"Maenad" also implies a marriage to the god. And in "Full Fathom Five" she remembers his "shelled bed." In all of these cases, she is sentenced to living out her life in terms of her daughterhood— as her father's priestess, votary, bride, queen.

This "marriage" has many elements in common with the "sacred marriages" discussed in *The Golden Bough* (and discussed to a lesser extent in *The White Goddess*). Frazer speculates about the motives underlying the sacred marriages, or "magical dramas," which occur at Whitsun, the beginning of spring:

. . . our rude forefathers personified the powers of vegetation as male and female, and attempted, on the principle of homeopathic or imitative magic, to quicken the growth of trees and plants by representing the marriage of the sylvan deities in the persons of a King and Queen of May, a Whitsun Bridegroom and Bride, and so forth. [P. 156]

Frazer suggests that just such an annual sacred marriage between the King and Queen of the Wood once took place in the sacred grove of Diana.

Since the married deities personify spirits of vegetation, like vegetation they are subject to death. So conceived, they are thought "to pass a certain portion of each year underground"; and they "naturally come to be regarded as gods of the lower world or of the dead. Both Dionysus and Osiris were so conceived" (p. 452).[6] In virtually all the dying god and mourning goddess myths, two gods marry or are divine lovers; then one dies and the survivor mourns and often searches for the lost "underground" partner, who is eventually reborn. In some myths the goddess 'dies' along with the god, or she may herself be the dying vegetation spirit (the 'death' of Persephone is explained in these terms).[7]

The theme of the fixed term of the sacred king (discussed by both Frazer and Graves) is clearly relevant to the "marriage" to her father (as well as to her marriage to her husband). Like Persephone, part of her life is given to a dead god ("The day you died I went into the dirt"). The priestess in "The Colossus," "married" to her god, tends the ruined monolithic remains of her dead father ("My hours are married to shadow").

The most complete and explicit portrayal of the daughter's marriage to the dead underground god appears in "The Beekeeper's Daughter"—obviously set in a sacred grove—which "recounts a key event in her *Vita Nuova*."[8] The grove provides the setting for an intense 'Freudian' drama; it possesses a suffocating and somehow unnatural lushness and fecundity:

> A garden of mouthings. Purple, scarlet-speckled, black
> The great corollas dilate, peeling back their silks.
> Their musk encroaches, circle after circle,
> A well of scents almost too dense to breathe in.

The speaker's (dead) father is presented as the priest-king of this grove, and the daughter depicts her total submission to him:

> Hieratical in your frock coat, maestro of the bees,
> You move among the many-breasted hives,
>
> My heart under your foot, sister of a stone.[9]

Plath's use of the epithet "many-breasted" may be yet another echo of *The Golden Bough*:

. . . in her sanctuary on the Aventine [Diana] was represented by an image copied from the *many-breasted* idol of the Ephesian Artemis, with all its crowded emblems of exuberant fecundity. [P. 163; italics added.]

Plath's sacred fertility grove also abounds in other "emblems of exuberant fecundity":

> Trumpet-throats open to the beaks of birds.
> The Golden Rain Tree drips its powders down.
> In these little boudoirs streaked with orange and red
> The anthers nod their heads, potent as kings
> To father dynasties. The air is rich.

In the "little boudoirs" of flowers, sexual union and conception occur. The bee grove is also a boudoir, inviting marriage and sexual union—incestuous union, echoed in the decadent overripeness and overabundance of the setting.

At the end of the poem the speaker, in the guise of "queen bee," "marries" her father, in his aspect of underground god. In doing so she depicts her assumption of the guilt for his death, since the male dies after mating with the queen (just as the God of the Waxing Year always must die):

> Here is a queenship no mother can contest—
>
> A fruit that's death to taste: dark flesh, dark parings.
>
> In burrows narrow as a finger, solitary bees
> Keep house among the grasses. Kneeling down
> I set my eye to a hole-mouth and meet an eye
> Round, green, disconsolate as a tear.
> Father, bridegroom, in this Easter egg
> Under the coronal of sugar roses
>
> The queen bee marries the winter of your year.

The grove as a setting for this "marriage" is both appropriate and ironic. It is a sacred marriage, and such marriages may be incestuous (as between kings and queens of ancient Egypt). Yet, as Frazer points out, the sacred grove of Diana was the place in which the crime of incest was expiated, since it was believed that incest would cause a dearth; therefore "atonement for the offence should be made to the goddess of fertility" (p. 163).

The queenship is "a fruit that's death to taste" not only for the father but for her, because marriage to him means going underground, entailing the death of her vitality. The poem suggests that the speaker would only end her mourning and recover her true self with the 'rebirth' of the god to whom she is married. That she is married to the "winter" of his year suggests that she hopelessly waits for 'spring' and the resurrection of this particular god; this is also intimated in the ironic reference to the "Easter egg," associated with spring and the rebirth of a god.

The attitude toward her father in "The Beekeeper's Daughter" and other earlier poems is usually mournful, nostalgic, and elegiac —but not bitter or vindictive. The speaker has resigned herself to the fixed, frozen relationship with her father and does not try to escape ("No longer do I listen for the scrape of a keel / On the blank stones of the landing," as she says in "The Colossus").

This resigned acceptance of the "marriage" contrasts sharply with the later mythology, in which she tries to break her father's hold (and, explicitly or implicitly, that of the other god, her husband). The 'Electra' who recites "Daddy" sounds quite different from the nostalgic, sorrowful speaker of "Electra on Azalea Path"; instead, she is bitter, determined, and even exhilarated. Not the 'rebirth' of her father but her own liberation is now her goal: the emphasis has shifted from mourning his absence, to reviling what that absence and mourning have done to *her*. The earlier bondage to her father, and the extremity of her earlier role as passive victim, are implicit in the violence of her determination to escape him.

The often extreme and intimate experiences dealt with in Plath's late poetry are given forms and meanings which make them appear as sudden revelations of ancient truths rather than particular biographical data. Perhaps what makes the late poems both shocking and seductive for many readers is precisely that "cries from the heart"[10] are communicated in mythic forms, whether or not these forms are recognized as a source of the poems' power. The remark that her last poems "have impressed themselves on many readers with the force of myth" acknowledges the impact of her poems without analyzing the cause: the poems have the force of myth because they are mythic, as a fuller grasp of their meaning, and a consideration of some of her influences and her use of them, make plain.

V

"Poem for a Birthday" and the
Imagery of Metamorphosis

Shortly before December 1959, when Sylvia Plath and Ted Hughes left the United States to settle in England, she wrote "Poem for a Birthday," a series of seven poems later published in the 1960 British edition of *The Colossus*. The series, written at Yaddo in the autumn of 1959, marked an important point in her poetic development, particularly with respect to the structure of the later mythology. In this series, she made a concerted attempt to mythicize her biography in terms of false self/true self, god/devil, and death/rebirth images. In fragmentary and embryonic form, these poems present a drama in which the heroine appears in both a mourning and a resurrected role. The ways in which the poem falls short of the finally accomplished mythology cast light on the nature of that accomplishment, and the series is also important in showing a new freedom in her writing.

"Poem for a Birthday" was written during a period in which, Ted Hughes notes, "she changed at great speed and with steady effort." His remarks on "Flute Notes from a Reedy Pond," the fifth poem in the series, apply as well to the series as a whole:

. . . like most of the pieces she wrote at this time, it is an elegy for an old order, the promise of a new. The sudden enrichment of the texture of her verse, and the nimble shifting of focus, were something new. . . . At this time she was concentratedly trying to break down the tyranny, the fixed focus and public persona which descriptive or discursive poems take as a norm. We devised exercises of meditation and invocation.[1]

In "Poem for a Birthday," she attempted to confront the painful subject-matter of her breakdown and hospitalization in 1953. Perhaps a catalyst for the series, which showed her how to enlist her own fantastically-populated inner world into her poetry, was her reading of Paul Radin's *African Folktales,* a collection of fantastic stories which straightforwardly present violent and miraculous events:

> She was reading [them] with great excitement . . . she found the underworld of her worst nightmares throwing up intensely beautiful adventures, where the most unsuspected voices thrived under the pressures of a reality that made most accepted fiction seem artificial and spurious. At the same time she was reading—closely and sympathetically for the first time—Roethke's poems. The result was a series of pieces, each a monologue of some character in an underground, primitive drama.[2]

In tales of hallucinatory intensity and immediacy, she found death, murder, dismemberment, betrayal, revenge, and resurrection portrayed with engaging simplicity as everyday occurrences. These characteristics of the *African Folktales,* and many of their specific images, appear in her poem.

Roethke's poetry, on the other hand, and particularly his "greenhouse" poems, is elegiac, celebratory, and nostalgic. Many of the poems deal with his childhood and with his dead father (whose Prussian background, 'pastoral' inclination, and name— Otto—are shared by Plath's father, a coincidence she would have found meaningful; and before Plath did so, Roethke had claimed, "The Moon's my mother").[3] Many of the "greenhouse" poems express in an extremely vulnerable and open way an empathy with what Roethke called "the minimal"—plants, roots, small insects, and animals. Just such vulnerability and openness, combined with the matter-of-fact presentation of the violent and the miraculous, characterize much of "Poem for a Birthday."

In many of his poems, Roethke had surmounted precisely that "fixed focus and public persona" which Plath had been struggling to break down. His is the frank and innocent language of child-

hood; it is a drastic regression *from* something and at the same
time a return or renewed access *to* something: the earliest emotions and, perhaps, also a sense of his underlying true self. For
example:

> I know it's an owl. He's making it darker.
> Eat where you're at. I'm not a mouse.
> Some stones are still warm.
> I like soft paws.
> Maybe I'm lost,
> Or asleep.
>
> A worm has a mouth.
> Who keeps me last?
> Fish me out.
> Please.[4]

Roethke and Radin were among the immediate influences which
came to fruition in "The Stones," the last, and the best, of the
"Birthday" series; and also, according to Ted Hughes, the last
poem Plath wrote in America:

Stones was . . . the only one [of the "Poem for a Birthday" series] not
obviously influenced by Roethke. It is full of specific details of her experience in a mental hospital, and is clearly enough the first eruption of
the voice that produced *Ariel*. It is the poem where the self, shattered in
1953, suddenly finds itself whole.[5]

That "The Stones" marked "the end of the first phase of her
development"[6] was a milestone that Plath herself recognized:

When she consolidated her hold on the second phase, two years later,
she dismissed everything prior to *The Stones* as Juvenilia, produced in
the days before she became herself.[7]

"Poem for a Birthday" charts Plath's breakdown, her view of
its source, and her recovery. Some of the same details, and many
of the same attitudes, appear in *The Bell Jar*, a version of which
Plath was probably thinking about and quite possibly working on
at this time.[8] She had, in a letter, referred to her experience of
1953 as a time of

. . . symbolic death, and numb shock—then the painful agony of slow rebirth and psychic regeneration.[9]

In *The Bell Jar* and in early poems she identifies her father's death as the source of the breakdown. These events, the main subject-matter of "Poem for a Birthday," are not, however, presented in terms of a single system of imagery. There are, instead, several separate systems of imagery among which attention is distractingly shuttled. The shifts from one image to another are of quite a different order in her late poetry, where they are the result of an elegant internal logic and do not give the effect of being fragmentary or undisciplined. The overabundance of images in "Poem for a Birthday" is a squandering of resources, rather than a variety of mutually reinforcing poetic strategies, and the literary sources, particularly Radin and Roethke, are only partly digested.

Since she had not yet conceived a symbol large and flexible enough to give shape to all she wanted to say, in "Poem for a Birthday" she bestows her attention in rotation, picking up—or improvising upon—first one strand of imagery and then another, with a consequent lack of continuity, within the individual poems as well as between the poems of the series.[10] "Witch Burning," for example, plays on the notion of purification by fire as part of a ceremony of rebirth. The speaker who undergoes the ritual appears variously as a wax effigy, a grain of rice, and a beetle, all of which are in some way 'taught the truth' by fire. Some logic connects all these images, but since it is not an adequate logic the many alternatives produce an incoherence. By distributing the first person voice among so many different personae, its power as an organizing device is undermined.

> *the death of [the] integrated self . . .*
> Sylvia Plath, "The Magic Mirror"

"Who," the first poem of the series, is spoken by a quiet, numb, stripped-down, nameless small voice:

> The month of flowering's finished. The fruit's in,
> Eaten or rotten. I am all mouth.
> October's the month for storage.

This shed's fusty as a mummy's stomach:
Old tools, handles and rusty tusks.
I am at home here among the dead heads.

Let me sit in a flowerpot,
The spiders won't notice.
My heart is a stopped geranium.

If only the wind would leave my lungs alone.
Dogbody noses the petals. They bloom upside down.
They rattle like hydrangea bushes.

Mouldering heads console me,
Nailed to the rafters yesterday:
Inmates who don't hibernate.

Cabbageheads: wormy purple, silver-glaze,
A dressing of mule ears, mothy pelts, but green-hearted,
Their veins white as porkfat.

O the beauty of usage!
The orange pumpkins have no eyes.
These halls are full of women who think they are birds.

This is a dull school.
I am a root, a stone, an owl pellet,
Without dreams of any sort.

Mother, you are the one mouth
I would be a tongue to. Mother of otherness
Eat me. Wastebasket gaper, shadow of doorways.

I said: I must remember this, being small.
There were such enormous flowers,
Purple and red mouths, utterly lovely.

The hoops of blackberry stems made me cry.
Now they light me up like an electric bulb.
For weeks I can remember nothing at all.

This is the shattered identity, the self at rock-bottom. The title poses the question of the speaker's identity, which appears to be minimal. The voice is disembodied, like that of a homeless spirit. The lack of developed and consistent imagery to characterize the persona confirms the lack of wholeness. Instead there is a multi-plicity of minimal identities ("I am all mouth"; "I am a root, a stone, an owl pellet") to answer "who."

A withdrawal, a shrinking inward or regression, has taken place. There is the sense of being buried, or stored away and forgotten. This is the "symbolic death" and the "numb shock" of her breakdown, but there is also the intimation of the eventual rebirth which is promised in the title of the series.[11] The storage shed is a tomblike place inhabited by "dead heads," but also womblike, "a mummy's stomach," suggesting not only a corpse, but a baby inside the stomach of a real 'mummy,' an embryo in a state of prebirth. (Since Egyptian mummies were stored and pre-served for eventual resurrection, the association of death with the promise of rebirth is reinforced.)

A dreamless "pellet" suggests a dead or traumatized and be-numbed condition, as well as the state of an embryo, or the con-sciousness of prebirth. The subsequent development of "Poem for a Birthday" continues the central identification of "symbolic death" with prebirth.

In "Who," the setting for the prebirth is apparently in some sense a mental hospital: the other residents of the shed are referred to as "inmates." The image of a hospital conveys the same sense of suspended activity, or of moratorium, conveyed by the images of the storage shed and the mummy's stomach. There are signs at the end of the poem that this suspended animation is reced-ing: the reference to amnesia-inducing shock treatments ("Now they light me up like an electric bulb. / For weeks I can remember nothing at all") nonetheless implies that light and life may even-tually replace deadness and darkness. The image also offers a new perspective on the blank and numb consciousness, which may now be seen as a sign of cure as well as a symptom of illness.

The final lines of "Who" refer implicitly to the split between the past (when the speaker was "small" and there were, she re-members, "such enormous flowers") and the present. Other poems of the series further develop the contrast between past and present.

In the second poem, "Dark House," an amorphous, underground voice speaks from the "house" which it has built:

This is a dark house, very big.
I made it myself,
Cell by cell from a quiet corner,
Chewing at the grey paper,
Oozing the glue drops,
Whistling, wiggling my ears,
Thinking of something else.[12]

This voice, like the speaker of "Who," seems almost without memory, history, personality, or gender—but it is now active and possesses a coherent form and consciousness. The speaker in "Who" felt *like* "a root, a stone, an owl pellet," while the one in "Dark House" *lives* in "the bowel of the root," *smells* "pebble smells, turnipy chambers," and *feels* "round as an owl."

"All-mouth,"[13] the father, has driven the speaker underground: "He's to blame" for this. Yet the dark house represents not only the state of breakdown, but also a safe, womblike place of healing.

Here the prenatal state is comprehended under the imagery of biological (specifically, insect) metamorphosis, which also appears or is implied in most of the remaining poems. The use of this extended metaphor shows that Plath was searching for a symbol to represent as interdependent the ideas of death and rebirth, and false and true selves, a symbol which would present the promise of rebirth as inherent in the death of the false self. This requirement is met by the symbol of metamorphosis; however, since this symbol does not include a way of referring to her other major motif, that of the male god, she needs another class of imagery as well, and for this purpose she relies on imagery she had, to a limited extent, already developed in slightly earlier poems such as "The Beekeeper's Daughter" and "Full Fathom Five." This anticipates the dying god and mourning goddess motif of the late poetry (which includes, in the one pattern, both the death of the god and the rebirth of the heroine). Together, these two classes of imagery fully define the outlines of the story she wants to tell, yet because the story is divided in this way (perhaps aggravated by the piecemeal telling of it), it cannot be presented as a unified whole.

Among her reasons for using the symbol of insect metamorphosis must have been that the poetic truth of her psychic death and rebirth was validated by an actual biological phenomenon which associates dormancy, or "symbolic death," with a process of "slow rebirth." Specifically, the metamorphoses she alludes to are those of the firefly beetle (in "Dark House") and the caddis fly (the ostensible subject of "Flute Notes from a Reedy Pond"). The metamorphoses of both firefly and caddis fly, like those of most insects, are marked by the sharply differentiated phases of larva (the caterpillar), pupa (also nymph or chrysalis) and imago (or adult). All three phases appear in "Poem for a Birthday," and each corresponds to a phase of "psychic regeneration."

Although the clues are not obvious, the speaker of "Dark House" is probably a firefly larva, an identification which at least coordinates many of the disparate details in the poem. The firefly larva or glowworm is often luminous, and the speaker of "Dark House" does apparently glow: "I see by my own light." The firefly larva "lives in the ground . . . and transforms to the pupa in an oval earthen cell";[14] perhaps this is the "dark house."

"Larva" derives from a word meaning "ghost, specter, mask," because the "larval stage of an insect masks or hides the true character or imago of the species."[15] This describes the speaker of "Dark House," who is certainly quite unlike the "adult" persona of "The Stones"; yet the structure of metamorphosis promises the birth of the adult, just as the "symbolic death" of the psyche anticipates its rebirth.

Because through metamorphosis one in a sense gives birth to oneself, as one does in "psychic regeneration," it is clear why the speaker of "Dark House" feels pregnant:

> Any day I may litter puppies
> Or mother a horse. My belly moves.

The larva is about to give birth to a new form of itself—the pupa.

The next two poems, "Maenad" and "The Beast," develop the theme of the loss of her father in terms which often parallel the imagery of dying god and mourning goddess. While developing this imagery, she temporarily puts aside the theme of metamorphosis.

In "Maenad," the speaker identifies herself as a woman, and for the first time discloses and relates to the present a crucial past event:

> Once I was ordinary:
> Sat by my father's bean tree
> Eating the fingers of wisdom.
> The birds made milk.
> When it thundered I hid under a flat stone.
>
> The mother of mouths didn't love me.
> The old man shrank to a doll.
> O I am too big to go backward:
> Birdmilk is feathers,
> The bean leaves are dumb as hands.

The death of her father has divided the golden age and "ordinary" magic of her childhood from what came after. An unloving mother caused her father to shrink away to a doll, a plaything of memory, bringing her childhood to an end. She cannot "go backward," having suffered—to use John Berryman's phrase to describe his similar trauma—"an irreversible loss"; and having, in consequence, suffered a blow to her "integrated self." Because of the split caused by her father's death, she retrogresses to a symbolic death which nevertheless has also the masked character of a prebirth, a prefiguration of a newly integrated self.

The lines "The mother of mouths didn't love me. / The old man shrank to a doll," suggest that since she was not loved by this mother, her father's death was in some sense her own fault. Such guilt is implicit in the line "The birds made milk," which comes from the title of a Xosa tale, "The Bird That Made Milk," collected by Radin. In this story a father makes his children swear not to reveal that he owns a milk-making bird which provides food for the whole family. But the children's playmates persuade them to tell the secret, and as a result the bird escapes. The children are therefore to blame for ending the magic. Plath's reference to this tale distinguishes the magical 'before' from the sorrowful 'after' of her childhood.[16] While her father lived, magic was commonplace and "The birds made milk"; but now that he is dead—for which she is somehow to blame—the magic has died with him, and "Birdmilk is feathers."

In "Maenad," the speaker is a worshipper of Dionysus, and this symbolizes her relationship with her dead father, who has changed from a father-god to a malignant ghost, an "all-devourer."[17] By the end of the poem the maenad has been caught up in the blood-rites,[18] the last line acknowledging both her loss of identity and her hope of recovering it:

> Lady, who are these others in the moon's vat—
> Sleepdrunk, their limbs at odds?
> In this light the blood is black.
> Tell me my name.

An earlier line, "I am becoming another," also intimates that she will recover her wholeness. The line may allude to "The Sun and the Children," another of the *African Folktales:*

The sun actually pierces the moon with his knife and that is why it decays. . . . [the moon] *went home to become another, a moon which is whole.* He again comes to life although it had seemed that he had died.[19]

The next poem, "The Beast," is ambiguous and overly private, but its general outline may be identified. Like "Maenad," it expresses the dying god and mourning goddess motif, contrasting an initially idyllic past with a present fall from grace:

> He was bullman earlier,
> King of the dish, my lucky animal.
> Breathing was easy in his airy holding.
> The sun sat in his armpit.
> Nothing went mouldy. The little invisibles
> Waited on him hand and foot.
> The blue sisters sent me to another school.
>
> . . .
>
> Mud-sump, happy sty-face.
> I've married a cupboard of rubbish.
>
> . . .
>
> Hogwallow's at the window.
> The star bugs won't save me this month.

I housekeep in Time's gut-end
Among emmets and molluscs,
Duchess of Nothing,
Hairtusk's bride.

The split between past and present also manifests itself as the difference between living aboveground and living underwater:

I bed in a fish puddle.
Down here the sky is always falling.[20]

The many types of beast may be incarnations of the godlike father, but might also represent the men in the speaker's adult life, in whom she tries but fails to find a substitute for her lost father. In either case, her father remains identified as the origin of her eventual breakdown and her marriage to this cupboard of rubbish (her father's memory, or his proxy) means that a part of her self remains buried with him.

After "The blue sisters sent me to another school," that is, after the death of the fabulous "bullman" (obviously a creature like the bull-god Dionysus—already alluded to in "Maenad"—or the Minotaur), the beasts degenerate to "Monkey," "Mumblepaws," "Fido Littlesoul," "Hogwallow," and "Hairtusk." The images represent in a sense the transformation of her father into the "rubbish" to which she is nonetheless married. If these less noble animals represent the other men in her life, they are no less substitutes for her father, who fall so far short of him that they only emphasize his irreplaceability.[21] Thus the speaker finally regresses to living among emmets and molluscs in a subterranean or underwater world.[22] Appropriately, in the following poem—"Flute Notes from a Reedy Pond"—which returns the series to the imagery of metamorphosis, dormant forms of life await underwater their new births:

Now coldness comes sifting down, layer after layer,
To our bower at the lily root.
. . .
. . . all things sink

Into a soft caul of forgetfulness.
The fugitive colors die.
Caddis worms drowse in their silk cases,
The lamp-headed nymphs are nodding to sleep like statues.

Puppets, loosed from the strings of the puppet-master,
Wear masks of horn to bed.
This is not death, it is something safer.
The wingy myths won't tug at us any more:

The molts are tongueless that sang from above the water
Of golgotha at the tip of a reed,
And how a god flimsy as a baby's finger
Shall unhusk himself and steer into the air.

The poem evokes the somnolent approach of winter, when pond-
life begins to die, to hibernate, and, as in the case of the aquatic caddis worms, to enter into the quiescent pupal phase, the
period of dormancy immediately preceding the final stage of adulthood.

Whereas the larval phases are usually active, the pupal phase
is a "state of rest or insensibility" while "an elaboration is going
on."[23] "Pupa" derives from a word meaning "a girl, a doll, puppet,"
and the poem speaks of the pupae as "Puppets, loosed from the
strings of the puppet-master." "Nymph," another name for the
pupal phase, derives from a word meaning "young wife" or "bride,"
which applies to Plath at that time in her life; and "chrysalis,"
still another common synonym for pupa and nymph, comes from
the word meaning "gold," and thus it is "also called . . .
aurelia."[24] Since "Aurelia" is the first name of Sylvia Plath's
mother, this etymology would support, in a private way, the
symbolism of giving birth to herself, of being her own mother.

"Flute Notes from a Reedy Pond" marks a break in the narrative; it is the only poem in the series which makes no explicit
reference to the story being told. It apparently springs from a
different impulse,[25] though sufficiently related to have been included in the series. In contrast to the other poems in the series,
it is elegiac and impersonal, the only one in which the pronoun
"I" never occurs. Its mood is of great quiet, the cessation of mo-

tion and thought, "indolence," "forgetfulness," waiting, imminence—all of which constitute not death, but "something safer" than death, a phase in which the creature awaits only the infusion of an animating force. The pupae of caddis worms particularly suggest readiness for a new birth, since they "are very much like mummified adults."[26]

The last two lines of the poem refer to an actual image of rebirth, shifting the perspective from the womblike pond to the larger world above. The mention of Golgotha introduces a reference to a dying and reviving god; and the caddis worms themselves, following their ageless pattern, emerge from the apparent death of pupation as flimsy gods.

"Witch Burning," the sixth poem in the series, also represents through metamorphosis the psyche on the verge of a new birth. At the beginning of the poem, the speaker acknowledges her affliction, and then submits, in various guises, to a ritual of purification by fire. The poem ends with images of light and air, where earlier poems in the series had dwelt in darkness and submersion.

WITCH BURNING

In the marketplace they are piling the dry sticks.
A thicket of shadows is a poor coat. I inhabit
The wax image of myself, a doll's body.
Sickness begins here: I am a dartboard for witches.
Only the devil can eat the devil out.
In the month of red leaves I climb to a bed of fire.

It is easy to blame the dark: the mouth of a door,
The cellar's belly. They've blown my sparkler out.
A black-sharded lady keeps me in a parrot cage.
What large eyes the dead have!
I am intimate with a hairy spirit.
Smoke wheels from the beak of this empty jar.

If I am a little one, I can do no harm.
If I don't move about, I'll knock nothing over. So I said,
Sitting under a potlid, tiny and inert as a rice grain.

They are turning the burners up, ring after ring.
We are full of starch, my small white fellows. We grow.
It hurts at first. The red tongues will teach the truth.

Mother of beetles, only unclench your hand:
I'll fly through the candle's mouth like a singeless moth.
Give me back my shape. I am ready to construe the days
I coupled with dust in the shadow of a stone.
My ankles brighten. Brightness ascends my thighs.
I am lost, I am lost, in the robes of all this light.

The readiness of the speaker to "construe the days / I coupled with dust in the shadow of a stone" indicates that she has begun to come to terms with her past. She understands that she has coupled with mere dust, that she has been enthralled by a ghost.

The firefly beetle about to become "a true representation or image of its species,"[27] on the verge of escaping the clenched fist of the "mother of beetles" (also the "black-sharded lady"),[28] represents the self on the threshold of finding itself whole, the imminent emergence from the pupal phase. (When the firefly's light, a natural symbol of the soul or spirit, is extinguished ["They've blown my sparkler out"] the state of breakdown, the dead self, is symbolized; with its light restored, the firefly represents the self made whole.) The image of the doll's body expresses the prior unwholeness, an experience of the body as an alien thing.[29] These images, together with the grain of rice which grows as the flames "teach the truth," and the witch purified by fire, embody the moment of breakthrough.

In "The Stones," the last and most successful poem of the series, "where the self, shattered in 1953, suddenly finds itself whole," the speaker appears as her adult self, her true representation; her sense of self, formerly dispersed and rootless, has found a home; her "shape" has been restored; and she has an answer to the question posed by "Who," the first poem of the series:

This is the city where men are mended.
I lie on a great anvil.
The flat blue sky-circle

Flew off like the hat of a doll
When I fell out of the light. I entered
The stomach of indifference, the wordless cupboard.

The mother of pestles diminished me.
I became a still pebble.

. . .

Only the mouth-hole piped out,

. . .

The people of the city heard it.
They hunted the stones, taciturn and separate,

The mouth-hole crying their locations.
Drunk as a fetus
I suck at the paps of darkness.

. . .

This is the after-hell: I see the light.

. . .

A current agitates the wires
Volt upon volt. Catgut stitches my fissures.

A workman walks by carrying a pink torso.
The storerooms are full of hearts.
This is the city of spare parts.

My swaddled legs and arms smell sweet as rubber.
Here they can doctor heads, or any limb.

. . .

Love is the uniform of my bald nurse.

Love is the bone and sinew of my curse.
The vase, reconstructed, houses
The elusive rose.

Ten fingers shape a bowl for shadows.
My mendings itch. There is nothing to do.
I shall be good as new.

Unlike the other poems, the imagery in "The Stones" successfully embodies complex themes, without straining the sense of
how the poem legitimately may develop. Many of the images
in the earlier poems crowded one another, making conflicting

claims; in "The Stones," the imagery, even when grotesque, is unitary and coherent, reflecting the coherence of the speaker, who has understood and ordered her experience. The earlier poems did of course reflect a still-traumatized and confused speaker, yet sometimes not only she, but also the poem itself, seemed confused.

Radin's *African Folktales* provided Plath with a ready-made analogy for "The Stones." From "The City Where Men Are Mended," she took the first line of her poem and the basic idea upon which she improvised.[30] A "city where men are mended"—where, in the tale,[31] two dead and mutilated girls are repaired—is not very different from a hospital, and so the city of Plath represents a place where the broken self is reconstructed.

The dispersed "stones" of the speaker's shattered self are gathered together and reconstructed, reenacting the myths of Dionysus (who is alluded to in "Maenad"), Osiris, and other gods who undergo dismemberment and resurrection:[32]

. . . Dionysus . . . resembled Osiris . . . and was said like him to have been torn limb from limb. [Frazer, p. 439]

. . . Osiris in his triple aspect as dead, dismembered, and finally reconstituted by the union of his scattered limbs. [P. 435]

In the case of Osiris, the parts of his body were widely scattered and his sister Isis made a long journey in order to collect them. "The people of the city" similarly collect and reassemble the parts of the speaker's self.

In "Maenad," the speaker's worship of her dead father suggests the ritual reenactment of Dionysus' death; the speaker in "The Stones" uses similar imagery to describe her own death and resurrection. In the late poetry the governing myth unites these two aspects: the Moon-heroine is now conceived as a dying and reviving goddess, and mourning (or celebrating) the death of her god is a part of her Moon-myth—though the emphasis is on *his* death and *her* resurrection.

"The Stones" came at the close of an important period in Plath's life, about a year after she had decided to "leave teaching and throw herself on writing for a few years." During this time devoted entirely to writing, she produced poems such as "Suicide Off Egg Rock," in which, "For the first time, she tried deliberately to locate just what it was that hurt." In the autumn of 1959, just before she wrote "The Stones," she had "changed at great speed and with steady effort." "Quite suddenly," says Ted Hughes about the writing of "The Stones," "she found herself free to let herself drop, rather than inch over bridges of concepts."[33]

"The Stones" foreshadows the mythology of the late poems in several ways. It organizes and interrelates the ideas of psychic death and reconstruction, of false and true selves, and relates them to her father's death.

Further, the "bald nurse," presumably at her bedside, clearly parallels the "disquieting muses" standing at the side of the crib— both presences later connected with the Moon-muse. Like the muses, the bald nurse is an ambivalent figure, both welcome and unwelcome; like the later Moon-muse, she is associated with both life and death.[34] Though a nurse supposedly aids recovery, her uniform—love—is also the speaker's curse. Plath further develops the connection between the bald nurse and the Moon in *Three Women*, where the Moon, associated with the sickness of barrenness and its cure, is "luminous as a nurse" whose white uniform 'glows': therefore, the Moon's white glow is a kind of uniform. (The interconnections between Moon, muses, and nurses, all bald and all ambiguously threatening as well as proprietary, are reflected throughout her poetry.)

The image of the bald nurse is not the only way in which Plath qualifies the absoluteness of the recovery. "I shall be good as new" sounds a wry if not ironic note, and raises the question whether being "reconstructed" really is being "good as new." Images of rebirth in *The Bell Jar* suggest the same qualification:

There ought . . . to be a ritual for being born twice—patched, retreaded and approved for the road. [P. 275]

But being "retreaded" does not quite amount to "being born twice." The description of the reconstruction of the self in terms of mechanical repair falls short of the symbol of a new birth. Later, when in "Daddy" she refers to her suicide attempt and breakdown, she writes that "they pulled me out of the sack, / And they stuck me together with glue." Being stuck together suggests a temporary repair-job that may again come unstuck. As Esther wonders in *The Bell Jar*, "How did I know that someday—at college, in Europe, somewhere, anywhere—the bell jar, with its stifling distortions, wouldn't descend again?" (p. 271).

The irony of the claim "I shall be good as new" is reinforced by images which are not really images of newness, and which, because they express a degree of doubt or tentativeness appropriate to a period of convalescence, still put the cure into question:

> The vase, reconstructed, . . .
>
> . . .
> Ten fingers shape a bowl for shadows.
> My mendings itch.[35]

What Plath attempted in "Poem for a Birthday" provides a perspective for viewing the later mythology. The imagery of metamorphosis, for example, was used to render accurately the experience of what she had described as her "time of darkness, despair, disillusion—so black only as the inferno of the human mind can be,"[36] and her symbolic death and psychic rebirth. Although metamorphosis and the image of a reconstructed vase do suggest psychic regeneration, their use precludes the mythic import of her experience, and this may explain why she abandoned the imagery of metamorphosis (promising as such) as an organizing device.[37] While metamorphosis is cumulative and transitional, the protagonist in the late poetry has two different aspects: in a sense she already *is* the queen bee, even while she acts the drudge. Her true self is always present and not merely a promise for the future; only it is suppressed, buried, or disguised. Eventually it is revealed or released, and not just evolved into.

She needed a myth which would allow her to express more than does the mere image of repair, the results of which *The Bell Jar* clearly describes. When Esther is about to leave the mental hospital, her mother says:

> "We'll act as if all this were a bad dream." . . .
> A bad dream.

I remembered everything.

I remembered the cadavers and Doreen and the story of the fig tree and Marco's diamond and the sailor on the Common and Doctor Gordon's wall-eyed nurse . . .

Maybe forgetfulness, like a kind snow, should numb and cover them. But they were part of me. They were my landscape. [P. 267]

In the late poetry, she no longer wants to claim her "landscape," but to transcend or discard it along with her false self. She wants to be, not "good as new," but really new, "Pure as a baby" ("Getting There").

A god such as Dionysus is not stitched and mended, but torn apart and revived. His myth no more celebrates his 'reconstruction' than Christianity celebrates Christ's 'reconstruction.' Plath's later poems are as absolute as this in their images of rebirth.

The evolution of the firefly imagery illustrates this movement toward absoluteness. An imitation of the firefly had appeared earlier, in "The Disquieting Muses," where the "muses" had intervened to prevent the speaker from taking part with her schoolmates in a pageant:

> Blinking flashlights like fireflies
> And singing the glowworm song, . . .

Then, in "Dark House," the speaker appears as an actual glowworm (the first stage of metamorphosis). In "Witch Burning," the adult firefly beetle is about to emerge, but it shares the reader's attention with the witch and the rice grain. Despite the first person voice in the poem, all of these images stand apart from and are referred to by the real speaker of the poem. In a poem such as "Lady Lazarus," there is no such distance; the real speaker and the ostensible speaker are one. It is toward the persona of "Lady Lazarus"—a phoenix, burning goddess, firebird, who engenders her own death, purification, and rebirth—that the earlier firefly images steadily progress.

The use in the earlier poetry of such a variety of metaphors to express the themes of false and true self, and death and rebirth, conveys the urgency behind her impulse to transform her biography into myth. In the "Poem for a Birthday" series, this impulse comes closest to fulfillment in "The Stones," which echoes the myths of dead, dismembered, and resurrected gods, not as an extraneous allusion, but as an integral aspect of the vision. In doing so it prefigures the late mythology in which, typically, mythological structures are completely appropriated into the poetic vision, and the speaker does not stand apart from the poem, but, rather, discloses her mythic character.

VI

The Mythic Biography in the

Late Poetry

Ritual has been described—by Frazer, among others—as the dramatization of myth. Frazer has also remarked that myth is to theory what magic and ritual are to practice (p. 770). Sylvia Plath's late poems can, with respect to the underlying myth, be roughly divided into corresponding classifications of 'theory' and 'practice.' Poems such as "Lady Lazarus" and "Daddy" express the 'theory' which underlies her late poetry; they paradigmatically refer to and present the source of her mythology and the interrelated motifs which make up the mythicized biography. The 'ritual' or 'practice' poems form the much larger group. Through them the underlying mythicized biography receives the envisioned dramatic or ritual resolutions required by its inherent conflicts. Such rituals, or acts of resolution, as the exorcism of her father's ghost, are nearly always rituals of rebirth or intermediate steps toward rebirth.

Since "Daddy" and "Lady Lazarus" also fit in this latter category, they are perhaps the two most important poems in defining her mythology. Most of the other poems which offer ritualized resolutions are not 'theoretical' as well but, as resolutions of the myth, they presuppose it. "Purdah," for example, ostensibly sparked by seeing or imagining the jade figurine of a woman, rapidly evolves, by a train of associations determined by the underlying 'theory,' into the ritual slaying of an oppressive bridegroom by a previously passive Moon-heroine who suddenly unlooses her true self. While the poem does not trace the origins of the mythology, it does present, as ritual, a symbolic resolution of that implicit past history.

"Little Fugue"

Not only because it was the first of the poems written after the "writer's block" of winter 1962, but also because of its effortless assimilation of mythic elements, free of the artificialities of earlier poems which contain mythological references, "Little Fugue" clearly stands at the beginning of Plath's late work.[1] It evinces the origins of her mythology and its related pattern of death-in-life. The "fugue" is really the life of the speaker, and its central theme is her dead father, a death never fully comprehended, outgrown, or successfully mourned. Her life, resembling in its repetitive involutions a musical fugue (a "little fugue," as opposed to Beethoven's *Grosse Fuge*), is a kind of torture, the claustrophobic, circular entrapment in a drama whose outcome is foreclosed, yet feared. The specter of her father appears everywhere; all other details, even those which seem at first incidental or occasional, receive their meaning in terms of him. The yew tree, her fingers, the baby, the clouds, all ultimately reveal themselves as portents or symbols of the dead god who rules her life, and though she does not explicitly mention him until halfway through the poem, his appearance modifies the earlier images: for they are soon mentioned again in relation to him and it becomes clear retrospectively that they have all along encoded his ghostly presence. (In other late poems, his presence is either taken for granted or stated more obliquely.) She makes plain that this mythic marriage trauma originates in her father's death:

> I was seven, I knew nothing.
> The world occurred.
>
> . . .
>
> I am lame in the memory.
>
> . . .
>
> This was a man, then!
> Death opened, like a black tree, blackly.

The poem elaborates the death-in-life which results from this; it thus not only states the origin of the myth, but presents a paradigm of the death-in-life (or false self) pattern.

The poem also refers to a different sort of fugue (one relevant to the belated entry of her father into the poem). "Fugue," in its psychiatric sense, explains the effects of her father's death and his persistent ghost. In this sense it means:

. . . a state of psychological amnesia during which a patient seems to behave in a conscious and rational way, although upon return to normal consciousness he cannot remember the period of time nor what he did during it; temporary flight from reality.[2]

Her father's death has given to not only the particular morning described in the poem but to her entire life the involutions and unreality of a fugue in both its senses. The poem suggests that its speaker, unlike the typical fugue victim, never enjoys periods of full recovery and "normal consciousness." Her amnesia results from a wound in her distant past, and she can no more repair her lack of a proper sense of relation to her dead father than a "trepanned veteran" ("Cut") can ever be truly whole. (The fugue is also in a sense the wound itself.) What she lacks, what she 'forgets,' is in effect her true self; rather than complete (though temporary) amnesia, she suffers partial (though chronic) fugue. She can attend to her daily life, minding her baby, and so on, but she always remains "lame in the memory," broken where she should be whole.

Many details of the poem reflect its affinity with the White Goddess mythology. Black—the color of "death and divination," and of Hecate to whom the yew is sacred—is peculiarly suited to the dead, oracular father. (His voice is "black and leafy.") White can signify birth and newness; but it can also have the sinister connotations of deathliness, of a corpse. Such whiteness symbolizes the speaker's sickliness, pallor, and blankness, which even the "marriage dress" shares. The repeated mention of the white clouds, which are vacuous, indistinct, and aimless, suggests that they represent to the speaker the ghostly insubstantiality of her present death-in-life. This contrasts with the definiteness and rootedness of the black yew and with her father's death, which is also "a black tree." And just as the blind pianist's fingers play Beethoven's *Grosse Fuge*, the yew's black fingers play out and on her life, which she follows by rote, like a familiar musical score. The blind pianist plays his fugue from memory—and so, in a sense, does she.

The yew symbolizes poetic destiny, and is therefore her tree, the poet's tree, as well as that of her dead father. (Both themes are combined in a line excised from the final draft: "a tree of poems, of dead men.") The same image which involves her destiny as a poet therefore also connects her with her father. (*The White Goddess* explains the underlying logic of this identification.)

A major section of *The White Goddess* discusses an ancient finger-alphabet, or "deaf-and-dumb finger-language" (p. 112), often used by Druidic poets, who sometimes "induced a poetic trance by treating their finger-tips as oracular agents" (p. 197). Perhaps Plath also found it significant that the vowel "I," symbol of the first person, was the "death vowel" or "yew-letter," sacred to the witch-goddess Hecate, and assigned to the little finger, which had "oracular [auricular] power" (p. 195). The transition can easily be made from the death- or yew-finger of a hand alphabet, to the whole hand as a yew tree which spells out messages. (Graves provides a visual model which facilitates this; he has several diagrams of hands with the appropriate letters written in along the fingers and finger joints.) For Plath the yew tree becomes a hand of "black fingers" speaking the "deaf-and-dumb finger-lan-guage" of poets and the oracular language of the dead:

> The yew's black fingers wag;
> Cold clouds go over.
> So the deaf and dumb
> Signal the blind, and are ignored.

The yew is a medium to her dead father (a line excised from the draft calls it a "go-between" that talks for the dead). Though the association of the yew with death is commonplace (parts of the tree are poisonous, and it has traditionally been planted in Eu-ropean graveyards), *The White Goddess* gives a coherence and mythic context to the image of the dead talking through it.[3] Trees belong both to the world of the living and also to that of the dead, their root-system being like an underground mirror-image of the daylight tree. Since these roots, among which the dead lie scattered, connect to the aboveground tree, it is the perfect "go-between," the roots carrying messages which the branches and leaves 'broadcast.' This is, in fact, like a telephone system; and later, in "Daddy," through a similar image—the black telephone "off at the root" so "the voices just can't worm through"—she breaks the connection which, in "Little Fugue," is still in working order.[4]

In the late poems, images of mutilation generally encode a reference to the emotional crippling caused by the death of her physically crippled father (he was an undiagnosed diabetic and died of complications following the amputation of his leg). In fact, virtually all images of mutilations, amputations, stumps, and the like, may be taken to incorporate such a meaning because of a totemistic association with her father. "Little Fugue" makes plain the connection between the speaker who is "lame in the memory" and the father who "had one leg."[5]

In this context, an amnesiac fugue might be described as an amputation of one's sense of reality. Literal and metaphorical images of a cutting off from the true self caused by the death of her amputee father pervade her poetry (a sense expressed not only by mutilation, but also by related categories of experience such as being sealed off by glass). Whether or not the absent 'god' is identified as the cause (in "Little Fugue" and "The Jailor" he is; in "Cut," he is not), the recurring symptoms imply the same underlying state of being—a paralysis of the true self.

A passage from *The Bell Jar*, eventually excised but almost certainly written before "Little Fugue,"[6] makes explicit the connection between her father's physical, and her emotional, crippling:

"I feel so cut off," I finished.

"No, no! It is not *you* who are cut off!" The doctor pointed to me dramatically. "It is your father's *leg* that was cut off!" And, with his right hand, he made a rapid, amputating gesture on his left thigh.

I was glad it was my father's leg, and not me, that had been cut off, and I was just about to ask, the way I always wanted to ask, what practical suggestions the doctor could give me to feel joined back again, when somebody tapped on the door.

The month after "Little Fugue," she wrote "Event" (first titled "Quarrel") where long-enduring "faults" in a marriage have "dis-membered" it. In both these poems, images of physical dismember-ment reflect the cutting off which, emotionally, death-in-life is; and both express longing for a lost wholeness. The same pattern of association holds true in a number of other poems, such as "A Birthday Present," where the speaker longs for the present to be given "whole" and not "come by the mail, finger by finger."

That *The White Goddess* devotes an entire chapter to types of lame dying and reviving gods was surely extraordinarily significant for Plath. "Little Fugue" identifies Christ, considered by Graves to be a 'lamed' god,[7] with the yew tree, which in the draft has "one foot"—one root (as the elm has a tap root)—and this is an icon for the speaker's one-legged father, a lame and mourned-for god:

> The yew my Christ, then.
> Is it not as tortured?
> . . .
> You had one leg, and a Prussian mind.

(In "Daddy," too, the father's one leg is "your foot, your root.")

The poem also implies the identification of tree and father in a more subtle and insistent way. The speaker addresses her father as "you," a homonym for the name of the tree and the poem's most persistent fugal element:

> The yew's black fingers . . .
> . . .
> Black yew, . . .
> . . .
> The yew my Christ, then.
> . . .
> And you, during the Great War
> . . .
> You had one leg, . . .
> . . .
> Do you say nothing?

(There may be another, private level of association for her, since "yew's" is also a near-homonym for her married name, "Hughes.")

The new clouds which now suffocate her life, "similar" to those which first appeared when her father died, "are a marriage dress," naturally bringing to mind her current marriage. The image expresses her present death-in-life as both an echo and a reenactment of the distant "marriage" to the father whom she has survived but to whom she is still bound:

> I survive the while,
> Arranging my morning.

It is also her *mourning* for her father that she 'arranges,' so that even minute details of her daily life are an expression of her grief. Her father affects the very meaning of her own bodily presence. When in the last stanza she says, "These are my fingers," the meanings already assigned to "fingers" make clear that even they are somehow possessed by her father's spirit. Like the yew's fingers they act as a medium through which he speaks.

The final lines of the poem suggest that she has survived a catastrophe:

> I survive the while,
> Arranging my morning.
> These are my fingers, this my baby.
> The clouds are a marriage dress, of that pallor.

If the elementary declarative phrases "These are my fingers, this my baby" suggest someone numbed with shock, they also suggest someone relearning the world, a disoriented survivor or convalescent. This idea recalls "this earth our hospital" (the phrase adapted from Eliot which she once used as an early title for one of her stories), the earth for her being a place of survivors.

In form and spirit Plath's line resembles "Inventory," a twelve-line poem by Günter Eich (referred to in an article by Hans Magnus Enzensberger), in which he speaks as a survivor of the Nazi terror. Plath very likely knew this translation:

This is my cap,
this is my coat,
here is my shaving kit
in a linen bag.
. . .
This is my notebook,
this is my groundsheet,
this is my towel,
this is my thread.[8]

The ending of "Little Fugue" employs the same strategy of simple declarative phrases to achieve similar ends (while the "clouds" suggest the cause).

Enzensberger says of "Inventory" that it was "written from the situation of a prisoner of war in a camp; but this situation simultaneously stood for the condition of all Germans." Enzensberger's concern is with German poetry "after Auschwitz"—that is, with poetry of survivors for whom the problem was that "the German language was debauched"; "After the entry of the Allies, Germany was mute, in the most precise meaning of the word, a speechless country." In Eich's poem, "paralysis has itself become language." Yet the poem

. . . simultaneously describes and overcomes the situation: . . . The poet is staking a claim to the absolute minimum that remains; to a material, spiritual, and linguistic remnant. His manner of writing corresponds to this. It is stripped down as far as poetry can be stripped. The text sounds like a man learning to speak; it is with such elementary sentences that language courses begin.[9]

The line in Plath's final stanza creates a similarly ambiguous effect, both appalling and hopeful: an effect of numbness and fresh simplicity, of a paralysis of language and a new beginning.

"Daddy"

No other poem, except "Lady Lazarus," so forcefully and completely recapitulates Sylvia Plath's myth as "Daddy." It weaves her three major polar motifs into a variation on the dying god and mourning goddess theme in which the persona (the "Electra" figure) rejects the role of mourning which perpetuates her false self.

The poem ends with an act of exorcism. The earlier recapitulation of the myth is a prologue to and part of this ceremony; the list of charges against Daddy supports the act of sentencing him to death. The culminating portrayal of the father as a devil who must be exorcised differs greatly from the way he appeared in "Little Fugue," written about six months earlier. The contrast reflects the different aims of these two chapters in defining his mythic identity. In "Little Fugue," he was a stifling, authoritarian figure, but also a suffering "dying god," like Dionysus or Christ. He was not regarded with the extreme bitterness and venom (counterpointed, implicitly but undeniably, by a love just as extreme) of "Daddy," in which his aspect of malignant underground god has come to dominate, becoming incarnate in stereotyped images of evil: Nazi, Fascist, brute, devil, vampire.[10]

The two differing portraits of her father parallel a shift in perspective. "Daddy" involves no question of feeling guilty or even of denying guilt, as does "Little Fugue" ("I am guilty of nothing"). She now rejects both guilt and suffering, seeing herself more as a vengeful victim. Her father's death is a crime *he* committed against *her*—a reversal of the view of poems such as "Maenad."[11]

In a note written for the BBC Sylvia Plath had commented on some psychological aspects of the poem:

Here is a poem spoken by a girl with an Electra complex. Her father died while she thought he was God. Her case is complicated by the fact that her father was also a Nazi and her mother very possibly part Jewish. In the daughter the two strains marry and paralyse each other—she has to act out the awful little allegory once over before she is free of it.[12]

This statement is completely consonant with the mythicized biography (though it may be a distortion of Sylvia Plath's own literal history).

In her attempt to free herself—to cure the paralysis, to be reborn—she symbolically reenacted the drama of victim and torturer by marrying her father in the form of another Nazi, who also "drank my blood" and then abandoned her, and whom she finally destroys along with her father. Rejecting her previous role as mourner, she emerges as a heroine who escapes from the devil, just as Persephone escapes from Pluto by being 'reborn.'

The history of the "girl with an Electra complex" runs in ten-year cycles, each decade marked by near-death and revival. This "Electra" says she was ten "when they buried" her father—a split in time which originated her false self and created a permanent need to complete the relationship with him. At twenty, she tried to repair her history by dying and rejoining him (a tacit reference to the theme of sacred marriage to an underground god). Although revived, she was not *reborn*, for she neither escaped his influence nor fully succeeded in 'getting back' to him. Now on the verge of completing a third cycle, she will finally resolve her relationship to Daddy by getting back *at* him, 'killing' both him and the husband whom she married as his proxy.

Nearly all the other late poems either directly express the patterns exemplified by "Daddy" (or variations on the theme, such as the reenactment of the pattern in relation to her husband), or are more generally conceived musings on liberation from her mythic drama. Aside from the 'theory' and 'practice' poems, most of the other late poems show the daily life of the protagonist. "Cut," "Poppies in October," and "The Couriers," for example, present neither the source nor the nature of the myth, nor are they ritualized resolutions of it. Instead, they show how the myth organizes the elements of daily experience, and they may therefore be called Plath's equivalent of 'occasional poems' in the special sense that each encounter with some element of daily life (her cut thumb, the blood-red poppies, her wedding ring) releases some aspect of the underlying motifs. Although these occasional poems do not describe the myth, they result from it and are chapters in the mythology, even if not key chapters from the point of view of defining it; but even the occasions for poetry are in a sense solicited by the myth itself.

"Lady Lazarus"

"Lady Lazarus" also alludes to the origin of her myth, and re-capitulates the cyclical pattern of dying and reviving:

> I have done it again.
> One year in every ten
> I manage it—
>
> A sort of walking miracle, my skin
> Bright as a Nazi lampshade,
> . . .
> I am only thirty.
> And like the cat I have nine times to die.
>
> This is Number Three.
> What a trash
> To annihilate each decade.
>
> What a million filaments.
> The peanut-crunching crowd
> Shoves in to see
>
> Them unwrap me hand and foot—
> . . .
> The first time it happened I was ten.
> It was an accident.
>
> The second time I meant
> To last it out and not come back at all.

"Lady Lazarus" was written not long after "Daddy" and may be considered a companion-piece to it. Like the speaker of "Daddy," Lady Lazarus must escape "Herr Doktor," "Herr Enemy" (although both epithets may be addressed to her father here, the pluralized reference at the end of the poem, when she threatens "men," probably includes her husband—whose "wedding ring" she leaves behind). In "Daddy," the portraits of father and husband centrally define their roles as villains and death-gods. "Lady Lazarus," how-ever, goes beyond this in showing what Electra becomes once she frees herself from their paralyzing influence, realizing her true identity as a triumphant resurrecting goddess, the fully liberated, fiery true self which is the protagonist, manifest or underlying, in most of the late poems.

"Lady Lazarus" presents the double nature of the male figure as both Sun-god and underworld god of the dead, as both "Herr God" and "Herr Lucifer," the two faces of a single divinity. The heroine has been married to these gods, each of whom has in some way died to her, resulting in her death-in-life; but now her aspect of mourning goddess has given way to that of dying and reviving goddess. Plath described Lady Lazarus as

. . . a woman who has the great and terrible gift of being reborn. The only trouble is, she has to die first. She is the phoenix, the libertarian spirit, what you will. She is also just a good, plain, very resourceful woman.[13]

This phoenix—an image of the reborn true self—possesses the magical self-sufficiency of the queen bee. While the queen bee gives birth to every other member of her hive, the phoenix is self-generating:

When it has completed five centuries of life, it . . . builds a nest . . . and ends its life . . . a little phoenix is born anew from the father's body, . . . When the nestling is old enough . . . it lifts the heavy nest . . . carries its father's tomb, its own cradle . . . till it reaches the city of the sun, . . .[14]

Although as a Sun-bird the phoenix may traditionally be male, Plath (like D. H. Lawrence, one of the writers she admired) sees it as female. Like the queen bee, mating with whom spells death to the male, Plath's phoenix "eat[s] men like air," and is clearly sister to "the White Goddess, or Muse, the Mother of All Living, the ancient power of fright and lust—the female spider or the queen-bee whose embrace is death." Graves mentions a type of Moon-goddess who ritually renews her virginity, usually after murdering her old consort and before taking on a new one. A case of this type is the "fate of the antlered king," where the goddess trans-forms her lover into a stag, hunts him to death, and then takes a new lover after having "refreshed her virginity by bathing naked in a sacred fountain" (p. 216). That Lady Lazarus was conceived along these particular mythic lines is made explicit in an earlier draft of the poem:

> Each time I rise, I rise a bloody virgin.
> Sweet whore

As in "Daddy," the recapitulation of her deaths (and the implicit reference to her myth) prefaces a ritual, in this case the rebirth with which the poem ends. The first half of the poem describes the heroine and her spectacular act. Details of her past are not mentioned until stanza twelve, and the Nazi-gods (who have in a sense caused her to exercise her power of dying and reviving, and who, if not directly responsible for her deaths, at least take proprietary pleasure in them: she is their "opus," their "valuable"), only appear in the final third of the poem. The threat that she will eat men like air suggests that although Lady Lazarus has undergone previous deaths and rebirths, she has never before, in her fiery resurrection, consumed her male oppressors, as this time she will. In her rebirth she will leave behind the ashes of the mourning goddess, the dead self, consumed along with the "men."

This poem, and the most dramatic and intense of her other poems—such as "Daddy," "The Bee Meeting," "Lesbos," "Fever 103°," "Ariel," and "Purdah"—were written within a few weeks in October and early November of 1962, when Plath was evidently at fever-pitch. Visions of despair alternate with the predominating visions of triumph and liberation. The two moods complement one another. The bitter cynicism of "The Applicant" counterpoints the murderous intent of "Purdah." The sense of imminent doom in "Death & Co." is the necessary counterpart—perhaps the fuel—of the vision of rebirth in "Getting There." Although the Moon-muse represents the nature of the drama which the protagonist tries to escape, even the death-goddess has other aspects; like the Moon, Plath's protagonist in poems of this period characteristically attempts to die into a new phase.

A number of other poems express the 'theory' of her myth in more limited ways, as variations on the thematic patterns of "Daddy" and "Lady Lazarus." Such poems do not recapitulate the myth as prologue to a ritualized resolution, but present a dramatic monologue in a specific setting (often an enclosed place —a jail, or kitchen or other room) and develop in terms of a dramatic situation (for example, Sherlock Holmes and Dr. Watson in "The Detective," inspecting a country estate for signs of a body and the murderer).

"Purdah," "The Jailor," and "The Detective" vary the theme of the heroine's relationship with her father, repeated with bridegroom, jailor, or husband—aspects of a figure who, though the proxy for and, in one sense, the reincarnation of her father (an underlying identity even when not explicitly stated), also partakes in the drama in his own right. Many more late poems explicitly involve the husband than the father; of course, implicitly (and in "Daddy," explicitly) the figure of the husband *is* a 'father figure.' "The Rabbit Catcher," "The Courage of Shutting-Up," and other poems suggest an unholy union, the mythic contrary to sacred marriage.

The similarity of the two figures becomes apparent in a comparison of "Daddy" and "The Jailor." In both poems the male figures oppress and diminish the heroine. She feels like "a foot / . . . poor and white" which has lived in the "black shoe" created by her attachment to her father, and she lives in the prison created by her attachment to the jailor. In both cases she experiences her attachment to these men as persecution by them.

But the father—though his influence persists—is dead. Ending his influence, killing him for good, is spoken of as putting a stake through a vampire's "fat black heart." Having served the purpose for which his daughter has conjured him up, the father's ghost can be allowed to rest in peace: "Daddy, you can lie back now." By contrast, the husband remains very much alive—his existence creating an entangling web of possibilities and fantasies which are a form of death-in-life.

VII

Resolutions of the Myth

RITUALS OF EXORCISM

"Daddy"

Poems explicitly about the protagonist's father, read in order of composition, show that the attitude toward him evolves from nostalgic mournfulness, regret, and guilt, to resentment and a bitter resolve to break his hold on her. "Lament," "All the Dead Dears," "Full Fathom Five," "On the Decline of Oracles," "The Beekeeper's Daughter," "Electra on Azalea Path," "Poem for a Birthday," "The Colossus," and "Little Fugue" attest to her enthrallment, and display the historical pattern (surviving without him is a kind of death) which ultimately requires his exorcism.

The recital of the myth in "Daddy" ends in a ritual intended to cancel the earlier "sacred marriage" which has suffocated her:

> You do not do, you do not do
> Any more, black shoe
> In which I have lived like a foot
> For thirty years, poor and white,
> Barely daring to breathe or Achoo.[1]

In this image of passive and victimized domesticity, the speaker implicitly compares her past self to the 'old woman who lived in a shoe' who 'didn't know what to do'; now, however, she makes it clear she does know what to do.

In a preamble to the exorcism, she recounts the development

of her father's image, beginning with his earlier status as a "bag full of God, / Ghastly statue" (that is, a godlike colossus—although the 'ghastliness,' the ghostly, deathlike, pallid nature of the statue, makes plain the revisions to come) and then introducing the revised images: "panzer-man," "swastika," "Fascist," "brute," "devil," "bastard." Daddy must be cast in this new light, transformed from god to devil, if he is to be successfully expelled, but there must also be some real basis for it. To be effectively exposed, he must first appear as godly. But the speaker soon shows that she now attributes his godliness in part to his authoritarianism and personal inaccessibility—qualities which became intensified through his death, and which later became transferred to "a model of you"—her husband. Both men are really variations on a familiar type, even a stereotype: the "god" who, like Marco the "woman-hater" in *The Bell Jar,* is "chock-full of power" (p. 120) over women precisely because of his deadness, or ultimate inaccessibility, to them. Loving a man literally or metaphorically dead ("The face that lived in this mirror is the face of a dead man" ["The Courage of Shutting-Up"]) becomes a kind of persecution or punishment; and so, by the end of the incantation, Daddy deserves to be exorcised. The "black telephone," now "off at the root," conveys the finality of the intended exorcism.

The 'venomousness,' ambiguous from the beginning, is not the whole story. "Daddy" is not primarily a poem of "father-hatred" or abuse as Robert Lowell, Elizabeth Hardwick, and others have contended. The need for exorcising the father's ghost lies, after all, in the extremity of the attachment to him. Alvarez very justly remarks that

The whole poem works on one single, returning note and rhyme, echoing from start to finish:

> You do not do, you do not do . . .
> . . . used to pray to recover you.
> Ach, du . . .

There is a kind of cooing tenderness in this which complicates the other, more savage note of resentment. It brings in an element of pity, less for herself and her own suffering than for the person who made her suffer. Despite everything, 'Daddy' is a love poem.[2]

The love is not merely implicit in the rhythm and sound of the poem, it is a necessary part of the poem's meaning, a part of the logic of its act.

The exorcism serves another purpose because through it she also attempts to reject the other 'god' and to reject the pattern of being abandoned and made to suffer by a 'god.' She creates an image or "model" of her father and marries this proxy. Then she kills both father and husband at once (the killing is, of course, figurative in both cases), magically using each as the other's representative.[3] Each death entails that of the other: the stake in her father's heart also kills the "vampire who said he was you"; and the killing of her marriage (for which she now claims to take responsibility, as she does for having allowed her marriage to perpetuate, by proxy, her relationship to her father), finally permits Daddy to "lie back now." Identifying herself as a formerly acquiescent victim, she now vengefully cancels that role. The marriage to and killing of her father by proxy are acts of what Frazer calls "sympathetic magic," in which "things act on each other at a distance through a secret sympathy" (p. 14). Such magic, which assumes that human beings can either directly influence the course of nature or can induce gods to influence nature in the desired way, nearly always constitutes the 'logic' of the rituals Frazer discusses. The ritual marriage of a Whitsun bride and bridegroom, for example, aims at sympathetically encouraging a marriage between the powers of fertility, thus assuring abundant crops. Likewise, diseases may be either inflicted or drawn off by sympathetic magic on the principle that "as the image suffers, so does the man" (p. 14).

Plath was familiar with and used such ideas, as is evidenced by her transcription, from Frazer, of the remark about the fertility or barrenness of a man's wife affecting his garden; and also by the line that she excised from "The Other," connecting the opening of doors and windows with the facilitation of childbirth. (And the 'lameness' of memory and self, associated with her father's lameness and death, is at once a homeopathic wound and a sympathetic attachment to him.) The notion that "as the image suffers, so does the man"—affecting the real subject through a proxy—nicely describes the marriage to a model of Daddy, and explains why, "If I've killed one man, I've killed two." The earlier attempt of the speaker in "Daddy" to recover her father also involved sympathetic magic; she had tried to rejoin him by dying and becoming like him:

> At twenty I tried to die
> And get back, back, back to you.

She finally exorcises her father as if he were a scapegoat invested with the evils of her spoiled history. Frazer's discussion of rituals in which the dying god is also a scapegoat is germane here. He conjectures that two originally separate rituals merged to form this combination, and the father in "Daddy" may well be described as such a divine scapegoat figure.[4]

The location of devils to be cast out is sometimes a place, but usually it is a person who is possessed. In Plath's mythology the heroine is not possessed by her father in this sense, but by the false self who is in his thrall. That is why the true self is released (as in "Purdah" and "Lady Lazarus") when the oppressor is made hateful, and thereby overthrown. Rituals of exorcism in Plath's poetry therefore inherently involve the idea of rebirth. Whenever exorcism, or attempted exorcism, of her father or his proxy occurs, it is always as a preliminary to a rebirth which also entails the expulsion of her false self and spoiled history. Conversely, even where the ritual of rebirth involves no explicit exorcism, it is usually implied.

The logic of sympathetic magic, which appears widely in Plath's late poetry, and not only in rituals of exorcism, might well be called one of the physical laws of the world of her poetry. (The motif of the external soul, shortly to be discussed, also depends upon sympathetic magic.) Such a logic is appropriate for a mythology. That the Moon-muse (or the rival) governs and affects her by a "secret sympathy" is natural to a mythic drama.

The pre-set motifs 'released' in her late poems themselves contain the potential for a sympathetic association of those details which express the same motif. Because the details are not incidental, called forth as they are by her mythology, the sympathy is in a sense guaranteed. The images of blood, violent death, and red poppies, all of which 'release' the death and rebirth motif, have the potential for sympathetically affecting one another through their family resemblance. "Tulips" contains an example of the secret sympathy which operates through family resemblance (that is, through expressing the same motif):

> The tulips are too red in the first place, they hurt me.
>
> . . .
>
> Their redness talks to my wound, it corresponds.[5]

The word "corresponds" refers both to the communication between tulips and wound and to their underlying resemblance. The tulips stand in the same relation to the incipient health or normalcy of the speaker that the poppies in later poems do to her suppressed true self, to (or with) which the poppies correspond. In a sense, this correspondence, and the contrast between it and the speaker's death-in-life existence, *is* the underlying motif in these poems.

It has already been suggested that the Moon-muse has a "sympathetic"—even though not entirely welcome—relation with the protagonist[6] (as mother, totem, familiar, emblem) which can be activated without her consent, just as in "Tulips" she cannot prevent her wound from corresponding with the red flowers. Similarly, the coldness and sterility of the Moon-muse may infect the heroine, causing and not merely representing her state of being. The Moon is thus both "emblem" and "real agent."

"Medusa"

"Medusa," like "Daddy," presents the exorcism of an oppressive parent—in this case the speaker's mother. As in "Daddy," the poem constructs a negative portrait of the presence to be cast out, treating the creation as a scapegoat laden with the evils of her spoiled history, a source and sustainer of her false self, who therefore deserves to be expelled. The poem is particularly significant because the literal mother does not appear elsewhere in the mythology, the role of mother being filled by the Moon-muse. Otherwise, the literal mother's role in the myth is conspicuous by its absence. Though peripheral to the myth, however, the maternal side of her history must be conjured up in order to exorcise it, to make a clean sweep of the past. The strategy is to undo her fate by canceling her historical parents and banishing from the portrait the affection which would only keep her tied to the past and thereby undermine her resolve to affirm a new birth.

The mother in "Medusa" both symbolizes and sustains her daughter's sense of alienation and death-in-life, much as a glimpse of the head of Medusa, the Gorgon of Greek mythology turned one to stone. And she resembles the Medusa jellyfish (named after the Gorgon), the sea-nettle whose poison can be paralyzing.[7] "Medusiform" means "in the form of a bell," and the image of the bell-shaped jellyfish is related to that of the suffocating bell jar (". . . your body / Bottle in which I live").

The many allusions to Catholic religiosity suggest that, like the mother in *The Bell Jar*, the speaker's mother is a Roman Catholic. The body of the jellyfish thus appears as a "ghastly Vatican," which, with its implication of paralyzing and overwhelming authority, parallels the image of her father as a "ghastly statue":

> Who do you think you are?
> A Communion wafer? Blubbery Mary?
> I shall take no bite of your body,
> Bottle in which I live,
>
> Ghastly Vatican.

The Communion wafer, through the eating of which one is mystically identified with Christ, is another reference to sympathetic magic, particularly that aspect of it which Frazer deals with under the heading of "eating the god." That the speaker refuses to take a "bite of your body" means that she does not want to incorporate what her mother means to her. A certain stifling martyrdom is suggested by the "red stigmata at the very center," a reference to Christ's wounds and to the marks, in imitation of these, of psychosomatic (hysterical) bleeding that appear on the skin of persons in a certain state of religious enthusiasm;[8] and by the notion of the mother offering herself up to be eaten in sacrifice. A stanza excised from the final version, but read by Plath for a recording (made on October 30, 1962), confirms this suggestion:

That martyr's smile!
That loony pivot!
That stellar jelly-head!
And a million little suckers loving me!

Another echo of *The Bell Jar* appears here. Esther recalls a remark of her mother's, made shortly before Esther left the mental
hospital:

"We'll take up where we left off, Esther," she had said, with her
sweet, martyr's smile. "We'll act as if all this were a bad dream." [P.
267]

Here, as in "The Disquieting Muses," the daughter feels that her
mother's outlook is a denial of her own experience of life.

"Medusa" pictures the state of death-in-life as a state of incomplete birth. The mother's embrace so stifles her daughter that
she cannot be completely born: the transatlantic "cable" is a birth
cord, a "barnacled umbilicus" (in the final spell of exorcism it becomes an "eely tentacle"—a terrifying image). When the mother
steams over the sea bringing her ministrations, the jellyfish becomes a poisonous placenta, from the grasp of which the daughter
must be delivered.

As in many other poems the true and false selves are represented in terms of a contrast of red with whiteness or paleness. The
heroine represents herself as a fuchsia, a purplish-red flower whose
bell-shape resembles the jellyfish, and her mother's inhibiting presence as

Squeezing the breath from the blood bells
Of the fuchsia. I could draw no breath,
Dead and moneyless,

Overexposed, like an X ray.

Since magnified blood-cells look like coins (as in Dylan Thomas'
"my red veins full of money"),[9] "moneyless" here also means
'without blood.' Lacking color, the fuchsia, a mere X ray of its true
self, would resemble the jellyfish.

To be finally and completely born as her true self she pronounces
her spell of exorcism:

Off, off, eely tentacle!

There is nothing between us.

Casting off the eely tentacle, cutting the "Old barnacled umbilicus, Atlantic cable," parallels the telephone imagery of the broken connection in "Daddy." Here, too, she is finally "through."[10]

RITUALS OF DEATH

The image of death in Sylvia Plath's late poetry usually encodes a deeper, hidden wish for rebirth, the birth of the true self. Certain poems contain clear images of rebirth; but even "Edge," "Death & Co.," and "A Birthday Present," which focus on actual or imminent death, envision death in such a way as to make plain that, although the poem does not overtly indicate its achievement, the ultimate motive for death is rebirth or transcendence. Robert Lowell's remark, in his foreword to the 1966 U.S. edition of *Ariel*, that Plath's poems "tell that life, even when disciplined, is simply not worth it," therefore misses the deeper significance of her death-imagery, and misses too the mythic import of her poems. (Lowell's comments are a useful point of reference, because their context has given them such wide currency and because, although Lowell himself may now feel otherwise, they have been so uncritically accepted. The context of these comments suggests that they should be taken as part of the introduction of the posthumous publication of a fellow poet more than as a final critical statement.)[11]

Lowell's foreword also misses the point in seeing death ever-present in her poetry while overlooking the impulse toward rebirth:

. . . her art's immortality is life's disintegration. The surprise, the shimmering, unwrapped birthday present, the transcendence "into the red eye, the cauldron of morning," and the lover, who are always waiting for her, are Death, her own abrupt and defiant death.[12]

The assumption appears to be that, because she did actually kill herself, "her own abrupt and defiant death" must be the meaning of what in the poems she seeks. But in the examples Lowell mentions nothing is "waiting" for her; it is *she* who actively seeks, invites, or demands, and the ultimate meaning of what she seeks here is not Death.

"A Birthday Present"

Although "A Birthday Present" concludes with an image of the speaker's death, its whole thrust is to express the desire for an envisioned resolution of the death-in-life that is caused by falseness—whether actual falsehoods, or a paralyzing uncertainty that makes life seem tentative and unreal, or the false self that is sustained by its attachment to the 'god' and which suppresses in turn the autonomous true self. The desire for death is then essentially a desire for the death of that condition in a new beginning.

If "the shimmering, unwrapped birthday present" is "her own abrupt and defiant death," it is so only in this very qualified sense. An earlier title of the poem—"The Truth"—indicates the real nature of what the speaker wants. It is a mistake to interpret the later title as simple irony (that she should want *death* for her *birth*day). The present, which can arrive by "annunciation," by "word of mouth," or "by the mail," is clearly a message or information of some kind, and the poem should be seen as expressive of a genuine wish that a miraculous rebirth might somehow result from the purifying confrontation with this truth, even though it be "death."

Uncertainty and irresolution poison the speaker's life. She must resolve her relationship to the "silver-suited" man (her husband) in order to be "let . . . go . . . whole," a phrase which applies not only to herself but also to the truth. Only by getting the whole truth can she hope to recover her whole (true) self; and perhaps only the certainty of a clean break can end her oppressed, paralyzed state of being.

Her present life, stifled and unreal, resembles life in a bell jar:

> If you only knew how the veils were killing my days.
> . . .
> . . . the clouds are like cotton—
> . . . They are carbon monoxide.

Only a real living in the present would dispel these clouds, and for this she requires the truth. The gift she now wants is, precisely, the vitality of the *present*—her days free of the smothering veils of uncertainty and the "cold, dead center / Where spilt lives congeal and stiffen to history" (not just the obvious "lives" that are spilt in sex, but their own lives—hers and her husband's).

To dispel the clouds she must know the whole truth, which her husband can give her—for him the veils (a conventional symbol of what hides Truth or God from the seeker; reality from the person clouded by illusion) are "only transparencies, clear air." Yet she does not want what she knows, the truth that "breathes from my sheets," to be confirmed. Although uncertainty kills her days,[13] she fears that really being let go will be intolerable, will be death.

In "A Birthday Present" (as in "The Jailor," "The Courage of Shutting-Up," "Purdah," and other late poems), the truth supports the true self (or the potentiality for the rebirth or recovery of the true self) while lies, deceits, and self-delusions elicit or reinforce the false self, or death-in-life. To destroy her false self, she must destroy the lie of the world she inhabits. Though that would be death, it would have "a nobility," for the subject of that death, the false self with the "cold, dead center," is in a sense already dead:

> After all, I am alive only by accident.

> I would have killed myself gladly that time any possible way.

Her state of suffocation, incompleteness, and falseness is expressed by images of whiteness or semitransparency (frost, "clouds," "cotton," "babies' bedding"), while transparency and clarity represent truth. These associations appear to be rooted in Greek mythology, in which false dreams pass through the white, semitransparent Gate of Ivory, one of the two gates through which dreams pass from the underworld into the world of sleep. While the semitransparency of the Ivory Gate falsifies dreams, they pass undistorted through the transparent Gate of Horn.[14] The poem specifically mentions "ivory" in this connection:

> Now there are these veils, shimmering like curtains,

The diaphanous satins of a January window
White as babies' bedding and glittering with dead breath.
  O ivory!

  It must be a tusk there, a ghost-column.

Since the present is veiled in white, it too appears to be white: "bones," "a pearl button," or "a tusk." But she cannot be sure. It is worth recalling here that the Moon and the rival are carriers of whiteness and are associated both with "pallor" and with ivory: the barren woman has an "ivory" body; the moon has "ivory powders." Their relation to the whiteness of falsity or death-in-life (exemplified by the veils and the clouds) is apparent.

The opposition of blurred and smothering uncertainty and falseness to the sharp and clear knowledge of the truth appears in the contrast between death by butchery and a death "pure and clean." Denial of full truth is denial of her true self: being cut off from her self is like being cut up, and she feels as if she were undergoing a prolonged mutilation, like an animal inspected, priced, and butchered alive piece by piece:

  . . . O adding machine—

Is it impossible for you to let something go and have it
  go whole?
Must you stamp each piece in purple,

Must you kill what you can?

She fears that the truth, too, will be mutilated and parceled out: "Let it not come by the mail, finger by finger,"[15] so that by the time she possesses the corpus of truth, she will be too old and too numb to make a new life. These images of butchery are quite unlike the action of the knife of truth envisioned at the end of the poem, which does not "carve," but 'enters' the side—painlessly and sacramentally—as if it were not a knife but a ray of light.

The relation between truth and falseness in "A Birthday Present" closely resembles that in Tolstoy's *Death of Ivan Ilyitch*. The numerous parallels between the two works suggest that Tolstoy's story influenced this and perhaps other of her writings.[16]

Ivan Ilyitch knows he is about to die, yet eventually this becomes less upsetting to him than the refusal of others to acknowledge the truth of his condition. Their refusal traps him in a life of falseness, a "ceremonial lie" maintained by his family and friends for their own convenience. He yearns for the "absolute truth [to] become manifest."[17] Only by resolving the falseness in this way can he die well. A similar contrast between a suffocating lie and the absolute truth occurs in "A Birthday Present," which also contains several stylistic and verbal echoes of *Ivan Ilyitch*, one of which is the repeated reference to the birthday present as "it." After admitting to himself that he will soon die, Ivan Ilyitch for a time thinks obsessively about "It." Although this preoccupation is eventually overshadowed by a preoccupation with the *truth* about "It," Death at first seems to persecute him:

Ivan Ilyitch perceived it, tried to turn his thoughts from it; but it took its course, and it came up and stood directly before him, and gazed at him: . . . he began . . . to ask himself,—
    "Is there nothing true save It?" . . .
    . . . other shelter came along . . . but . . . grew transparent, as though It became visible through all, and nothing could hide it. . . .
    . . . suddenly It gleamed through the shelter: he saw *It*. It gleamed:
. . . he cannot forget it, and It clearly gazes at him from among the flowers.[18]

Similarly, in "A Birthday Present," the undisclosed but partly perceived "it"—the specter of truth which 'gleams'—gives to the world the translucency of a veil, symbolizing suffocating uncertainty and half-suspected truth. Plath's repetition of "it"—like Tolstoy's—conveys the insistent everpresence of what is hidden:

What is this, behind this veil, is *it* ugly, is *it* beautiful?
It is shimmering, has *it* breasts, has *it* edges?

I am sure *it* is unique, I am sure *it* is just what I want.
. . .
But *it* shimmers, *it* does not stop, and I think *it* wants me.
. . .
Let us sit down to *it*, one on either side, admiring the gleam,

The glaze, the mirrory variety of *it*. [Italics added.]

The "it" here refers, however, not so much to Death as to the truth. When the speaker says

> If it were death

> I would admire the deep gravity of it, its timeless eyes.
> I would know you were serious. . . .

she uses death (or rather killing, the giving of death) as a metaphor for delivering brutal truth, contrasting the authenticity of such an act with the inauthenticity of evasion. The victim of this "death" would be the false self.

Ivan Ilyitch's eventual death exemplifies the achievement of transcendence when a dying person relinquishes (false) hope, a process described by Russell Noyes:

With the end of uncertainty, anxiety falls away and the event of death itself is faced with calm. Poe . . . related this emotion to *the losing of uncertain hope.*[19] [Italics added.]

As long as one struggles in the face of imminent death one suffers in false hope, but the acceptance of death leads to a transfiguring reconciliation. Noyes quotes the death scene of Ivan Ilyitch as an illustration of such transcendence:

. . . it became clear to him that all he had been tortured by and been unable to throw off was now falling away of itself, falling away on two sides, ten sides, all sides at once. . . . He searched for his accustomed terror of death and could not find it. Where was death? What was death? There was no fear because there was no death. There was light instead of death.[20]

The logic of "A Birthday Present" is not identical with that of *Ivan Ilyitch*, but analogous to it. The speaker is attached to and suffocated by a false hope: not of life, but that somehow what is probably an illusion in which she has invested her life is not false. Because the "adding machine" does not let her go whole, she remains enmired in an impossible situation and false hope maintains her false self. The resolution she envisions parallels Ivan Ilyitch's relinquishing of false hope (of life in his case) and his achievement of transcendence.

The details of the sacrifice with which the poem concludes reveal it as essentially a ritual of purification and rebirth:

> And the knife not carve, but enter
>
> Pure and clean as the cry of a baby,
> And the universe slide from my side.

Two other of the late poems connect the truth with the image of a knife. In "A Secret," the secret is "A knife that can be taken out / To pare nails, / To lever the dirt." The poem makes clear that, above all, the secret is something *true*, and from this it derives its power and threat. The idea of truth as a knife that might kill occurs also in a line excised from "Burning the Letters": "You know I would die on truth like a straight kitchen knife." In this poem, too, the power of truth contrasts with the paralyzing effect of uncertainty and false hope, and an image of liberating violence concludes the poem. (In both "Burning the Letters" and "A Birthday Present," the association of knife, truth, and kitchen suggests that the kitchen is a peculiarly appropriate setting for rituals intended to resolve a mythic domestic drama.)

While the heroine may imply that only the lack of confirmation of the truth—the truth that would finally kill her false hope—keeps her from killing herself, she still demands that confirmation: not because she seeks death, but because only by really letting go can she achieve transfiguration. The phrase "the universe slide from my side" embodies this duality, for it represents at once the ebb of consciousness—the loss of her world—as the loss of blood; and the loss of ego (or false self) and the consequent achievement of a transcendent unity, as the giving of birth.

The knife-wound which draws forth the universe from her side might suggest the spear-wound in Christ's side, also associated both with death and resurrection. The heroine therefore resembles both Christ and Mary; early in the poem she ironically awaits the "annunciation" of a miraculous birth, tacitly comparing her adherence to the rules of cookery ("Measuring the flour, cutting off the surplus, / Adhering to rules, to rules, to rules") with the purity of Mary. The birth of purity from impurity—of her true self ("the universe") from her false self—would be miraculous, like the birth and resurrection of Christ.

Several critics have seized on the sexual imagery of the knife-wound—which does of course exist: the phallic entry of the knife does produce a "baby"—"the universe." But this is a superficial level of meaning in the poem, which the obvious sexual metaphor alone does little to explain.

Many readers are disconcerted by Plath's frank interest in images of death and perhaps this is why a poem such as "A Birthday Present" is so easily misjudged. The awareness that Sylvia Plath actually did kill herself, together with the centrality of death in her poems, seems by some curious logic enough to foreclose for those readers the issue of what such imagery (and even her suicide) means. Possibly, too, the current anxiety and consequent taboos about death (the fruit of a world-view that denies the possibility of transcendence and denies therefore the meaningfulness of death—and, ultimately, of life) have something to do with the view of her poetry as obscenely morbid, and with the morbid fascination it holds for some. Such readings of "A Birthday Present" ignore what the poem—and her poetry in general—clearly and steadily implies.

"The Bee Meeting"

In primitive society the theme of rebirth often ·finds concrete representation in the ancient and widespread notion of the separable or external soul. This theme, mentioned in *The White Goddess*, is perhaps the major theme in *The Golden Bough*, the golden bough being the embodied representation of the soul of the sacred priest-king at Nemi. The bough, probably a branch of mistletoe, was plucked by a challenger for the sacred office, who would properly succeed the incumbent by slaying him. The defeat of the old king in a duel to the death demonstrated his inadequacy to continue the kingship and the victor's right to succession. The sacred kingship continued unaffected through this change and thus it continually renewed itself, just like its embodied representation (through sympathetic magic), the golden bough.

The office of the kingship, rather than the individual bodily or ego form of the incumbent, was the incumbent's true self. Faith in his sacred office was faith in his true immortality. A priest-king would fight for his life as a sacred duty, but not—if he had faith— out of fear for his life, for even if he were defeated, the immortality of his true self, the sacred kingship resident in the golden bough, was guaranteed. Whether he lived or died, it was an equally sacred event. The meaning of such a life is properly called transcendent.

Plath's work contains several instances in which, as a means of expressing her mythic sense of rebirth, a separable or external soul embodies the true self. Allusions as well as direct references to this idea occur throughout her poetry. (The use of this idea to express the notions of true self and rebirth does not of course require a belief in literal immortality.)

Her interest in this theme was established as early as her under- graduate thesis, in which the idea of a separable soul was an or- ganizing principle; in it she treated the theme as a variation on the interrelated motifs of false and true selves and death and rebirth. Her thesis cited Otto Rank's essay "The Double as Immortal Self," which traces the origin of the double as harbinger of death to—and finds it a degenerate form of—belief in the double as one's immortal (and separable) soul.

Something like a separable soul appears in "The Stones":

> The vase, reconstructed, houses
> The elusive rose.

Similarly, the poem "In Plaster" depicts a woman encased in plaster who thinks of herself as the "soul" of the "new absolutely white person" (the cast):

> I gave her a soul, I bloomed out of her as a rose
> Blooms out of a vase of not very valuable porcelain, . . .

In "Last Words," the speaker does not "trust the spirit" because it "escapes like steam / In dreams," and she therefore wryly declares her allegiance to "things." In "Surgeon at 2 a.m.," the surgeon observes the "white light" of the operating room, and then, think- ing of the anesthetized patient, says:

> . . . The soul is another light.
> I have not seen it; . . .
> Tonight it has receded like a ship's light.

Frazer mentions that the separable soul was often depicted as a light (he refers, for example, to a witch whose "life" was a "light" kept in an egg). In the late poem "Stopped Dead," the speaker asks her fellow accident victim:

> Where do you stash your life?
>
> Is it a penny, a pearl—
> Your soul, your soul?

Next only to the Moon, the most compelling and complex embodiment of the separable soul in Plath's late poetry is the queen bee, which might (like the Moon in some cases) be called a totem of the protagonist. According to Frazer, totems are "the receptacle in which a man keeps his life" (p. 800). The substance of totemic death and resurrection rituals "consists in extracting the youth's soul in order to transfer it to his totem. . . . The lad dies as a man and comes to life again as an animal; the animal's soul is now in him, and his human soul is in the animal" (p. 802). Something akin to this ritual appears to have occurred between Plath's heroine and the queen bee.

All of Plath's "bee" poems are charged with special significance because the bee is her family emblem, both in her life (Otto Plath was an entomologist, an authority on bumblebees), and in her mythology; and the mention of bees implicitly involves the origin of her myth (the death of her beekeeper father) and its pattern (the struggle to escape death-in-life or the false self, through the recovery of her true "queen bee" self).

The symbol of the queen bee in Plath's poetry fulfills its function with even greater justice than did the golden bough in representing the sacred office at Nemi. The golden bough exemplified continuity and regeneration. The queen bee provides as well a dramatic reenactment of mythical rebirth, for younger queens will fight duels to the death with the incumbent, just as did the challengers at Nemi.

The idea of the queen bee as the separable soul or totem of the protagonist was incipient in "The Beekeeper's Daughter": in it she depicts her attachment to her dead father as the marriage of a queen bee. The idea comes into its own in the *Ariel* poems, particularly in "The Bee Meeting" and "Stings" (part of her cycle of five "bee" poems: "The Bee Meeting," "The Arrival of the Bee Box," "Stings," "The Swarm," and "Wintering," all of which were composed within a single week). Both these poems begin with a search for a queen bee and end with the disclosure of a mysterious sympathetic identification between the speaker and the queen.

Several levels of meaning operate in "The Bee Meeting," a particularly easy poem to misinterpret because even its overt level has an air of unreality. A group of good folk from an English village (the midwife, the secretary of bees, the sexton, the rector, and others), all of whom are familiar to the speaker, convene for a "bee meeting." The poem does not explain why all of them are needed for the "operation" they perform—which results in the protection of the queen bee from the virgins who would kill her when they emerged from their cells. The virgins are taken away and "there will be no killing." The old queen is not seen, either before or after their removal.

The speaker's motives for participating in this event are not clear; her presence seems both voluntary and passively helpless. Despite her protective clothing she remains terrified of the bees. When the removal of the virgins is complete, she feels exhausted, and 'blacks out' as bees swarm around her. She next sees the villagers removing their protective covering and shaking hands with one another, and she wonders, "Whose is that long white box in the grove, what have they accomplished, why am I cold."

Though that is the overt meaning of the event, its significance for the heroine is anything but straightforward. Ominous and dream-like from the start ("Who are these people at the bridge to meet me? They are the villagers"), what on one level is a fear of the bees is on the dream-like level a fear of the villagers, who are unrecognizably transformed in their protective gear; even "Their smiles and their voices are changing." The dream-like event in the "grove" to which they are leading her may perhaps be a sacred ritual (appropriately, the performers include the sexton and the rector, transformed with the others from their mundane roles into sacred functionaries, "knights in visors") in which the heroine is the initiate; or, instead, "Is it some operation that is taking place?" In either case, its meaning is that "they are making me one of them."

The poem sustains nearly to its end the ambiguity of the dream-like level, that is, the uncertainty whether to view the event as a sacred ritual or some surgical operation. The speaker's acquiescence, despite her fear, in whatever is in store for her could evince equally the attitude of a patient being led to surgery or that of an initiate into a sacred mystery:

> They are leading me to the shorn grove, the circle of hives.
> Is it the hawthorn that smells so sick?
> The barren body of hawthorn, etherizing its children.
> . . .
> It is the surgeon my neighbors are waiting for,
> This apparition in a green helmet,
> Shining gloves and white suit.
> Is it the butcher, the grocer, the postman, someone I know?

The "shorn grove" could just as well echo the ritual depilation of the initiate or the preparatory shaving of the surgical patient. What seemed at first to be "blood clots"—an ominous portent of surgery—revealed themselves to be bean flowers, "scarlet flowers that will one day be edible"—a promised metamorphosis with ritualistic associations. Moreover, as Graves mentions, beans are associated with rebirth—they were thought to contain new souls. The barren hawthorn "etherizing its children"—perhaps this is what is happening to her—is associated with death, as beans are with birth. Graves says that the hawthorn was "the tree of enforced chastity" (it would therefore be "barren"), and associated with death. (Cardea, a form of the White Goddess, cast spells with hawthorn and could enlist it to destroy children.) Plath's emblematic colors (and those of the White Goddess)—red, white, and black—characterize the scene. Here black (the color of death) and white (the color of birth or sickness) dominate.

The true character of the action is finally disclosed in terms of what the villagers do to the heroine's external soul, the queen bee.

The event has not been a sacred ritual, but something both secular and profane. At the overt level, what (for all the poem tells us) is an act of mercy, the saving of the life of the "old, old, old" queen bee by the well-meaning villagers, is at the dream-like level of the event the subversion of a sacred order. In "Stings," the companion poem to this, such a queen bee

> . . . is old,
> Her wings torn shawls, her long body
> Rubbed of its plush—
> Poor and bare and unqueenly and even shameful.

In the terms of sacred kingship, only one test can determine such a queen's worthiness for her office.

The priest-kings at Nemi owed their incumbency to craft as much as strength. But (as Frazer says of the sacred kings of Shilluk) when the challenger appeared, "it was a point of honour with the king not to call the herdsmen [the only people nearby] to his assistance" (p. 312). The queen bee of the poem might be "hiding, . . . She is very clever. / She is old, old, old, she must live another year, and she knows it." That is, she might survive another year by the stealth she already displays. When external intervention saves her: "The old queen does not show herself, is she so ungrateful?"—only the understanding that the queen bee is the incumbent of a sacred queenship can make sense of this question. The answer must be the same as it would be if some sentimental and faithless meddlers had so 'saved' the priest-king at Nemi. The word "duel" conveys the ritualistically appropriate meaning. The "murderess" will "inevitably" (in the sacred order—but not if the sacred order is subverted) "win," to fly freely "into a heaven that loves her."

The speaker thus learns just how "they are making me one of them." The villagers' act is one of faithlessness; it represents the evasion of the fearful, not the transcendence of fear. Though she suddenly achieves the courage to face the fearful ("Pillar of white in a blackout of knives. / I am the magician's girl who does not flinch"),[21] the event has gone in the opposite direction. It has not been a sacred ritual, but a surgical operation. Like members of a surgical team unmasking after an operation and congratulating one another, "The villagers are untying their disguises, they are shaking hands." Now it is clear "Whose is that long white box in the grove, what have they accomplished, why am I cold."

Though the speaker was prepared to undergo a ritual ordeal in order to realize her true self, and though she did experience a moment of identification with the sacred queenship, which implies personal fearlessness as a manifestation of transcendence, the event turned out to be an act of surgery; instead of exorcising her false self, it excised her principle of vitality. So she is left "cold," unlike Lady Lazarus whose unflinching confrontation of death ends in a fiery virgin rebirth.

The villagers represent the forces in the life of the speaker which undermine its principle of vitality (in the name of life, which is really death-in-life) just as they subvert the 'inevitable' defeat and succession of the old queen bee by her virgin rival. In this they are like zealous missionaries who sabotage a bloody savage ritual, the transcendent meaning of which is beyond their comprehension.[22]

"Death & Co."

Sylvia Plath described "Death & Co." as a poem

. . . about the double or schizophrenic nature of death—the marmoreal coldness of Blake's death mask, say, hand in glove with the fearful softness of worms, water and the other katabolists. I imagine these two aspects of death as two men, two business friends, who have come to call.[23]

In this poem, Plath parodies two conventional representations of physical death, the abstract aspect of finality and the tangible aspect of decay. The first becomes in her poem a cold, cadaverous, condor-like businessman who delivers a sales pitch, urging "how sweet / The babies look in their hospital / Icebox," insinuating that death might do as much for her, make her that pure and that sweet. His colleague, who parodies the idea of Death as Lover or Bridegroom, is sleazy and repellent: a phony, theatrical, sexually ambiguous character, presumptuously smiling and smoking.

The last five lines of the poem sound an ominous, apprehensive note:

> The frost makes a flower,
> The dew makes a star.
> The dead bell,
> The dead bell.
>
> Somebody's done for.

This final incantation conjures up notions of perfection or completeness achieved through images of transformation—in essence, metamorphoses. The images in the lines "The frost makes a flower, / The dew makes a star," record the transformation of something from a transitory into a relatively more permanent state, and the passage of time, from night (frost) to morning (dew). When dawn finally arrives, "the dead bell" is doubtless ringing for her. What that death may mean has been encoded in the preceding transformations (from frost to flower, from dew to star), each alluding to a familiar religious attitude toward death. The first intimates a pantheistic reabsorption into nature, and the second suggests the way some mythological characters become constellations when they die.

Perhaps the speaker will also take a more permanent form and 'make' something new, achieving the finality and perfection of a work of art, her death the magical third in the series of transformations. The symmetry of the final lines, and the poem's association of death with the change from night to day, suggest that it may. But though these images imply transcendence through reference to the mythic meanings of death, they do not ultimately constitute more than a feeble protest ("I do not stir") against an inevitable physical doom. In this respect—though this might not at first be apparent—"Death & Co." differs considerably from "Edge," in which the physical aspects of death are irrelevant—or if relevant, unequivocally transcended.

"Edge"

The heroes of Shakespeare convey to us through their looks, or through the metaphorical patterns of their speech, the sudden enlargement of their vision, their ecstasy at the approach of death: . . . They have become God or Mother Goddess, the pelican, "My baby at my breast," but all must be cold; no actress has ever sobbed when she played Cleopatra, even the shallow brain of a producer has never thought of such a thing. The supernatural is present . . . the thermometer falls, . . . There may be in this or that detail painful tragedy, but in the whole work none. I have heard Lady Gregory say, rejecting some play in the modern manner sent to the Abbey Theatre, "Tragedy must be a joy to the man who dies."

W. B. Yeats
"A General Introduction for my Work"

The poem "Edge" presents the final scene of Sylvia Plath's drama as the concluding tableau in a ritualistically staged tragedy. It does not itself constitute a ritual so much as present the outcome of some ritual:

> The woman is perfected.
> Her dead
>
> Body wears the smile of accomplishment,
> The illusion of a Greek necessity
>
> Flows in the scrolls of her toga,
> Her bare
>
> Feet seem to be saying:
> We have come so far, it is over.
>
> Each dead child coiled, a white serpent,
> One at each little
>
> Pitcher of milk, now empty.
> She has folded
>
> Them back into her body as petals
> Of a rose close when the garden
>
> Stiffens and odors bleed
> From the sweet, deep throats of the night flower.
>
> The moon has nothing to be sad about,
> Staring from her hood of bone.
>
> She is used to this sort of thing.
> Her blacks crackle and drag.

The protagonist and her history lie immune to further change, completed and perfected. Though there is death, the vision is not of mere physical extinction, as in "Berck-Plage." The aspect of extinction is curiously neutralized by the movement of the poem from the dead woman to the "visiting moon," raising the meaning of the event to another level.

Insofar as "Edge" embodies the final scene of a drama, it asserts transcendence through completion (rather than through a more literal rebirth). "It is over,"[24] and the details of the poem confirm this. Everything appears fixed and permanent, surveyed from a great height, as if under the aspect of eternity. Both the Moon, the guiding spirit of the drama, and the speaker share this celestial perspective which was dramatically indicated in an early version of the first line:

> *Down there* the dead woman is perfected.
>
> [Italics added.]

The Moon illuminates the woman in her white toga, and the dead 'white serpents,' the children whose whiteness also identifies them as participants in the lunar drama. The Moon-muse has reclaimed her daughter just as the daughter has reclaimed and reabsorbed her own children. In this frozen and eternal tableau, death is not imminent but an absolute condition. Nothing hints that, like Lady Lazarus, this woman will suddenly be resurrected. "Edge" presents a different kind of transcendence.

Several details indicate that Sylvia Plath conceived the dead woman to be someone like Shakespeare's Cleopatra. Both are associated with Greece and Rome. The dead woman wears a Roman death-gown with the "illusion of a Greek necessity." Cleopatra, too, is identified with both Greece and Rome. (Her connection with Rome is more apparent; but she was also a Greek, a member of the Ptolemy family: "it is a mistake to think of her as an Egyptian.")[25] Further, the dead children, coiled serpents who lie at the breasts that once nursed them, recall the serpent (the asp) which Cleopatra put to her breast to kill herself, and which she spoke of as her child:

> Dost thou not see my baby at my breast,
> That sucks the nurse asleep?[26]
>
> [V.ii.312–13]

For Cleopatra, death will perfect and fix the meaning of her life; likewise the speaker in "Edge" claims that death has "perfected" the woman, a theme reiterated in the line—later excised—"Now nothing can happen." Cleopatra expressed a similar sentiment that death would perfect her life, not only protecting her from the danger of ending it in a degrading captivity, but insuring it forever against all contingency:

> . . . and it is great
> To do that thing that ends all other deeds;
> Which shackles accidents and bolts up change; . . .
>
> [V.ii.4–6]

Since death completes the meaning of her life, Cleopatra places a high value on dying nobly and well:

> . . . what's brave, what's noble,
> Let's do it after the high Roman fashion,
> And make death proud to take us.[27]
>
> [IV.xv.86–88]

Shakespeare's Cleopatra is also, according to Robert Graves, an incarnation of the Moon-goddess:

> . . . poets can be well judged by the accuracy of their portrayal of the White Goddess. Shakespeare knew and feared her. . . . He shows her . . . in *Macbeth* as the Triple Hecate presiding over the witches' cauldron, for it is her spirit that takes possession of Lady Macbeth and inspires her to murder King Duncan; and as the magnificent and wanton Cleopatra by love of whom Antony is destroyed. [P. 424]

These two manifestations of the White Goddess correspond to the witch-like Moon (whose "blacks crackle and drag") and to the dead heroine.

Shakespeare's Cleopatra acknowledges the moon as her planet in disowning it when, determined to die, she renounces change:

> My resolution's plac'd, and I have nothing
> Of woman in me; now from head to foot

I am marble-constant; now the fleeting moon
No planet is of mine.

[V.ii.238–41]

Plath, in an early draft of "Elm," had identified the Moon as "that gold Cleopatra." Like that of the Moon as the heroine's mother, the association appears both among the first and the last of the late poems.

Cleopatra as a White Goddess heroine (who 'destroys' men) has a natural affinity with other such types of the Goddess, as well as with the queen bee and Lady Lazarus aspects of Plath's protagonist. Such figures are self-sufficient, giving birth either to themselves or to their worlds. The dead woman in "Edge," reversing the process of birth, has reabsorbed her world and her children, an act which emphasizes the perfectedness of her life. The Moon has, similarly, absorbed the woman's fate back into itself.

The children emblemize a certain aspect of the heroine's history, and to that extent they are implicated in their mother's death; perhaps they have drained her, or "[sucked] the nurse asleep." By reabsorbing them she reconciles herself to them and to the life they represent, in a way that goes beyond judgment or blame:

> She has folded
>
> Them back into her body as petals
> Of a rose close . . .

Here she does not see the children as other than herself, not as mere creations which have turned on her, nor as two roses 'handed' to her, but as an inalienable part of herself.[28]

Although "Edge" presents a vision of death, the terms in which it is envisioned contradict the superficial reading that Plath is merely morbidly fascinated with the prospect of personal annihilation—one would not think of calling Cleopatra a morbid suicide. Cleopatra's obstacles were, of course, external, and many of the afflictions in Plath's poetry—and life—are not. It is nevertheless significant that in her poems death so often appears in noble, mythic terms. "Edge" may be a harrowing poem for its note of finality (together with the extraneous knowledge that it was one of the last two poems Plath wrote before she killed herself),[29] but it cannot be called a depressed poem. Its pervasive clarity and calm have been widely acknowledged. Plath's dying heroines, in poems such as "A Birthday Present" and "Edge," have little in common with stereotypes of suicidal women (in whose actions a sense of the *meaning* of death does not even figure), and a great deal in common with tragic heroines who die calmly and nobly.

RITUALS OF REBIRTH

All of the late poems which involve mythic rebirth were written within a period of a few weeks, in the autumn of 1962, when Plath was at her most prolific. A few of the very last poems consider the possibility that even a new mythic self might ultimately only present the same problem, that even striving for the same *type* of self—'me, only different'—might be self-defeating, and that to achieve the desired rebirth the very forms of self and drama might have to be transcended. Poems which approach this more radical form of rebirth will be discussed in the chapter titled "Beyond Drama."

"Stings"

In "Stings," the speaker achieves the rebirth denied her in its companion poem, "The Bee Meeting." Both poems identify her true self with the sacred queenship; in "Stings," it is the queenship that is immortal rather than the individual queen bee, as is borne out by the line, "Is she dead, is she sleeping?" Even though the queen bee may be "dead," the heroine still has "a self to recover, a queen." (The queen has, in a sense, been dead; but now she flies "over the engine that killed her.") In this way Plath uses the idea of the queenship with its ongoing immortality to express that the true self can always be recovered, however dormant or dead, while the false self (the apparent vehicle of the true self) can *really* be permanently killed or altered.

The recovery of the true self with which "Stings" ends signals rejection of the role of "drudge" mentioned earlier in the poem in the lines:

> I am no drudge
> Though for years I have eaten dust
> And dried plates with my dense hair.
>
> And seen my strangeness evaporate, . . .

These powerful images of abasement, describing her previous condition (once she ate dust, the curse visited upon the serpent who had tempted Eve), counterbalance the fierce and exultant recovery of the queen bee self which also implies victory over the male to whom the false self has been servile—a reversal of Mary Magdalene's case. Drudgery—washing Jesus' feet with her tears and drying them with her hair; repentance; submission to the god and normalcy; losing her "strangeness"—is Mary Magdalene's salvation. For the speaker of "Stings" it is death-in-life.

Identification of the true self with the sacred queenship assures escape from drudgery. A queen bee, in entomology a 'perfect female,' can start a new hive independently. The domesticated "drudges" (the worker bees), 'imperfect females' who "work without thinking" and "only scurry," represent the rejected, slavish role—for them the main topics of interest are household information and sexual gossip: "Whose news is the open cherry, the open clover."

The role of queen bee entails the destruction of male bees, the drones—in particular, the one with whom she mates. Not only does this represent the heroine's triumph over husband and father, but also over the domesticity of "The mausoleum, the wax house"[30] —a wax museum where everything is lifelike but dead.

The husband is tacitly rejected at the end of the poem, and perhaps he and her father are both exorcised earlier in the guise of the scapegoat. On the overt level, the victim of the stings appears to be a stranger—or is it that the speaker willfully excludes him: "He has nothing to do with the bee-seller or with me," meaning also that *she* wishes to have nothing to do with him. Yet despite his magical, other-dimensional ghostliness, he also acts as "scape-goat" and as such must have enough of a connection with her to make him appropriate to carry off her sins. The sympathetic link exists at least partly through a sort of male drudgery:

> He was sweet,
>
> The sweat of his efforts a rain
> Tugging the world to fruit.
> The bees found him out,
> Molding onto his lips like lies,
> Complicating his features.

His "efforts" parallel her domestic drudgery (his "sweat . . . a rain" resembles her tears, implied in the Mary Magdalene parallel), including childbirth—although his "tugging the world to fruit" is a false and empty imitation. These lines strongly imply a composite husband/father scapegoat, as in "Daddy." One tugs her world to fruit by making her bear fruit—by fathering her children (and perhaps this image also implies her dependence on him if *she* is the world); and the other brings forth her world by fathering *her*. Bees, too, have a dual function in defining the scapegoat as a husband/father. The figure in the poem has an interest in bees (his "efforts," at least in part, appear directed toward them), and this suggests her father; but the same bees that link her to her father (and through him to the larger pattern of mourning the god) also avenge her within the pattern by stinging the scapegoat —'finding him out,' sacrificing themselves in order to expose him. (On the biographical level, a letter of hers describes an episode in which bees set upon her husband.) It is this example she declines to follow—refusing to identify herself with the self-sacrificing female bees (males are stingless), or to martyr herself for the sake of the "wax house" (both her past and present houses—in relation to these two males—being a kind of death):

> They thought death was worth it, but I
> Have a self to recover, a queen.

The heroine in "Stings" achieves rebirth by a sudden sympathetic identification with the queenship of a hive she herself owns, and which (in sharp contrast to the passive, terrified initiate in "The Bee Meeting"), she controls:

> It is almost over.
> I am in control.

The color of the queen bee's "lion-red body" signifies recovery of the true self. Comparing the bee to a lioness adds a heroic dimension which is awesome ("terrible"), threatening ("red scar"), and supernatural ("red comet"). There are related associations in both "Ariel" ("God's lioness, / How one we grow") and "Purdah" ("I shall unloose . . . The lioness"), in which the color red also figures, and where the lioness represents either a sacramental recovery of a purer self (the speaker of "Ariel," identified with "God's lioness," plunges into "the red / Eye, the cauldron of morning"), or a violent release of the suppressed true self (the "lioness" in "Purdah" who threatens a bloody death).

"Stopped Dead"

Not only "Stings," but "Stopped Dead," "Lady Lazarus," and "Purdah" all present, in terms of the three pairs of motifs, a ritual of rebirth accompanied by the downfall of a male, along with whom the speaker's false self also dies. In "Stopped Dead," this pattern is 'released' through an imagined motor accident, a confrontation with death in which rebirth is implicit, as the first two lines make clear:

> A squeal of brakes.
> Or is it a birth cry?

The speaker and her traveling companion, an "Uncle, pants factory Fatso, millionaire," have squealed to a halt over the edge of a cliff and are "hung out over the dead drop." The uncle's case is hopeless: he is awkward, fat, and in any case "out cold"; but she has a chance for a miraculous escape:[31]

> I'll . . .
> Simply open the door and step out of the car
> And live in Gibraltar on air, on air.

The accident provides her opportunity to escape from an oppressive life—"There's always a bloody baby in the air." And she does not seem to mind that the uncle cannot be saved. She imagines that he suspects her—perhaps rightly—of harboring murderous impulses toward him, and so, by means of ironical, rhetorical questions (addressed to his unconscious form), she tells him that she, unlike Hamlet, does not plan murder:

> Who do you think I am,
> Uncle, uncle?
> Sad Hamlet, with a knife?

The next lines make clear that although the uncle's physical body may die, he could be saved through rescue of his separable soul:

> Where do you stash your life?
>
> Is it a penny, a pearl—
> Your soul, your soul?

The word "stash" recalls Frazer's remark that a totem is like a bank in which one can deposit one's soul for safekeeping. Plath presents the uncle's body as the gross "receptacle" (Frazer's term) for his soul, a pure, tiny object. Implicitly, the speaker can likewise, through a liberating confrontation with death, leave behind her body—"out cold" (in a sense, this is what has occurred in "Edge")—shedding as well her oppressive life, the screaming babies, and the emotional excess represented by the scenery:

> Is that Spain down there?
> Red and yellow, two passionate hot metals
> Writhing and sighing, . . .
> . . .
> It's violent.

A common type of separable soul story tells of a queen or princess held captive by an evil male (a giant, ogre, or bad magician) whose external soul makes him appear invulnerable. He hides this "soul, heart, life, or death (as it is variously called)" (Frazer, p. 775) in some object outside his body, such as a stone, bird, or fish. In this type of tale the princess often pretends great concern for the ogre, and so tricks him into revealing the hiding place. To reassure her that he is safe from death, he gives her a complete account of his invulnerability, describing in detail where he hides his soul. She or her rescuer can then find and destroy it and effect her escape.

In "Stopped Dead," too, the speaker expresses concern and asks, "Where do you stash your life?" (the question echoes many fairy stories, including the tale mentioned by Frazer in which "an ogre is asked by his daughter, 'Papa, where do you keep your soul?' " [p. 776]). Perhaps the speaker in "Stopped Dead" really does intend to "carry it off" to safety, but the clear parallel to the princess and the ogre sort of story argues that she regards him as some sort of symbol of her oppression. Free of him (or of what he represents), she might have a new life, living on air and fulfilling the new birth promised in the opening lines.

There is another possible interpretation, that the poem describes the rebirth of a male speaker and his imagined liberation from domesticity, the screaming babies and—or—a burdensome history, which for him is a false life; and his desire for rebirth into an existence where he can be without responsibility and can live on air. (The attitude toward the babies is more in keeping with the interpretation that this is a male persona.) This would be similar to adopting the perspective of the husband in "Amnesiac" who achieves an ironic sort of new life by conveniently forgetting his old one—his "Name, house, . . . little toy wife . . . Four babies and a cocker!" If the speaker in "Stopped Dead" is male, then the offer to "carry it [the soul] off like a rich pretty girl" is a fantasy of eloping with the millionaire uncle's "life"—with his money (the soul *is* negotiable currency, a "penny" or a "pearl" that can be 'stashed')—as he would elope with a beautiful rich girl.

The ambiguity of the speaker's gender may have been deliberate, for the poem would then cut both ways—portraying the woman's envisioned rebirth, her freedom from the false self caused by her absent mate, as well as pointedly parodying the husband's fantasy of freedom from domesticity, or his escape or absence which has precipitated *her* desire for rebirth. In either case, the important point is the sense of a strong identification with a speaker (as with the male speaker of "Paralytic"—the "Amnesiac" cannot really be called the speaker of that poem because he only says the last three lines) who undergoes, or is about to undergo, rebirth.[32]

"Lady Lazarus"

In his "Memoir" on Sylvia Plath, Alvarez mentions her "queer conception of the adult as a survivor, an imaginary Jew from the concentration camps of the mind," and that she "sardonically felt herself fated to undergo [death] once every decade" as "an initiation rite qualifying her for a *life* of her own":

> God knows what wound the death of her father had inflicted on her in her childhood, but over the years this had been transformed into the conviction that to be an adult meant to be a survivor. So, for her, death was a debt to be met once every decade: . . .[33]

The involvement with survival, both in her life and in her poetry, is necessarily also an involvement with rebirth. In "Lady Lazarus," confronting death purges away the "trash" of the past.[34]

From this rebirth emerges the queen bee aspect of Plath's protagonist, the type of goddess who ritually murders her consort. Her "red hair" may also reflect traditional mythic elements. On the literal level the red hair of the woman is the blazing plumage of the phoenix. But Plath may also have recalled that red-haired victims were often preferred for sacrificial burning because they resembled the spirit of the ruddy grain, the god to whom they were offered, and so the red hair of Lady Lazarus allies her with a type of dying and reviving divinity.

Though Lady Lazarus proclaims that "dying is an art," her real art is "the great and terrible gift of being reborn." She acknowledges that "It's easy enough to do it and stay put"; that is, it's easy enough to die. Her real specialty is the "Comeback in broad day." Possibly this sideshow resurrection act of Lady Lazarus was inspired by the central character in Kafka's story, "A Hunger Artist," who practices "professional fasting" for a crowd of spectators. (In an earlier version of the poem, Lady Lazarus likewise speaks of her "profession.") The Hunger Artist retires into his cage to fast (like Christ in his retreat to the desert) for forty days—the time-limit set by his "impresario"—and when he emerges to break his fast, a grand public ceremony takes place, with flowers, a military band, and pretty girls to prop him up. Similarly, the "peanut-crunching crowd" in "Lady Lazarus" "Shoves in to see / Them unwrap me hand and foot— / The big strip tease." It is a "theatrical comeback." Her act, like the Hunger Artist's, is ironically identified with Christ's resurrection. "Gentlemen, ladies, / These are my hands / My knees. / I may be skin and bone, / Nevertheless, I am the same, identical woman" parodies "Behold my hands and my feet, that it is I myself" (Luke 24:39).

Like the Hunger Artist with his "impresario" and "overseer," Lady Lazarus is a Resurrection Artist, a 'hot property' of "Herr God, Herr Lucifer," and "Herr Enemy":

> I am your opus,
> I am your valuable,
> The pure gold baby
>
> That melts to a shriek.
> I turn and burn.
> Do not think I underestimate your great concern.[35]

But this opus turns on her creators, destroying them as she destroys their creation, her false self. Her first two 'deaths,' whatever else their meaning, were implicitly attempts to mend her relationship with her dead father (a type of "Herr God" and "Herr Lucifer"); finally death becomes her means of escaping such 'gods' while liberating her true self.

The Hunger Artist's talent may seem miraculous to the outside world, but "he alone knew, . . . how easy it was to fast. It was the easiest thing in the world."[36] For Lady Lazarus, too, dying and being reborn, however difficult it may be for others, is a natural talent ("I guess you could say I've a call")—and in its way, a curse. With his dying breath, Kafka's Hunger Artist confesses to his overseer that he ought not to be admired:

Because I have to fast, I can't help it, . . . I couldn't find the food I liked. If I had found it, believe me, I should have made no fuss and stuffed myself like you or anyone else.[37]

Perhaps, like the Hunger Artist, Lady Lazarus might say that if only she had found the life she liked, she would have made no fuss, and that this is what she is trying to achieve. An observation made about Kafka (by Milena Jesenská, in a letter to Max Brod) might also be applied to this and to other of Plath's poems:

. . . he does not oppose *life,* but only *this kind of life:* that is what he opposes.[38]

"Purdah"

"Purdah," like "Lady Lazarus," tells of the heroine's rebirth, the destruction of her male oppressor, and the corresponding recovery of her true self. The speaker—initially passive and submissive, a mere object—resembles Lady Lazarus in being the "valuable" property of a male:

> Jade—
> Stone of the side,
> The agonized
>
> Side of a green Adam, I
> Smile, cross-legged,
> Enigmatical,
>
> Shifting my clarities.
> So valuable.
> How the sun polishes this shoulder!

Even in her master's absence, she exists only in terms of him: "Even in his / Absence, I / Revolve in my / Sheath of impossibles." Yet she retains a certain wry self-awareness as she describes her enslavement and sense of unreality. When at the end of the poem she casts off her false, doll-like self and becomes a "lioness," it is clear that all along this true self has been latent.

Her bridegroom is "Lord of the mirrors";[39] she, only a mirror, does not initially reveal her underlying true self but reflects her Sun-god, just as the Moon reflects the Sun, her true self lying hidden behind the mirror of her false self, and the mirror thus acting as a sort of veil. The word "purdah" actually means "veil" (it is a Persian word for curtain, and derivatively a Hindi term for a veil, curtain, or screen for the seclusion of women). As in "A Birthday Present," the veil symbolizes the false self (or the true self smothered by it) and its death-in-life existence. The veil prevents the heroine from expressing her true nature, and her bridegroom from perceiving it. Foolishly he assumes that an identity which he has imposed or encouraged is her true, entire nature; to him the veil signifies only "I am his."

In initially describing herself as a jade statuette, the speaker acknowledges the extent to which she has become reified. She is a part of her husband: having been born from the "agonized / Side of a green Adam,"[40] she is therefore a jade Eve. She also thereby reveals her origins in sympathetic magic. (Similarly, the "stone of the side"—jade—was believed to cure pain in the side. As a jade Eve made from a green Adam, she can cure the pain which may initially have been caused by carving her out of him.)

Being of Adam's substance, a natural sympathy exists between them; in a sense, then, she is his external soul. Since, "as the image suffers, so does the man," what happens to her will happen sympathetically to him. When she unlooses her true self, "the lioness," and destroys her false self, the "jeweled doll," he will also be destroyed because that false self *is* his separable soul—that is why he "guards [it] like a heart." (As in "Stopped Dead," the separable soul connects the murder or death with the liberation.)

Her false self is *his* separable soul, while the Moon is hers—her "indefatigable cousin" embodying her true self and symbolizing the story of a Moon-heroine who ritually murders in his bath her Sun-god or Sun-king. Her bridegroom, clearly enough a god of this kind, is also in an earlier draft called a "Sun-god." Graves considers Clytemnestra's murder of Agamemnon to be just this kind of killing:

Sacred kings often meet their end [in the bath] . . . for example . . . Agamemnon, the sacred King of Mycenae, at the hands of Clytemnestra . . .[41] [P. 321]

The last three lines of "Purdah" allude to this murder. The Cassandra of Aeschylus, prophesying the event, calls Clytemnestra a "two-footed lioness" (*Agamemnon*, l. 1218)—this, too, fits in with her mythology, though the metaphor is natural enough. The "shriek in the bath" is Agamemnon's death-cry and "the cloak of holes" the raiment in which Clytemnestra enmeshes him and through which she stabs him:

> And at his next step
> I shall unloose
>
> I shall unloose—
> From the small jeweled
> Doll he guards like a heart—
>
> The lioness,
> The shriek in the bath,
> The cloak of holes.

The ritualistic repetition and magical abbreviation of the emblems of Agamemnon's murder lend the fatedness of Greek tragedy to the visionary certainty of the final pronouncement.

"Getting There"

"Getting There" has frequently been viewed as the expression of a death-wish, as in this remark by Eileen Aird:

'Getting There,' one of the most openly anguished poems, sees the progress of living as the journey of a train carrying wounded soldiers, mutilated, bleeding, despairing, yet still surviving, towards a death which offers the only possibility of peace: . . . However the only stillness which the traveller of 'Getting There' can hope for is in the complete immobility of death, disturbingly seen as a birth into purity: . . .[42]

But the trip is more metaphorical and less disturbing than this— it is the death of the self that identifies with enduring the sufferings of life; and the death in the poem, far from being absolute, is an intermediate step toward rebirth. The speaker's tortured existence—the nightmare journey through entanglement, confusion, and suffering—culminates not in a death seen as birth into purity, but in a purification which prepares her for rebirth (of her true self) and her return, purified of her past history, to the "you" addressed at the end of the poem.

The nature of this journey is symbolized by Lethe, "a river in Hades . . . *its water was drunk by souls about to be reincarnated,* so that they forgot their previous existence."[43] The name of the river derives from a word meaning oblivion or forgetfulness. Lethe bestows the oblivion required for rebirth, and is therefore not synonymous with death but associated with it as an intermediate stage between death and rebirth. For Plath to have used "the black car of Lethe" merely to signify death (or the purity of death) would have been an imprecision uncharacteristic of her. Her etymological usages are usually quite deliberate; there may be irony (as in "Lesbos") or deliberate distortion or "iconotropy," but not vagueness or inaccuracy.

"Lethe" has the same usage in other poems of hers such as "Amnesiac," and the earlier poem "Two Campers in Cloud Country," where Lethean forgetfulness precedes a new awakening:

> Around our tent the old simplicities sough
> Sleepily as Lethe, trying to get in.
> We'll wake blank-brained as water in the dawn.
> ["Two Campers in Cloud Country"]

Graves explicitly mentions Lethe as a guarantor of rebirth, noting that if one is to "escape from the Wheel" of rebirth, one must *not* drink of Lethe. The Orphics were determined

. . . not to forget, to refuse to drink the water of cypress-shaded Lethe however thirsty one might be, to accept water only from the sacred . . . pool of Persephone, and thus to become immortal Lords of the Dead, excused further Tearings-to-Pieces, Destructions, Resurrections and Rebirths. [P. 139]

The "black car of Lethe" has been interpreted in still other ways. In a review, Gary Kissick writes:

The box car which Plath rides in "Getting There" is a last desperate hope for peace and an end to destruction. But because Plath *is* in a *box-car*, we know her hope to be false—as false as the hope of the Jews box-carred for "resettlement." Thus, those last four lines present us with a tremendously bitter and sarcastic comment on the chances of man's history ever recording a chapter that is not replete with suffering.[44]

Although Plath was of course well aware of what Kissick calls "the terrors of the modern world"—she considered herself to be a political person—the poem does not show the speaker, like the Jews, to be a victim of deluded hopes. By the end, the ride in the boxcar—her (death-in-) life—has been transformed: the death-carriages become cradles, and she a baby. This image represents a transfiguration and transcending of history—of the war, the train, the death-camps, and the "old bandages, boredoms, old faces."

It is significant that the speaker willingly undergoes the train ride (just as in "The Bee Meeting" the heroine also voluntarily participates in the terrifying ritual in the hope for rebirth). In fact, she fears that the train will leave her behind on the battlefield:

> There is mud on my feet,
> Thick, red and slipping. . . .
> . . .
> I cannot undo myself, and the train is steaming.
> . . .
> . . . why are there these obstacles—

The narrative of the poem should be understood as the enactment of a willingly undertaken purgatorial ritual, in which the true self, purified by Lethe of all false encumbrances, finally emerges. This theme is further echoed in the other images of rebirth clustered at the end of the poem:

> I shall bury the wounded like pupas,
> I shall count and bury the dead.
> Let their souls writhe in a dew,
> Incense in my track.
> The carriages rock, they are cradles.

The pupas lie in a quiescent "mummified" state; soon they will metamorphose into their true forms. Probably the dead are counted when buried because there will be a resurrection in which they will be accounted for. Their souls (on the way to reincarnation) trail the heroine, "Incense in [her] track," as she travels through Lethe to rebirth.

In the final image of the baby, her history has been stripped away, leaving only her purified essential self:

> And I, stepping from this skin
> Of old bandages, boredoms, old faces
>
> Step to you from the black car of Lethe,
> Pure as a baby.

Discarding the "old bandages" also symbolizes resurrection: mummies were preserved in bandages for just such an eventual rebirth. (For Lady Lazarus, the bandages have a similar meaning. Part of her rebirth ceremony consists in her being 'unwrapped' in a "big strip tease"; there are literal strips here—the pieces of mummy-cloth, which resemble bandages.)

There may be in the journey of "Getting There" an allusion to the descent of Aeneas to the underworld (where he observes souls drinking of Lethe before their rebirth) and his return to the world of the living.[45] Perhaps "Getting There" implicitly alludes to the particulars of this journey. Aeneas meets his father's ghost in the underworld, and Plath may have intended such a reference. Nevertheless, the "you" at the end of the poem is very likely the speaker's husband, whom she rejoins after purification (in this case, she is not a vengeful goddess).

The poem's dimension of sexual symbolism supports this reading. Unlike other of Plath's poems which use sexual imagery in a primarily metaphorical sense in order to express something else, the sexual references in this poem are self-contained. The overall emotional logic of the poem is that of a sexual act:

> How far is it?
> How far is it now?

The association of death (loss of the sense of self or ego) with orgasm is a natural one; and the sense of destination expressed in the title and in the poem could apply to the sexual dimension as well. The self-oblivion attained through Lethe has something of the sense of relief and the dispelling of pent-up tension of sexual release. The description of the train seems also to suggest this interpretation. Its headlight is seen as

> . . . a minute at the end of it
> A minute, a dewdrop.

And the war imagery works in this way as well:

> Thunder and guns.
> The fire's between us.

The recognition of this sexual dimension makes clear the significance of the death and purification with which the poem ends (and it precludes the sort of interpretation proposed by Eileen Aird and Gary Kissick).

It becomes plain that "Getting There" encodes a spiritual death and rebirth when it is considered in the context of other poems which Plath knew, such as Lawrence's "The Ship of Death" and Eliot's *Four Quartets*, which also treat these themes through the symbol of a journey. Though diverging in sensibility and vision, both portray a process of "getting there": in Eliot, as in Plath, there is a train journey; in Lawrence, the journey is by sea, and his poem offers a lyrical exhortation to what "Getting There" presents as dramatic ritual:

> And it is time to go, to bid farewell
> to one's own self, and find an exit
> from the fallen self.
> . . .
> Build then the ship of death, for you must take
> the longest journey, to oblivion.
>
> And die the death, the long and painful death
> that lies between the old self and the new.
> . . .
> Piecemeal the body dies, and the timid soul
> has her footing washed away, as the dark flood rises.
> . . .
> And yet out of eternity, a thread
> separates itself on the blackness,
> . . .

. . . there's the dawn,
the cruel dawn of coming back to life
out of oblivion.

. . .

A flush of rose, and the whole thing starts again.

The flood subsides, and the body, like a worn sea-shell
emerges strange and lovely.

. . .

. . . and the frail soul steps out, into her house again
filling the heart with peace.

These last lines in particular may be echoed in the final stanza of
"Getting There."[46]

There is also, in Plath's allusion to Eliot, a suggestion of a more
absolute transcendence of the life-drama. In "Burnt Norton,"
Eliot writes of

. . . the still point of the turning world.

"Getting There" clearly echoes this:

Is there no still place,
Turning and turning in the middle air,
Untouched and untouchable.

Eliot further elaborates the sense of the "still point":

The inner freedom from the practical desire,
The release from action and suffering, release from the inner
And the outer compulsion, yet surrounded
By a grace of sense, a white light still and moving, . . .

But one must move, one must get there in order to be still:

. . . In order to arrive there,
To arrive where you are, to get from where you are not,
    You must go by a way wherein there is no ecstasy.
In order to arrive at what you do not know
    You must go by a way which is the way of ignorance.
. . .
In order to arrive at what you are not
    You must go through the way in which you are not.[47]

["East Coker"]

Eliot uses the metaphor of a journey to state that the self which identifies itself with its experiences in time is not the true self, but that the "still point" is:

> . . . the train starts, and the passengers are settled
> . . .
> Fare forward, travellers! not escaping from the past
> Into different lives, or into any future;
> You are not the same people who left that station
> Or who will arrive at any terminus,
> . . .
> Fare forward, you who think that you are voyaging;
> . . .
> Here between the hither and the farther shore
> While time is withdrawn, consider the future
> And the past with an equal mind.
> . . .
>
> ["The Dry Salvages"]

The speaker of "Getting There" can be described as one who only *thinks* she is voyaging—proceeding as if the self undergoing the journey were her deepest identity—but who also recognizes that she only thinks this and wonders why she cannot achieve the still place from which she would see the adventures of that other self in a different light. Plath's theme of "destinations" should also be considered in this context:

> What do wheels eat, these wheels
> Fixed to their arcs like gods,
> The silver leash of the will—
> Inexorable. And their pride!
> All the gods know is destinations.
> I am a letter in this slot—
> I fly to a name, two eyes.

The slot—distinct from the "I"—is the time-bound finite self. A more essential self, not identified with its "slot," allows the possibility of getting off the track entirely by uniting with the still place. While some destinations may be unalterable, the traveler in "Getting There" at least intellectually acknowledges another possibility, for she recognizes, as Eliot says, that ideally:

. . . the end of all our exploring
Will be to arrive where we started
And know the place for the first time.

["Little Gidding"]

And

. . . O voyagers, O seamen,
You who come to port, and you whose bodies
Will suffer the trial and judgment of the sea,
Or whatever event, this is your real destination.

["The Dry Salvages"]

Plath's annotation to these lines in her volume of Eliot's poems reads, "temporal destination doesn't matter—*real* destination," which nicely sums up one level of concern in her poem. Eliot's "still point," Plath's "still place," is the *"real* destination"—the metaphor of a conventional journey (to a place; through life) offering an ironic counterpoint to the idea that in some sense there may be no "there" to get to. A direct living apprehension of this insight is what the speaker of "Getting There" wants—even as she proceeds toward another sort of destination. Rather than enacting a journey toward death, the poem portrays a journey to rebirth and a new self at the incarnate level by one so caught up in that journey that she can spare only a fleeting recognition of the real destination, as is reflected by the way in which the lines

Is there no still place,
Turning and turning in the middle air,
Untouched and untouchable. . . .

bring the driving momentum of the poem to a sudden, though temporary, halt.

The echoes of Eliot imply the desirability of attaining, not just in order to rejoin a particular "you," but for its own sake, a self untouched ultimately by any drama. Other poems which primarily enact rituals of rebirth also hint, though less obviously, that the sought-for rebirth may be of this more absolute kind. However, several poems written at the very end of Plath's life explicitly entertain the possibility of purifying oneself not just for the sake of a new start between people, but for a new way of being.

VIII

Death, Rebirth, and Transcendence

In order to appreciate the meaning of death in Sylvia Plath's poetry (and to situate properly the knowledge of her suicide, insofar as this affects how one interprets her work), it must be kept in mind that not all acts of suicide have the same meaning, either to their agents or to others. For instance, there is the noble death of Cleopatra; the utilitarian suicide of someone suffering from a painful incurable disease; the Japanese ritual *seppuku*, which establishes the agent's honor beyond question; the self-killing which is an absurd Dada joke; and also the sort of suicide which, to use Lowell's phrase, tells us that life "is simply not worth it."

Given all this, it would be presumptuous to assume that one's actual suicide, or images of self-inflicted death in one's art, are inherently sick or morbid. Where a culture lacks a transcendent or sacramental dimension, death will be a taboo subject; people would rather not be reminded of it, and suicide in such a culture will be considered an embarrassment.

The notoriety of Sylvia Plath's suicide, in a culture where death has become an obscenity, often prejudices the interpretation of death in her poetry. It must also be kept in mind that the extraneous knowledge of her suicide may cloud what the poems actually say (and that the suicide does not *determine* what they say, although explaining the work in terms of it is common). Readers may tend to view all of her poems in which death or suffering appear in any form as suicidal or sensationalistic or degenerate, as if her interest in the theme of death could not have another, or larger, significance.

Any poet who dwells on death in other than an impersonal or lyrical way runs the risk of being thought morbid. Yet this may be more the problem of a culture that does not want to see than that of Plath, who wants to look. In her case, the judgment of morbidity is often automatic, a function of the peanut-crunching anticipation brought to her work because of her sensational death. Thus people may read even poems that have nothing to do with death primarily as statements foreshadowing suicide. But had she somehow survived her attempt to kill herself and had she undergone the transformation that she sought, the poems would have foreshadowed that 'rebirth' as clearly as they appear to foreshadow her suicide.

Studies of near-fatal accidents, in which people have suddenly and apparently irrevocably been confronted with death, have demonstrated that there is a capacity to experience a dissolution of or a detachment from the ego (the subject of one's personal history). The sense of ego yields to a sense of unity with the world and consequently of eternity. Such confrontations, when survived, can so drastically alter the perspective on one's former life that one is completely changed, and such experiences are rightly called experiences of rebirth. Premonitions of such experiences are abundant in life and art.

One explanation of a longing for death might, then, be the instinctual sense that in confronting death one can recover from a spoiled history. A reflection of this intuition runs through Plath's late poetry. Such a connection between (near-) death and rebirth is not a mere literary device, nor does it reflect the logic of a disordered mind;[1] it reflects, rather, the envisioning of an experience for which the human species has an innate capacity. A deliberate confrontation of death can, then, be considered in a sense a 'rebirth' ritual. It is not necessary to offer this interpretation as a theory of her suicide (though this, too, might be done as an alternative to Alvarez's speculations) to see its relevance to the meaning of death in her poems.

The effects of a sudden apprehension of imminent death have been explored by Russell Noyes and Albert Heim.[2] They have found that such confrontations often trigger the experience of the splitting off of one's ego and "bodily representation" from some

more essential consciousness which remains, perceiving the splitting off, and feeling itself merged with the universe. Such experiences, Noyes says, are essentially experiences of rebirth in the form
of "mystical, transcendental, cosmic, or religious" consciousness:

> . . . persons who have experienced mystical consciousness, . . . have
> expressed what happened to them in terms of death and rebirth. This
> "death" experience has been described as pleasurable and has led to
> removal of fear of death . . .[3]

An indispensable condition of such experiences is that the
person be convinced of the imminence of death. Those who qualify
include not only accident victims, but intended suicides:

> Victims of drownings, falls, automobile accidents, anaphylactic reactions,
> even suicides, may regularly have these experiences.

Further:

> Persons who have decided to kill themselves have also reported that
> acceptance of death is accompanied by a tremendous sense of peace.[4]

Noyes has noted three stages in the "rapidly unfolding experience that terminates in a mystical state of consciousness"; these are
"resistance, life review, and transcendence."[5] Albert Heim's account
of his fall from a cliff in the Alps provides a model of this experience. As he fell his past life and the self which participated in it
split off from another aspect of "self" which remained as specta-
tor:

> . . . I saw my whole past life take place . . . as though on a stage at
> some distance from me. I saw myself as the chief character in the per-
> formance. Everything was transfigured as though by a heavenly light
> and everything was beautiful without grief, without anxiety, and with-
> out pain. The memory of very tragic experiences I had had was clear but
> not saddening. I felt no conflict or strife; . . . Elevated and harmonious
> thoughts dominated and united the individual images, and like magnifi-
> cent music a divine calm swept through my soul.[6]

He concludes:

> Those of our friends who have died in the mountains have, in their last
> moments, reviewed their individual pasts in states of transfiguration.

. . . they were under the sway of noble and profound thoughts, heavenly music, and a feeling of peace and reconciliation.[7]

Noyes says that in the phase of transcendence the individual

. . . may feel as though he were outside of time, in eternity, or beyond the past and future. . . . A related characteristic is that of transcendence of space and of individual identity. A sense of oneness or unity with other human beings and the entire universe develops.[8]

As a concrete example of this phase, Noyes offers Jung's account of his experience following a heart attack:

. . . I had the feeling that everything was being sloughed away; . . . the whole phantasmagoria of earthy existence, fell away or was stripped from me—. . . I can describe the experience only as the ecstasy of a nontemporal state in which present, past, and future are one. Everything that happens in time had been brought together into a concrete whole. . . . One is interwoven . . . and yet observed it with complete objectivity.[9]

Noyes writes that

Transcendence is, in a large measure, achieved by removing many of the artificial divisions which people impose upon the world in their effort to simplify and master it.[10]

The ego (a self-constituted distinction between self and non-self) is primary among the "artificial divisions" which, when removed by an apprehension of imminent death, disclose a mystical or transcendent identity. Sylvia Plath obviously sensed that if one were to experience imminent death, the inessential aspects of self and personal history could separate from and be regarded by the permanent true self, leaving a sense of eternity and unity with the world. This helps to explain the logic of the imagery of the separable soul, and of the apparent detachability of the false self from the true, and it explains why the subject who undergoes death is symbolized as the body. This logic is implicit in Plath's description of a near-fatal accident:

> A squeal of brakes.
> Or is it a birth cry?
>
> ["Stopped Dead"]

Death possesses a similar duality in "A Birthday Present." The logic of such poems derives in part from a desire to dispense with all that is illusory and inessential (particularly the false self, the subject of the protagonist's spoiled history and death-in-life).

Because her spoiled history seems impossible of completion in its own terms, the imagined act usually takes the form of a more literal rebirth, a new beginning. But in several of the last poems Plath begins to extend the notion of the false self and to consider that any self at all, whether spoiled or not, which participates in a drama is an artificial limitation. The focus then shifts to absolute transcendence (not just 'rebirth' in order to leave behind the spoiled history).

Mere bodily extinction would not really resolve anything. It offers only a parody of completeness, as in "Berck-Plage": "This is what it is to be complete. It is horrible." The speaker here seems to flirt with the horror of the old man's death, viewing it as a switching off of life, which leaves the corpse as an item that must be made presentable along with the other furnishings of the death room.

But mere physical death completes a history only in the limited sense that no new initiatives can be taken; the significance of a past life, say of a public figure, can be retrospectively altered, but its subject is then purely at the mercy of fortune. Simply cutting off life cannot complete or resolve a spoiled history (the death in "Edge," since it is by no means a mere physical death, is different).

Nor does remaining alive while forgetting the past represent a satisfactory solution. Plath does consider this theme, however, since it pertains to her concern with wiping out history. Amnesia can 'erase' an unwanted past from consciousness (in the poem "Amnesiac"), but such a solution has no connection with the problem which still, in a sense, remains forever preserved in the past, like a freak of nature in formaldehyde. Some principle of continuity must connect the problem and the solution. The confrontation with imminent death provides this continuity through the shock whereby inessential elements fall away; the person who miraculously survives lives on with a changed perspective, effecting the necessary continuity. The same sort of continuity exists in cases of religious conversion (St. Augustine's, for example) in which the whole spoiled past is quite different from the reborn person, yet is not forgotten, and has its place as something 'fixed in a parenthesis' (to adapt Plath's phrase). Although repudiated, the past leads into, and so completes itself in, transcendence.

That Plath associated the risk of death with the shedding of the past and the achievement of a state of transcendence (or rebirth) is reflected in a number of poems ("I do it so it feels real" in "Lady Lazarus"; also "Ariel," "Getting There," "Fever 103°"). Such poems assume that the particular circumstances of a life are not the essential self and that an individual history can be transcended. This helps to explain why "Stopped Dead" begins with a promisingly traumatic event, a narrow escape from death which transforms mundane existence. (Although this can easily be mistaken for a morbid fascination with death, the fascination has a very different focus.) As in many of her other late poems, the very fact that it can be shed reveals the dispensability of the old self.

Such poems in which Plath's protagonist confronts death, or contemplates dying or suicide, are essentially envisioned rituals whose ultimate motive is to kill the false self along with the spoiled history and to allow the true self to be reborn—that is, simply to be disclosed; for as Noyes says of transcendence, it is largely a matter of "removing . . . artificial divisions."

Within Plath's poetry can be distinguished two senses of rebirth —the term is inherently metaphorical, having (in this context) no serious literal sense; as a metaphor it does, however, have a more and a less literal sense, both of which signify forms of experience. The more literal of these, which might be called mythic rebirth, is closer to the sense of physical death and reincarnation. "Lady Lazarus" and "Purdah" present examples of this sort of rebirth which, within the terms of the myth itself, resolves the specific 'problem' of the mythic drama. To absorb a biographical problem into mythic terms is to envision its resolution, given that the myth is of a cyclical nature, such as a myth of a dying and reviving goddess. Mythic rebirth involves a story, a drama with a protagonist and other characters; and the projected rebirth involves the relationship with those characters.

The other, less literal sense of rebirth is absolute transcendence of self. When Noyes speaks of the confrontation with death leading to the experience of "rebirth," he has the less literal sense of the term in mind. This kind of rebirth, egoless transcendence, is an identification not with individual forms of self, but with the larger, impersonal "Self" of the universe. Not only the false self, but the mythic true self as well (insofar as its selfhood is a limitation or barrier) are transcended.

The line between these two kinds of rebirth—egoless transcendence (an identification of the self with the eternal, without limitation) and the more literal (mythic) rebirth (an identification of the self with a timeless mythic order, though with limitation)—is not a firm one. Either form could believably be imagined as resulting from a confrontation with death. An intimation that confronting death can result in rebirth could, then, easily provide Plath with a sufficient logic both for the theme of mythic rebirth in her drama and for the theme of egoless transcendence. Intimations of this more complete kind of transcendence occur in many of Plath's characterizations of the more literal form of rebirth (as in "Getting There"), although egoless transcendence may not be presented as a specific aim in such poems.

Nearly all of the poems of mythic drama were written in Devon, in surroundings still associated with her recent past, after her husband left but before Plath moved to London to take up her new life and independence. By early December nearly all the mythic poems had been written. After her move later that month she was occupied with settling into her new flat and she apparently wrote no new poems until the end of the next month. Then, between January 28 and February 5 (the day she apparently wrote her last poems) she wrote "Totem," "Paralytic," "Mystic," "Words," "Contusion," "Edge" (among others), many of them frightening, but each nevertheless strikingly distanced and calm. They do not for the most part seem to be spoken dramatically by the mythic heroine; a poem like "Contusion" seems quite different in kind from the mythic poems. And in fact none of these poems was in her manuscript of *Ariel*, which included nothing written after "Death & Co." on November 12. The manuscript, as she arranged it, framed a story which began ("Morning Song," occasioned by the birth of her first child) with the word "Love" and ended ("Wintering") with the word "spring." Having identified with the queen bee (in "The Bee Meeting" and "Stings"), finally "The bees are flying. They taste the spring," as they rise renewed from their wintering.

Now, clearly on her own and for the first time in seven years living in a place not shared with her husband, her poetry seems increasingly to reflect a recognition that she must finally confront the patterns that had dominated her life and her very conception of self. She might in retrospect have seen in the writing of the mythic poems an attempt at self-hypnosis. Now that she was alone in London the images of mythic rebirth evaporated under the onslaught of a grim reality. The need she felt now seems not to have been rebirth or triumph in terms of the drama, but to inquire whether it might be possible to detach herself from it: another version of the false self / true self dilemma. Her last themes include the dissolution of the ego into a larger Self and the difficulty of integrating this experience of timeless ecstasy into ordinary life. Poems such as "Paralytic" and "Mystic" deal with 're-birth' as an actual experience of some sort; whereas the rebirths which occur in "Lady Lazarus" or "Getting There" do not claim to be experiences, but are metaphors which although more literalistic in form are also more literary.

IX

Beyond Drama

There are two lives, the natural and the spiritual, and we
must lose the one before we can participate in the other.

> William James
> *The Varieties of Religious Experience*

On the border . . . of the conscious and unconscious circles
of the mind is born the Self which grows in proportion as the
false self . . . dies down. . . . The disintegration of this
illusory self . . . before the true Self . . . is born, is filled
with danger.

> Christmas Humphreys
> *Zen Buddhism*

Stigma (of Selfhood)

> Sylvia Plath
> note on manuscript of "Elm"

The false self, which must be overthrown, is manifested in the
late poems in a variety of forms:

> A living doll, everywhere you look.
> It can sew, it can cook,
> It can talk, talk, talk.

["The Applicant"]

> I am your opus,
> I am your valuable, . . .

["Lady Lazarus"]

> . . . I could draw no breath,
> Dead and moneyless,

Overexposed, like an X ray.

["Medusa"]

If you only knew how the veils were killing my days.

["A Birthday Present"]

. . . I have lived like a foot
For thirty years, poor and white, . . .

["Daddy"]

. . . for years I have eaten dust
And dried plates with my dense hair.

["Stings"]

I am lame in the memory.

["Little Fugue"]

The fingers were tamping a woman into a wall, . . .

["The Detective"]

The constriction killing me also.

["The Rabbit Catcher"]

. . . the small jeweled
Doll he guards like a heart—

["Purdah"]

In poems which involve the "stigma of selfhood," the stigmatic
"I" (the self as ego) which suffers very often appears as disposable
or inessential—frequently as some sort of superficial covering;
often the body itself symbolizes this selfhood. In relinquishing this
selfhood, one relinquishes suffering:

. . . I unpeel—
Dead hands, dead stringencies.

["Ariel"]

And I, stepping from this skin
Of old bandages, boredoms, old faces . . .

["Getting There"]

(My selves dissolving, old whore petticoats)—

["Fever 103°"]

When these inessentials fall away—when one gets beyond not only self but selves—a purer and more fundamental state of being remains. This differs from mythic rebirth where the achieved state of being will only be "the same self" (in the sense of yet another selfhood) and the rebirth only provisional.

Transcendence (of ego or selfhood) avoids further rebirth into yet another drama of selfhood, because, when the self is transcended, there is nothing to be 'reborn.' William James, whose *Varieties of Religious Experience* Plath knew and refers to in her earlier poetry,[1] discusses, in his chapter on "Mysticism" (underlined and annotated in Plath's copy of the book), many experiences in which the mundane self is felt to die and a higher or larger self recovered—recovered, since it is seen to have been there all along:

. . . to return from the solitude of individuation into the consciousness of unity with all that is, to kneel down as one that passes away, and to rise up as one imperishable.[2]

The temporary loss or overcoming of the sense of personal identity through such an experience as riding a horse (as in "Ariel") may be an experience of ecstasy, through which one joins this larger self or deeper consciousness.

The fundamental problem in Plath's late poetry is first, the problem of that particular selfhood (in which false and true selves are tied up with an absent god), and ultimately the problem of any selfhood, which absolute transcendence or spiritual rebirth would reconcile. To state the distinction in another way, "it is not that the ego *has* a problem, but that the ego *is* the problem."[3] Most of the poems in which the mythic drama is central imply that the ego *has* a problem—the spoiled history, oppression by male 'gods,' the false self—which can be overcome and resolved by mythic rebirth into a new phase. Yet even when not explicitly stated, there is a growing awareness (reflected in a comparison of, say, "Totem," written two weeks before her death, and dramatic mythology poems such as "The Detective" and "Stings," written four months earlier), that

. . . the cause of the suffering is self. Where self exists there is suffering; where there is suffering there is a self to suffer. . . . For the suffering self there can be no therapy. Worries, quarrels, futile argument—the whole gamut of love and hate, all these and their attendant medicines will fade away when the cause of them is removed, and not before. . . . we cannot heal a problem as such. But we can . . . remove the factor which made it a problem, the wants and the fears and the loves of 'I'.[4]

Although this perspective is often unemphasized or undeveloped in many of the poems of mythic drama, it is nonetheless incipient in "A Birthday Present," "Lady Lazarus," and "Getting There"; and a few of her very last poems directly consider the ego or selfhood as the problem. The theme of absolute transcendence is an explicit concern in "Totem," "Mystic," and "Paralytic," written two weeks before her death within a period of three days:

> There is no terminus, only suitcases
>
> Out of which the same self unfolds like a suit . . .
>
> ["Totem"]
>
> Once one has seen God, what is the remedy?
> . . .
> Is there no great love, only tenderness?
>
> ["Mystic"]
>
> The claw
> Of the magnolia,
> Drunk on its own scents,
> Asks nothing of life.
>
> ["Paralytic"]

These poems reflect a crisis involving the "natural" and the "spiritual" lives, acknowledging the limitation of the "natural" life and doubting whether a free and powerful true self could be recovered in these terms simply by asserting that self; and considering what value the "spiritual" perspective might have, and whether she might achieve it. (The reflection of this crisis in her poems has been confirmed by Ted Hughes, who remarked in conversation that several times during the last two or three weeks of her life she said something to the effect that "I have seen God, and he keeps picking me up" and "I am full of God.")

"Fever 103°"

In "Fever 103°," Plath's myth appears with the trappings of farce, yet the farce ends in an image of transcendence. At the outset, it is uncertain how seriously the speaker will entertain the theme of purity and its related theme of transcendence.

The speaker initially experiences her high fever as a kind of hellfire or as flames of punishment, and then, by free association, the poem gradually rises both in temperature and seriousness. She introduces some images playfully, as if they were little more than amusing metaphors: "I am a lantern," or "Does not my heat astound you. And my light. / All by myself I am a huge camellia." Yet the "heat" and "light" ultimately become identified with transcendence, whereas initially they were identified only with punishment and fever.

Earlier, farcical lines ("dull, fat Cerberus / Who wheezes at the gate," or "The sheets grow heavy as a lecher's kiss") do not anticipate the final image of transcendence, which itself is at first somewhat ludicrous:

> I think I am going up,
> I think I may rise—

The speaker rises like a Japanese lantern by power of its candle— a hot-air balloon. It is as if the Virgin Mary were hoisted up to heaven by visible ropes. In this spirit the speaker, with her cargo of dime-store props parodying the conventional representations and emblems of the Assumption, ascends:

> . . . I, love, I
>
> Am a pure acetylene
> Virgin
> Attended by roses,
>
> By kisses, by cherubim,
> By whatever these pink things mean.

Beneath the farce, however, lies the powerful and threatening image of the pure acetylene virgin who, like Lady Lazarus, will transcend even her old "selves." The joke about the kisses and cherubim falls away, as the speaker, in the final lines of the poem, assumes another, more serious tone. Both her mundane selves and her earlier attitudes have altered, and the theme of purification by fire is finally realized:

> Not you, nor him
>
> Nor him, nor him
> (My selves dissolving, old whore petticoats)—
> To Paradise.

Even here a trace of the farcical element (the "old whore petti-coats") persists: but now the vision of transcendence clearly dominates. The farce in a sense rises by its own levity above itself. The fire which dissolves the selves reveals them for what they are: false, inessential forms.

"You," and the several other males left behind ("him" and "him")[5] are part of what she transcends, for they do not attend her. In leaving them, she implicitly abandons the roles she once played in relation to them (roles such as mother, daughter, wife), which must figure among her dissolving selves. This movement from the particular problems of self to the general question of selves parallels that from her feverish sufferings to suffering ("under-going," as in "Getting There") in general.

The imagery which portrays both the suffering and the resolving purification is one of the elements in the poem which belie, and are in tension with, the overt joking tone. A note Plath wrote for the BBC describes the serious thematic level in "Fever 103°":

This poem is about two kinds of fire—the fires of hell, which merely agonize, and the fires of heaven, which purify. During the poem, the first sort of fire suffers itself into the second.[6]

"Fever 103°" is only one of several poems in which fire brings a purity equivalent to transcendence. Plath's use of the phrase "fires of heaven" would seem to confirm this. (Frazer refers to such fires.)[7] Plath's "fires of heaven" dissolve not only sin (a problem the ego has) but the mundane "selves" (a problem the ego is). This function could not have been performed by the ineffectual fires of hell, which are "dull, . . . / Incapable / Of licking clean / . . .

the sin" and inflict punishment and agony rather than consume the self which sins. The smokes of the fires of hell do not rise, but their heat ignites the fires that do.

Insofar as the fires of hell exist to punish sins they are identified with the world of drama and the self which sins.[8] On the other hand, the purifying fires of heaven do not confirm but destroy the drama of suffering and sin, by destroying the selves which enact it. It is in this respect that the poem depicts transcendence as something won through suffering ("the first sort of fire suffers itself into the second"), for the mundane selves also suffer themselves into a purified form. The virgin who ascends to Paradise here, unlike Lady Lazarus, is not reborn as a new phoenix into her familiar world of drama, but enters another order of existence. While the reference to Paradise may be a joke at the farcical level of the poem, at the serious level it indicates transcendence.

"Ariel"

"Ariel," which Plath wrote on her birthday, October 27, is a powerful dramatic expression of an experience of ecstatic unity. Unlike "Fever 103°," this experience does not grow out of a reverie in which the mind is flooded with ingenious and, in a sense, extraneous images (fires of heaven and hell, Japanese lantern, Cerberus, etc.), which distract the reader's attention from the experience they signify. "Ariel" draws the attention into the sense of this central experience, which the images unify and from which they do not detract. Godiva, the split furrow, the hooks of the berries, the cauldron of morning all directly evoke the sense of ecstatic transcendence.

The fourth and fifth lines of the poem, "God's lioness, / How one we grow," refer to the speaker's horse Ariel (the name of a horse Plath used to ride), whose name contains a key to the poem. Although the horse's name (and the title of the whole collection in which the poem appears) has generally been taken to refer to the sprite of Shakespeare's *Tempest*—and though the speaker of the poem does feel airy and insubstantial—this is not the primary reference; the name as Plath uses it is actually a quite specific biblical reference, alluding to fiery sacrifice, purification, and transcendence. In Isaiah it is "A cryptic name for Jerusalem"[9] ("Ariel, the city where David dwelt!" 29:1). The derivation of the name may be either "lion (lioness) of God" or "altar [hearth] of God,"[10] and

> Regardless of the ultimate derivation . . . the meaning of Isaiah 29:1–2 seems to be that Jerusalem, here (prophetically?) called Ariel, is to become like the altar, i.e., a scene of holocaust.[11]

Also:

> The altar of holocausts is called the "ariel of God" . . . on this altar burned the perpetual fire that was used to consume the sacrificial victims (Lev. 6:12).
> Jerusalem is called Ariel by Isaias in the prophecy in which he describes the capture, the destruction and the divine preservation of the Holy City . . . the prophet sees Sion awaiting the impending invasion of Sennacherib like an altar on which the immolated victims will be consumed by fire.[12]

The horse in the poem is actually called "God's lioness" (and Plath wrote "lioness of God" at the top of the manuscript), and the poem also includes the other meaning, the "altar" or "hearth" of God. The speaker, identifying herself with Ariel as a fiery sacrifice, enacts her own "holocaust," becoming a "whole burnt-offering," a "sacrifice or offering entirely consumed by fire,"[13] as she plunges "Into the red / Eye, the cauldron of morning."

The process of shedding her inessentialities begins early in the poem, and as her feeling of unity intensifies, she becomes increasingly free and pure:

> Nigger-eye
> Berries cast dark
> Hooks—
>
> Black sweet blood mouthfuls,
> Shadows.
> Something else
>
> Hauls me through air—
> Thighs, hair; . . .

The "hooks"—like the mundane life she leaves behind—have no more claim upon her than does her own past, the next thing she sheds:

> White
> Godiva, I unpeel—
> Dead hands, dead stringencies.[14]

By temporarily identifying herself with Godiva, she expresses as the experience of a mythic heroine—and not just as an abstract feeling—the sense of purifying herself of the inessentials which include her self, and the reference indicates the extremity of her wish: even Godiva's nakedness does not suffice, and she unpeels still further, shedding "dead hands, dead stringencies," until there is nothing left for her to unpeel, and then "I / Foam to wheat, a glitter of seas." At the start of the poem, though already growing one with the horse, she is not completely merged with the world (the berries still try to catch her with their hooks). But soon she does become one with the landscape as well—the sea of wheat—and her transmutation continues until finally she merges into the sunrise.

The Godiva image probably encodes not just the process of transcendence, but the shedding of the mythic drama. Robert Graves claims that the Godiva legend derives from a disguised form of a White Goddess procession—Godiva actually being a white goddess of Love and Death, specially associated with the death of the sacred king.[15] (In this connection, it is worth noting that an earlier draft of the poem referred to shedding "dead men.") Although Godiva is associated with the White Goddess, she differs strikingly from figures such as Lady Lazarus and the woman in "Purdah," who do not grow one with anything, but, instead, recover their mythic true selves and are reborn in the more literal sense. That sort of unpeeling is exemplified in "the big strip tease" of Lady Lazarus, which can now be seen as less radical than what Godiva undergoes, for it only effects the loss of the spoiled past and the particular false self engendered by it; while the speaker of "Ariel," as Godiva, sheds the *form* of the personal self.

The emblematic colors black, white, and red encode this entire experience. "Stasis in darkness"—black—represents a traumatized yet expectant deadness. White suggests death-in-life, but also a kind of purity; and the image of "white Godiva" implies the nakedness of truth. Godiva nonetheless has "dead hands" and "dead stringencies" to shed, so her whiteness may also be an affliction. The color red—the fiery sunrise—is the color of rebirth and final purification. The sequence of colors tells the story of the poem: black stasis yields to the white of Godiva (an intermediate stage of purification, as the "substanceless blue" is an intermediate brightening of the landscape), and this in turn yields to the arrow and the dew which fly into the red eye of transcendence.

The "stasis in darkness" with which the poem begins helps precipitate the rider into her headlong rush toward selflessness. Plath uses "stasis" in its narrower, more specialized sense. In pathology, it means "a stopping of the blood in some part of the circulation."[16] Stasis, therefore, does not indicate just any suspension or stagnation, but one of a critical nature, where what is normally in motion has been unnaturally and dangerously interfered with. It is as if the initial darkness in which the rider finds herself is a state of trauma, requiring resuscitation—"then" giving way to the reviving "blue." The rider herself is at first like the stopped blood which, suddenly released, surges forward. The dissolution of stasis into motion anticipates the merging of the small white "I" into the "red eye"[17] (two separate 'I's' becoming one).

On the level of sound, this merging is reinforced by an increasingly frequent repetition of the long 'i' sound. In the first eighteen lines, this sound occurs four times ("lioness," "I," the "nigger-eye" berries, and "thighs"). In the concluding thirteen lines of the poem (once the speaker has identified herself as "Godiva"), the rhyme occurs eleven times:

> White
> Godiva, I unpeel—
> Dead hands, dead stringencies.
>
> And now I
> Foam to wheat, a glitter of seas.
> The child's cry

Melts in the wall.
And *I*
Am the arrow,

The dew that flies
Suicidal, at one with the drive
Into the red

Eye, the cauldron of morning.

Although the personal "I" merges with the eye of the rising sun, this is not a suicidal death-wish. The dew identified with the rider is called "suicidal" because, true to its nature, it flies or evaporates into the sun. But this image expresses mystical union or transcendence,[18] 'sui-cide' in that it represents the death of the (personal) self—the little "I"; or the (conventional) longing of the soul for union with God.

The end of "Ariel" represents neither "images of anarchic forces and centrifugal destruction," as Annette Lavers suggests, nor a sexual sublimation:

. . . the ecstasy of love, which is suggested by the gallop of a horse, is always evoked in a strangely passionless manner, which leads one to suggest that a blue and transparent transfiguration is preferred to a more personal feeling, as being psychologically safer. In 'Ariel' the horse is indeed pulsation conquered on 'stasis in darkness'; but it leads not to a fever of blood but to a pearly ecstasy:

I foam to wheat, a glitter of seas

and a happily suicidal wish. We deal here with a sublimation, the idea of love rather than actual love.[19]

That "a blue and transparent transfiguration is preferred to a more personal feeling" does not really need apology, though it may be difficult to recognize such a theme and to view it sympathetically and as other than a Freudian sublimation. Lavers, reversing the difficulty of two degrees of 'letting go,' implies that the desire for mystical union is an escape from erotic emotion.[20] If Plath's imagery here (no doubt consciously) suggests the "ecstasy of love," it does so because of the conventions of mystical or religious language. As William James says:

It is true that in the vast collection of religious phenomena, some are undisguisedly amatory—e.g., sex-deities and obscene rites in polytheism, and ecstatic feelings of union with the Savior . . . Religious language clothes itself in such poor symbols as our life affords, . . .[21]

The rider's headlong plunge into the sun, like the fatal falls which Albert Heim wrote about, involves surrender, a final letting go of self which yields an ultimate reconciliation. The rider does not regret leaving behind her self and history, for they are dead. Her mourning (for the lost 'gods,' the "dead men," for her dead history, and the "dead hands"), along with her personal self, is dissolved and transformed in the "cauldron of mo[u]rning." Consumed in the fiery sunrise, the rider, like Ariel/Jerusalem, has been both sacrificed and preserved.

"Years"

"Years," like "Ariel," treats the theme of transcendence, but rather than enacting it, offers a skeptical contrast between a static, boring eternity and a transcendence that can be achieved only through suffering—in its broadest sense of 'undergoing'—in time.

The speaker views Christ's crucifixion as a confirmation of this boring eternity, for it is his godhood, his eternal aspect, and not his suffering and death (represented by spikes of holly) that she is thinking about:

> They enter as animals from the outer
> Space of holly where spikes
> Are not the thoughts I turn on, like a Yogi,
> But greenness, darkness so pure
> They freeze and are.
>
> O God, I am not like you
> In your vacuous black,
> Stars stuck all over, bright stupid confetti.
> Eternity bores me,
> I never wanted it.[22]

What pains her is the thought of Christ's eternity (suggested by the frozen greenness of the holly). This is what she turns on—

first, in the sense of 'musing about,' but also in the sense of being
'impaled upon,' and in the sense of 'attacking':

> And you, great Stasis—
> What is so great in that!
> Is it a tiger this year, this roar at the door?
> Is it a Christus,
> The awful
>
> God-bit in him
> Dying to fly and be done with it?

The God-bit of a "Christus" (its bit of stasis) is only "dying"
(in two senses of the word) to rejoin its amorphous, vacuous eternity, as if living in time, in the world, and being incarnate, were
not real. She, however, does not think the "great Stasis" is "so
great"; she would rather suffer and die ("What I love is / The
piston in motion— / My soul dies before it") in order to be continually reborn in time, in moments of ecstasy—her suffering (in
its broad and narrow senses) continually redeemed by the death
of the soul or personal self. "Ecstasy," Ted Hughes says, was
Plath's favorite word.[23] Clearly she had the original sense of
the word in mind, the sense of transcending herself, losing herself,
standing outside of herself, in life. This is what "Years" celebrates
—in an earlier draft the speaker says the piston puts her in
ecstasy. In the final lines, the motionless red berries are "themselves," self-contained and "very still." Through their conventional association with Christ's blood, they also represent his
achievement: the surmounting of history by stasis. This is opposed
by the horses' hooves, which "will not have it"; and opposed by
the moving pistons before which the speaker's soul dies and she
stands outside herself, in ecstasy.

The theme of "Years" was very likely influenced by the depiction of the relation of time and eternity in *The Years* by Virginia
Woolf, one of Plath's favorite writers. The novel, in presenting the
history of a family, offers two distinct levels or perspectives. The
passages which introduce the chapters (each dealing with a different
one of the "years") depict timeless or impersonal or general aspects
of the world: wind, waves, sunlight, a rainstorm, falling leaves; or

the bustle of a city street. These passages almost never mention the characters. Yet when the lives of the characters are taken up, they in some sense incarnate aspects of the impersonal, of continuity, change, and so on. Without the historical level to embody these qualities, there would be no story, no action; there would be only stasis.

This is, precisely, the poem's objection to undifferentiated eternity. The years of one's life might be seen as momentary embodiments ("animals" which arrive from "outer space," eventually to be reabsorbed, like the Christus, into static eternity). Unembodied eternity is nothing—a great bore. It even bores itself— in a draft of the poem, the "great Stasis" is "secretly in love" with the "sound track" of history, echoing Blake's "Eternity is in love with the productions of time."[24]

Woolf's novel ends with an affirmation that eternity can be known only in time; "Years," too, presents this view of the relation between eternity (stasis) and ecstasy (ec-stasis). (In slightly different form, the same theme appears in both "Totem" and "Mystic.")

When the speaker says that her soul dies before the piston in motion, she means that at such a moment she feels reborn. This ecstatic transcendence, possible only by being open to suffering, is eternity grasped in the moment, and the potential for such rebirth exists in each living moment. In the draft, the speaker says that "foulnesses peel" from her "every day," another way of asserting continual redemption rather than a final experience like Christ's. This insight was familiar to Plath from numerous sources, including Eliot ("the time of death is every moment" ["The Dry Salvages"] to which Plath added the notation "birth every moment, too"); and probably also from her personal experience.

"Totem"

"Totem" approaches the problem of the meaning of life in the face of death; the idea that death must be confronted without sentimentality. Everything is death to something else, and everything in the end gets eaten by death:

The engine is killing the track, the track is silver,
It stretches into the distance. It will be eaten nevertheless.

Its running is useless.
At nightfall there is the beauty of drowned fields,

Dawn gilds the farmers like pigs,
Swaying slightly in their thick suits,

White towers of Smithfield ahead,
Fat haunches and blood on their minds.

There is no mercy in the glitter of cleavers,
The butcher's guillotine that whispers: "How's this,
    how's this?"

In the bowl the hare is aborted,
Its baby head out of the way, embalmed in spice,

Flayed of fur and humanity.
Let us eat it like Plato's afterbirth,

Let us eat it like Christ.

Can one therefore make sense of killing and eating (living and dying)? There seems to be no sacramental aspect to the killing done by the butchers: it is mere butchery, part of their profession. Their acts have been devalued, "flayed of . . . humanity." When she says, "Let us eat it *like* Plato's afterbirth," "*like* Christ," she invokes the ancient sacramental act of "eating the god," a reminder of life and death with sacred meaning. Yet meaning can no longer be found in such mystical participation, for the answers or examples of the gods are no longer adequate. Christ and Plato deny death —or at least to some degree sentimentalize it in denying its 'destroyer' aspect. Pathetic and ineffectual, they hang "On a stick that rattles and clicks, a counterfeit snake,"[25] reduced not only to mere mortals, but to toys. Redemption cannot be found through metaphorical eating of Plato and Christ—through mystically participating in the being of "important" men—because their importance is empty, dead, counterfeit, and harmless: devoid of essential power, just as they are. Their "grimaces" and "round eyes" suggest their childlike inadequacy. Sacramentally partaking of them would be an empty ritual.[26]

That Plato and Christ are counterfeit snakes suggests that a genuine snake—the real cobra—is an emblem of authenticity. The image discloses a vision which acknowledges and puts in perspective the destroyer aspect of existence. When one 'looks death in the eye,' one sees life eternally threading itself through death:

> Shall the hood of the cobra appal me—
> The loneliness in its eye, the eye of the mountains
>
> Through which the sky eternally threads itself?

With its outstretched hood, the head of the cobra resembles the head of a needle; and the thread of the sky eternally passes through its eye. Everything which lives, lives by virtue of passing through the eye—of incarnation and therefore of death—without which there would be no point of reference, no shape, no meaning to history or to individual life. It is as if personality, individual incarnation, were space sifting through forms. The sky would be infinite, blank, and static, were there nothing through which it threaded itself; but passing through the cobra's eye it becomes an image of time and being manifested in particular histories and lives. The cobra's eye is the particular 'now' through which eternity threads itself and death is accomplished. In representing the organizing principle of the universe, it is an image of the source of reconciliation, and may in fact allude to another such image. In the poem, the eye of the cobra is also "the eye of the mountains." And, on Mount Sinai, "Allah showed himself to Moses . . . through the opening the size of a needle."[27]

The same play on the words "eye" and "I" that occurs elsewhere in Plath's poetry is also a part of the meaning of the appalling "loneliness" in the cobra's eye. The poem here alludes to the seemingly impersonal bleakness of the perspective represented by the image of the cobra, an aspect that has sometimes been referred to as 'the loneliness of God.' Nevertheless, the impersonality of the perspective represented by the cobra reinforces the sense of it as an authentic vision, one which takes death into account.

Plato and Christ were seen in grotesque close-up, as counterfeit snakes or sticks; but the image of the sky threading itself through

the cobra's eye offers a detached view of the universe, a view
from the aspect of eternity—sharply contrasted with the lines
which immediately follow it:

> The world is blood-hot and personal
>
> Dawn says, with its blood-flush.[28]

If the cobra describes the universe in a timeless and impersonal
way, dawn exists in and delineates time on a more intimate level,
bringing the message that while death, abstractly considered, may
be impersonal, the death of each individual is, for that person,
an intensely blood-hot and personal prospect.

The image of the spider, a mad, unstoppable, relentless force,
unites the aspects of personal and impersonal death:

> I am mad, calls the spider, waving its many arms.
>
> And in truth it is terrible,
> Multiplied in the eyes of the flies.
>
> They buzz like blue children
> In nets of the infinite,
>
> Roped in at the end by the one
> Death with its many sticks.

A spider is multiplied in the compound eyes of a single fly, in the
collective eyes of many flies, and also in their 'I's'—or selves.
But despite such multiplication, and though there might be as
many spiders as there are flies, for an individual fly the spider
that eats it is for it *the* spider, *the* death. And in general there is
only *one* impersonal death, with its many sticks, its many instru-
mentalities, even if the flies do not see it this way (and perhaps
this is why they are "roped in," in the sense of being fooled). Death
manifests itself both as the spider, the predator, which ends each
blood-hot and personal experience of self by spreading its nets
over "the infinite" (a web which covers and defines blank eternity),
and as the cobra, the symbol of eternity as perpetually embodied
in living forms, phenomena, which are therefore impersonally and
universally condemned to death or decay.

In a sense, each personal death is really only a version of the same impersonal death which in one guise or another will conclude each life; and each individual life or story is a version of the same story eternally reenacted:

> There is no terminus, only suitcases
>
> Out of which the same self unfolds like a suit
> Bald and shiny, with pockets of wishes,
>
> Notions and tickets, short circuits and folding mirrors.

These lines suggest that there is no completion either for the general process or for the individual. What if, just as life, under the aspect of eternity, eternally moves through the cobra's eye, achieving form, each individual life must likewise eternally move through different bodies, without release? This is of course the *other* view of rebirth: not the optimistic perspective of the mythology (rebirth, literal or metaphorical, as the goal), but something akin to the view of Hindus and others, where transmigration is to be transcended. Not the optimism of the eternal phoenix, but the despair of the immortal Tithonus (and possibly, in the reference to dawn, Plath echoes this myth), sentenced to an unending selfhood.

"Totem" presents such a vision, of "no terminus," no finality, only a suitcase (the body) with which one travels, and out of which "the same self unfolds like a suit" (the one laundered in Lethe and then re-used). The wishes, tickets, and short circuits are all emblems of incompletion; places unvisited, things left undone. The suitcase with its same suit also suggests the true, eternal, and universal Self embodied, imprisoned, and disguised by the individual personality and selfhood.

This problem of the incompleteness of an individual life, or the incompleteness of a process which involves endless repetitions of the same self, has been dealt with in just these terms many times before, as in the Brihadāranyaka Upanishad (Ted Hughes, in conversation, said Plath had encountered Yeats's translation of the Upanishads in the latter part of 1962):

When the knowing Self masters the personal self at death, the personal self groans, . . .

When body grows weak through age or disease, the Self separates itself from the limbs, . . . man hastens back to birth, goes, as before, from birth to birth.[29]

And Shankaracharya states:

. . . The body is born, dies, is eaten by birds, turns into earth, is destroyed by weapons, fire and so forth, and suffers from disease and so on. I have entered this body as a bird enters a nest, . . . when this body perishes, I shall enter another body as a bird enters another nest when its previous one has been destroyed. Thus I am in beginningless transmigratory existence. I have been abandoning . . . bodies . . . and I have been getting other new bodies over and over again. I am forced . . . to rotate in the incessant cycle of birth and death as in a waterwheel. . . . I am tired of this rotation . . . so I have come . . . in order to end the rotation in the wheel . . . Therefore I am eternal and different from the body. The bodies come and go like a person's garments . . .[30]

Stating the problem in this way requires the solution of transcendence:

Death after death attains he who thinks he sees manifoldness in this world.

That imperishable, constant one must be perceived only with the mind; (it is) the unborn, great, constant Self, free from impurity, higher than the ether. . . . For the . . . enlightened man, complete liberation is obtained upon the death of the body . . . he is not reborn.[31]

Graves likewise mentions the problem of "escape from the Wheel"—release from the "same self," from the "stigma of selfhood." Just as with Shankaracharya, Graves, and many others, "Totem" shows Plath's concern with a nexus of problems which only transcendence can resolve.[32]

"Paralytic"

"Paralytic" treats the predicament of a particular life and of personal suffering concretely, as "Totem" does not. It presents the experience of a totally paralyzed man for whom the issues of the personal and the larger Self, and the theme of rebirth, become the only way to come to terms with his reality. Paralysis raises these issues as does illness or patienthood in several other poems, because it enforces the separation of thought from action, or of an essential from a mundane self, and so the paralytic finds himself naturally at a point which another might reach only through deliberate effort and discipline. Such a context might easily facilitate an experience of rebirth. A person incapable of action in the world, or someone who already feels that mundane identity has "[sunk] out of sight" ("Tulips"), may more readily experience the illusoriness or transitoriness of possessions, body, self, and drama. Having, to an extent, already been forced into this experience, such an individual—if the ultimate aim is letting go—will have the advantage of having less to hold on to.

In a draft of the poem, the speaker anticipates the ending when he says, "I am learning to let go." This letting go—the experiencing of a certain perspective—does not appear as an impersonal musing, but neither is it presented in terms of Plath's myth. She distances herself from the subject to the extent of presenting the story, outside her mythicized biography, of a man in a special position to give up his attachments to the world (because he can more easily relinquish the illusion of his mundane self as the ultimate protagonist) and to achieve transcendence.

The draft of the poem says, "There is no sin but acts. / They blacken the heart like vultures," a statement which implicitly opposes self-conscious, self-important acts, to *being*. The immobility of the paralytic reduces his participation in a drama, and therefore his sense of a self or an "I" which participates. He is thus as if 'sinless' in the Hindu sense that 'No act clings to him.' Plath probably eliminated the line "There is no sin but acts" for the same reason she excised "I am learning to let go": in both cases, what these lines had earlier flatly stated is, at the end of the poem, dramatically illustrated by the experience of the paralytic.

The paralytic does not undergo various conventional sorts of spiritual travail: his paralysis is at once trial enough, and also the very thing which places him where he must inevitably consider letting go, as there is really nothing else for him to do. And so movement toward transcendence, grace, and reconciliation reveals itself as immanent in a situation where one would least expect it. In an extreme sense, "Paralytic" illustrates William James's remark that we must lose the natural life before we can participate in the spiritual one; or that there is an "opposition between the men who *have* and the men who *are*."[33]

Since the body of the man in the poem is alienated from his sense of self, the world in which the body cannot participate also seems alien. His self really is, in effect, only his mind, for he has no active presence in the world, even though he continues to have a stake in it until he lets go. His former life is visible to him in his wife and daughters:

> Photographs visit me—
> My wife, dead and flat, . . .
> . . .
> Two girls
> As flat as she, who whisper 'We're your daughters.'

But this life is inaccessible to him in much the way that the past is inaccessible to the speaker of "A Life," who has "one too many dimensions to enter" it. For the paralytic, for whom "the day outside glides by like ticker tape," life consists of "tapestries" of random sights and sounds which he can lie on, like a "dead egg," but "cannot touch."

Plath's mention of "saintliness" and "saint" several times in the draft suggests that William James's chapter on "Saintliness" may have contributed to her portrayal of the paralytic,[34] whose experience is certainly illuminated by what James says of this quality:

The transition from tenseness, self-responsibility, and worry, to *equanimity, receptivity, and peace,* is the most wonderful of all those shiftings of inner equilibrium, those changes of the personal centre of energy, . . . and the chief wonder of it is that it *so often comes about,* not by doing, but *by simply relaxing and throwing the burden down. This abandonment of self-responsibility* seems to be the fundamental act in specifically religious . . . practice.[35] [Italics added.]

The point at which the paralytic breaks with life comes almost audibly, with the word "crack":

> The still waters
> Wrap my lips,
>
> Eyes, nose and ears,
> A clear
> Cellophane I cannot crack.

Having nothing else to do—and accepting the necessity of relinquishing self-responsibility—he smiles, and his experience of transcending selfhood, of oneness, appears in conventional mystical terms:

> I smile, a buddha, all
> Wants, desire
> Falling from me like rings
> Hugging their lights.

Having thrown down the burden (of wants, desires, and attachments), he feels "An immense elation and freedom, as the outlines of the confining selfhood melt down."[36]

The poem, while sympathetically presenting the paralytic's discovery of his transcendent self, ends with an image which, while it expresses self-sufficient "saintliness," might appear to contain a qualifying note:

> The claw
> Of the magnolia,
> Drunk on its own scents,
> Asks nothing of life.

One meaning of the image is that the flower—naturally *being*, with nothing to strive for—is juxtaposed with the man—who has both a problem and the consciousness of it (of not unselfconsciously being). But perhaps the image of the magnolia claw suggests a kind of narcissism. While fascinated by the prospect of absolute transcendence of selfhood and attachment, Plath might understandably have been made uneasy by the prospect of an experience which in a sense cuts the ground from under the self that contemplates it. To one who has not experienced such a state, it might seem grotesque; or one might be able to imagine giving up attachment to one's selfhood and its manifestations, yet be unable to see how one could, say, continue to love one's children in a way satisfactory to the person asking the question.

Whether or not Plath intended the magnolia claw as a qualifying note, the comparison of the paralytic with a buddha whose wants and desire have fallen away presents a straightforward image of the discarded self and drama. The image reflects descriptions of transcendence that occur widely in religious literature, as in the Upanishads:[37]

When all desires of the heart are gone, mortal becomes immortal, man becomes Spirit, even in this life.

As the skin of a snake is peeled off and lies dead . . . so this body falls and lies on the ground; but the Self is bodiless, immortal, full of light; he is of Spirit, he becomes Spirit. . . . He, whose Self lying in this mysterious uncertain body is awakened, becomes Spirit. He becomes the maker of the world, . . . he is the world itself.[38]

"Paralytic" similarly defines the concepts of false self and drama so that they refer not only to the speaker's particular condition, but to all such dramas and selves; and when the mundane self is let go, a transcendent identity is disclosed.[39]

"Mystic"

"Mystic," written just after "Totem" and "Paralytic," deals more straightforwardly than any other poem with the problem of transcendence. It illustrates a perennial religious or mystical crisis, that of the 'dark night of the soul'—although whether the ending of the poem presents a resolution to the problem (that is, whether or not an epiphany occurs) is ambiguous.

The poem begins with the speaker pondering the transitoriness of religious, ecstatic, or mystical experience. One may be "seized up" in "the sun's conflagrations," but the moment of ecstasy does not endure. Having "seen God," how can one settle for anything less? The poem asks whether one's only recourse is, then, to feeble rituals which cannot re-create the ecstasy or to "memory" which cannot reproduce it—for memory can no more recapture such an experience than the sea can "remember the walker upon it." Both the *immediacy* of the experience and its *sense of truth* 'leak' away. The "great love" or ecstatic union with God abates to "tenderness."

Plath had read accounts of mystical experience in James's book; and excerpts from such accounts, and his own observations about such experiences, clarify the nature of Plath's questioning in the poem. According to James the characteristics of mystical experience are ineffability, immediacy, passivity—with the will in abeyance, and a "noetic quality" or quality of truth. Such states of consciousness must also be "directly experienced"; for they "cannot be imparted or transferred to others" and are always transient.[40] These very characteristics constitute the problem presented in "Mystic"—the immediacy of the experience and its noetic quality being precisely what leak away. From this point of view, one might say that for Christ himself (insofar as he was a mystic), his experience was personal, essentially incommunicable, and evanescent. Mystical participation in Christ through the "pill of the Communion tablet" would avail nothing—it could not enable another to see God.

An earlier title, "Woodcut," and the original opening line of the poem ("This little woodcut of the Inquisition is so beautiful") suggest that Plath was looking at a depiction of an auto-da-fé or a scene that reminded her of one. This is useful in reconstructing the context in which the poem was conceived, and also suggests that the "hooks" of questions may possibly have a basis in the woodcut (aside from their being personal questions, hooks on which the speaker is caught) as a visual rendering of inquisitional fires, or perhaps a visual representation of the air. In either case, the hooks or questions would have been associated with religious ecstasy and the suffering it enables one to endure.

In its final form, "Mystic" begins with the oppressive "air . . . a mill of hooks— / Questions without answer," which afflict the speaker like flies

> Whose kiss stings unbearably
> In the fetid wombs of black air under pines in summer.

The reverie continues:

> I remember
> The dead smell of sun on wood cabins,
> The stiffness of sails, the long salt winding sheets.

The remembered "dead smell," "stiffness," and "winding sheets" also represent the deadness of memory itself, an insight then related to the earlier questions about the experience of the mystic:

> Once one has seen God, what is the remedy?

The question is asked only because the experience of God does not endure. What is one to do after being

> . . . seized up

> Without a part left over,
> Not a toe, not a finger, and used,
> Used utterly, in the sun's conflagrations, the stains
> That lengthen from ancient cathedrals . . .

The speaker ironically lists a series of obviously ineffectual remedies for the aftermath of such an experience, which include:

> The pill of the Communion tablet,
> The walking beside still water? Memory?
> Or picking up the bright pieces
> Of Christ in the faces of rodents,
> The tame flower-nibblers, the ones

> Whose hopes are so low they are comfortable—
> The humpback in her small, washed cottage
> Under the spokes of the clematis.

These feeble expedients are far removed from the actual ecstasy of being "seized up . . . in the sun's conflagrations."

The religious problem expressed in "Mystic" is the major theme of St. John of the Cross:

The best-known feature of St. John's mystical writings is his description of the dark night of the soul . . . By "the dark night" he principally meant the extreme sense of desolation and despair that overcomes the soul after its first illumination by God. This illumination is not the highest state, for eventually the soul will achieve a perfect, lasting union with God—the Spiritual Marriage. . . . It thus appears that the dark night is brought on by the deprivation felt when the mystical state of illumination ceases.[41]

This is Plath's formulation of the problem:

> Does the sea
>
> Remember the walker upon it?
> Meaning leaks from the molecules.

Since "meaning leaks from the molecules," it must be continually re-created and experienced in the present. It cannot be inherited from Christ. But the lines also suggest that the present (the ecstatic present expressed in "Years") might be no less miraculous or sacred than the past.

The ending of "Mystic" might imply that a tentative answer has been found through an epiphany. The sun has risen, and the world is fresh, created anew, suggesting the perpetual rebirth of the self, its changeless underlying purity. It is a celebration of ecstasy:

> The chimneys of the city breathe, the window sweats,
> The children leap in their cots.
> The sun blooms, it is a geranium.
>
> The heart has not stopped.

The poem does end with a sunrise, possibly signifying that the "dark night" is over.

These final lines seem to intimate a vision of all process as epiphany. The city—and, by extension, the world—is an organism which breathes, sweats, and leaps; and the sun is its heart. "The" (not "my") heart is the heart of the sun and of the speaker as well. It has not stopped, for both hearts are identified with the life of the world. The simplicity and directness of these lines enhance the sense of ecstasy continually enacted. That the sun is a geranium (which blooms every day) depicts a world continually sacrificed to itself and reborn. A wide variety of images found elsewhere in Plath's poetry support the view that the morning sun—the fiery red geranium—symbolizes transcendence, or spiritual purification.

Its redness and fire (as with similar images in "Fever 103°," "Lady Lazarus," and "Ariel") represent both the process of recovering the true self and the self that is recovered.

As a red flower that "blooms," and as the heart of the world, the sun is identified with vitality and life. There are similar associations in "Poppies in October," in which a woman's heart "blooms" through her coat; and in "Tulips," in which the heart of the speaker "opens and closes / Its bowl of red blooms." A red flower directly represents a stage in the progression toward transcendence in "Fever 103°," where the speaker is a fiery, "glowing" camellia. The sun in "Mystic" is particularly reminiscent of the fiery morning sun (in a draft of that poem even called a "red heart") into which the rider plunges in "Ariel." In "Poem for a Birthday," "My heart is a stopped geranium."

Herbert Fingarette points out that:

> . . . the self which is lost in mystic enlightenment is not the self essen-
> tial to the practical carrying on of one's ordinary daily activities. . . .
> when we speak of enlightenment, we are not talking of an existence
> divorced from the "everyday world." On the contrary, it consists of
> life within this world.[42]

This statement lends support to a view of the end of "Mystic" as an affirmation, a vision of ecstasy and celebration of "life within this world," the beginning of the incorporation of the meaning of the mystical experience into the course of everyday life.

The ending of Virginia Woolf's *The Years* contains a number of elements strikingly similar to the ending of "Mystic." Eleanor Pargiter, now an old woman, has been at an all-night family gathering, during which she has dozed off lightly. When she awakens,

> She felt extraordinarily happy . . . this sleep, this momentary trance,
> . . . had left her with nothing but a feeling; a feeling, not a dream.
> . . . Her feeling of happiness returned to her, her unreasonable exalta-
> tion. It seemed to her that they were all young, with the future before
> them. Nothing was fixed; nothing was known; life was open and free
> before them.

She dozes off again, and again awakens:

She half opened her eyes. But where was she? In what room? . . . She opened her eyes wide. Here she was; alive; in this room, with living people. . . .

There must be another life, she thought, . . . Not in dreams; but here and now, in this room, with living people. She felt as if she were standing on the edge of a precipice with her hair blown back; she was about to grasp something that just evaded her. There must be another life, here and now, she repeated. This is too short, too broken. We know nothing, even about ourselves. . . . She held her hands hollowed; she felt that she wanted to enclose the present moment; to make it stay; to fill it fuller and fuller, with the past, the present and the future, until it shone, whole, bright, deep with understanding. . . . It's useless, she thought, opening her hands. It must drop. It must fall. And then? she thought. For her too there would be the endless night; the endless dark. She looked ahead of her as though she saw opening in front of her a very long dark tunnel. But, thinking of the dark, something baffled her; in fact, it was growing light. The blinds were white.

This records the beginning of the transfiguration of a London dawn, which takes place in the last few pages of the novel:

The sun had risen. The sky between the chimneys looked extraordinarily blue. . . .

Eleanor . . . was looking at the curtained houses across the square. . . . Everything looked clean swept, fresh and virginal. . . . the roofs were tinged purple against the blue; the chimneys were a pure brick red. An air of ethereal calm and simplicity lay over everything.

Eleanor's "dream," the almost-grasped vision, leaves her in a heightened state, creating a rhythm which is completed in an ordinary event, answering a question which the book as a whole has been posing:

. . . Eleanor . . . was watching a taxi that was gliding slowly round the square. It stopped in front of a house two doors down. . . . A young man got out; he paid the driver. Then a girl in a tweed travelling suit followed him. He fitted his latch-key to the door. "There," Eleanor murmured, as he opened the door . . . "There!" she repeated as the door shut with a little thud behind them.

She then turns to her brother, her repetition of the word "now" complementing the eternality of the dawn described in the last line of the novel:

Then she turned round into the room. "And now?" she said, looking at Morris, who was drinking the last drops of a glass of wine. "And now?" she asked, holding out her hands to him.

The sun had risen, and the sky above the houses wore an air of extraordinary beauty, simplicity and peace.[43]

It is as if her "now," and the eternal—the "present day" (the title of this final section), and "the years" which at the beginning of the novel were impersonally "wheeling, like the rays of a searchlight, . . . [passing] one after another across the sky"—are, for Eleanor, finally experienced as one.

The ending of "Mystic" is open to another interpretation, according to which no epiphany occurs. As Eileen Aird puts it:

The dilemma of 'Mystic' . . . is that of harmonising ecstasy and normality, for the insights of the mystic bring him only pain. . . . Various reactions to normality are examined but rejected and the greatest pain strikes with the reluctant return to the new day with its muted beauty; . . .[44]

The final lines would record the speaker's reentry into mundane life following the ecstatic or mystical experience alluded to at the beginning of the poem; an experience, however, insufficient (in terms of intensity or integrity) to transform the speaker's perspective on that life and on her experience of her mundane self. Or to put it another way, the ultimate "Spiritual Marriage" has not yet taken place. (Even so, one would not say that the experience of the mystic brings *only* pain.) Such a reading would, apparently, be supported by a line excised from the draft of the poem, "It is only the sun that rises, the one transfigurer . . . it is not enough." (However, given Plath's unusually extensive reworking of the ending of this poem, this line may well represent a final attitude or resolution for the poem momentarily considered and then rejected.)

Here, the ending would, it seems, exemplify the continuing

problem outlined earlier in the poem through the series of questions, "Once one has seen God, what is the remedy? / . . . Memory? . . ." If so, Plath is dealing, from the mystical perspective itself, with one of the age-old problems of mysticism:

> . . . it is not amnesia which appears after the ecstasy any more than it was complete unconsciousness during it; the mystic remembers perfectly, but he does it through the belittling and dividing forms of the understanding which once more oppress him.[45]

Whether or not there is an epiphany at the end of the poem, its entire movement is within the bounds marked by the polarities of faith and despair. To see in the poem an attitude simply of despairing rejection, of sarcasm, or mockery toward mystical experience is to be oblivious to the evidence of religious crisis.

"Mystic" has nonetheless been taken as a poem which flatly rejects the mystical experience. For some readers, the theme of transcendence seems to be foreclosed; and Plath is read as if her poems were only an extension of her immediate domestic and private concerns, and as if broader themes did not enter her poetry. This sort of view shrinks the mystical experience referred to in the poem to a possible palliative, considered by the poet Sylvia Plath, who weighed and rejected it in her pride of torment. Such readers have either been unaware of the implications of Plath's concern with transcendence or have a limited notion of what mystical experience is.[46] Joyce Carol Oates, in a review of *Winter Trees*, says:

> All [the poems] take us through a personality-disguised-as-the-world, in which the terrifying question is asked: "Is there no way out of the mind?" ("Apprehensions"). There are tentative replies to this question, but all are burdened with their own kinds of terror. In "Mystic," the poet speculates upon the possibility of being "seized up" by God . . . and finds this "remedy" inhuman; . . .[47]

The question "Is there no way out of the mind?" is indeed a central one, but Oates treats Plath only as a 'confessional' poet with particular personal problems (in the same review she says Plath is "our acknowledged Queen of Sorrows" and that *Winter Trees* "affirms death"), and she does not see the impersonal or universal aspect of this question. She writes elsewhere of the poem's attitude toward mystical experience that

. . . even a tentative exploration of a possible "God" is viewed in the old terms, in the old images of dream and terror. . . . "questions without answer" . . . led her briefly to thoughts of God. Yet whoever or whatever this "God" is, no comfort is possible because the ego cannot experience any interest or desire without being engulfed: . . . "Used": the mystic will be exploited, victimized, hurt. He can expect no liberation or joy from God, but only another form of dehumanizing brutality.[48]

But the woman in "Mystic" desires this experience; the thought that the ego will be "engulfed" does not trouble her, but attracts her. "Once one has seen God" puts the experience firmly in the (hypothetical) past, stating the problem as one of continuing to live after the mystical experience, not as one of overcoming a brutalizing engulfing. The mystic is hurt only in being unable to maintain the experience (or to have its meaning transform mundane life).

The contrast between actually having a mystical experience (*being* a mystic, getting out of the mind) and having been a mystic, parallels Plath's statement about herself as a poet:

I find myself absolutely fulfilled when I have written a poem, when I'm writing one. Having written one, then you fall away very rapidly from having been a poet to becoming a sort of poet in rest, which isn't the same thing at all.[49]

(Writing *can* take one out of the mind, but this ecstasy, too, fades as one returns to everyday life.)

Whatever the ambiguities of the poem's ending, whether or not the dark night of the soul continues, transcendence nonetheless remains the central concern of "Mystic," and only by recognizing this can the poem—and the direction in which Plath's poetry was moving during the final weeks of her life—be brought into focus.

The Moon and Transcendence

"Edge" apparently envisions the last act of the mythic drama. One may wonder how, having written it, Plath could have gone back to the mythology—the poem seems so final. Yet its imagery serves a dual function, portraying the death of the mythic protagonist and the completion of the mythic drama, but also implying a more metaphorical death of the self, thereby implicitly challenging the ultimacy of the drama, and reconciling it.

The symbol of the Moon in particular represents the fate of the heroine, but also the general availability of a transcendent perspective on life-as-drama, through the death of the ego. Since it reconciles all the opposites it contains—birth and death, old and new, black and white—the Moon is "used to this sort of thing." The next step is for the speaker to share this perspective. The implication might be, the *Moon* has "nothing to be sad about"— why should I?

It is not that Plath rejects her earlier Moon-symbolism, but that all along the Moon had a double function (at least implicitly), suggesting both transcendence and the particulars to be transcended. As in "Lesbos" and "The Detective," it can represent the mythic drama of losing and mourning the god, and also a detached perspective beyond drama, "Hard and apart and white." The Moon is therefore both cruel and indifferent: the true Muse; and the attitude toward it might be said to be like holding God responsible in the short run for one's immediate sufferings, yet recognizing union with God as the solution, in the long run, of the predicament of the finite self.

The woman in "Edge" *is* dead, but the perspective with which the speaker (clearly in some sense the woman's proxy) identifies herself—and thus the dead woman's perspective on herself—is eternal or transcendent. To the degree that the speaker does seem to be the dead woman's proxy, the poem entails the paradox of a dreamer dreaming of herself, viewing her self'—which is not, however, her real self. Here is the splitting off of some essential self (identified with the imperturbable Moon) from that which must die in order to end the drama. The dual function of the Moon, which both represents the drama and is a natural symbol of a transcendent perspective, brings again to mind the Moon's function as the protagonist's double (her totem, familiar, mother, muse, cousin, and so on).

Otto Rank explores the connection between such associations in his essay "The Double as Immortal Self," which Plath, who cited it several times in "The Magic Mirror," sums up in this way:

> Otto Rank . . . analyses the gradual shift from the conception of the Double as the immortal soul to that of the Double as the symbol of death.[50]

Rank's essay provides a clear definition, as well as numerous concrete examples, of the double as representative of the mortal and the immortal (and separable) self:

> Originally conceived of as a guardian angel, assuring immortal survival to the self, the double eventually appears as precisely the opposite, a reminder of the individual's mortality, indeed, the announcer of death itself. *Thus, from a symbol of eternal life in the primitive, the double developed into an omen of death in the self-conscious individual of modern civilization.*[51] [Italics added.]

The symbol of the Moon has for Plath precisely this ambiguity, for while it is harbinger of the 'death' of the protagonist of the mythic drama, it also represents her immortal or transcendent self.[52]

The Moon is in fact a conventional emblem of transcendent or enlightened mind. Right at the beginning of the late poems, in "The Moon and the Yew Tree," Plath wrote: "This is the light of the mind, cold and planetary," and the light represents not just a particular mood of the speaker, but a symbolic quality. The "light of the mind" as the Moon's light is not mere embellishment, even though its potential is not developed.[53] Although the poem's ending involves a personified Moon ("She is bald and wild"), earlier the Moon suggests something impersonal.

Plath was familiar with many of the writings and contexts in which the Moon is associated with mind. In Yeats's mythology, for example, aspects of mind and personality are identified with various phases of the moon. The Moon also represents illumined mind in some of the writings which interested him (such as works of Indian philosophy and mysticism), which Plath encountered through Yeats and also elsewhere.

In Zen Buddhism—with which she was acquainted—the Moon

is a symbol of enlightened mind, the "mind of emptiness" in which dualities are reconciled:

Absence, extinction, and unoccupancy—these are not the Buddhist conception of emptiness. . . . It is Absolute Emptiness transcending all forms of mutual relationship, of subject and object, birth and death, God and the world . . . it is a zero full of infinite possibilities, it is a void of inexhaustible contents. . . . Sometimes the [Zen] master is more poetic and compares the mind of "emptiness" to the moon, calling it the mind-moon . . . An ancient master . . . sings of this moon:

> The mind-moon is solitary and perfect:
> The light swallows the ten-thousand things.
> It is not that the light illuminates objects,
> Nor are objects in existence.
> Both light and objects are gone,
> And what is it that remains?[54]

For Buddhism, the Moon's mirrorlike reflecting of light (a characteristic seen by some critics to be evidence of the Moon's negative meaning in Plath)[55] is precisely what makes it a suitable symbol of enlightened mind, of pure, natural, unspoiled Self,[56] exemplifying positive emptiness—a freedom from preconceptions, prejudices, automatic intellectualizing of experience, and pre-set ways of perceiving the world. It represents complete stainlessness.

A dead yet eternal planet, the Moon also emblemizes the death of the mundane self, the Buddhist 'true death.' It looks down upon the dead woman as if it were an eternal Self overlooking the incarnated "selfhood" it transcends. The coldness, hardness, and mercilessness of the Moon which make it a perfect symbol of implacable fate in a mythic drama also represent a desired state of being, the self which the drama does not really touch. Because the Moon in this way foreshadows both disaster and transcendence, it is at once—and particularly in "Edge"—an object of both threat and longing.

While Plath's strong sense of sympathy with the Moon may have been based partly on literary and other sources, these meanings and associations must have been rooted in a profound direct intuitive identification with the actual moon. She must have found in its nightly reappearance a silent companion and personal emblem, 'mother' of her mythic drama, her spiritual life, and possessor of a luminous and imperturbable calm. Seeing the moon clearly engendered in her a deep sense of communion, which James would surely have described as a feeling of a mystical nature.

Though "Edge" may seem merely a straightforward suicide note, and while this is one of the levels in it, it is an extremely complex and ambiguous poem. What does the death mean? The death of whom, or what? Does the poem signify the finality of a phase of life—does it represent being beyond the drama of marriage, through a clean break? Or does it represent an identity ultimately beyond all drama?

Even taken as a suicide note, "Edge" is clearly the imagining of a state of grace or transcendence. The motivation for such a concern entails the threat of disintegration. As Fingarette puts it:

We should not be surprised if, frequently, the motivation sufficient to continue such a painful effort is a threatening sense of personal disintegration on a massive scale as the only alternative to success. Such a struggle, while not inevitable, should be relatively common among mystics.[57]

But the aim is transcendence, not death, as is well expressed in the anonymous medieval guide to spiritual meditation, *The Cloud of Unknowing:*

Now you ask me how you can destroy this pure awareness and feeling of your own being. Perhaps you think that if it were destroyed all other hindrances would also be destroyed; and if you think that, you are correct. . . . All men have reason for sorrow, but most particularly does he . . . who knows and feels that he *is.* . . . And yet, in all this sorrow, he does not desire to cease to exist; . . . But he does desire unceasingly to be rid of the awareness and the feeling of his being.[58]

That suicides, according to Noyes, report a sense of great peacefulness and calm might be brought to mind in this context: the act is born of despair, but the fruit of despair is peacefulness—for them, this extremity is the only way they have of letting go; but they do let go, and experience a transfiguration.

"Edge" contains both despair and, motivated by it, the envisioning of grace—Plath's actual suicide marking the failure to achieve within life the faith she envisioned. To take the moon's perspective is to take the perspective of faith itself, for faith *is* a belief in completion, salvation not in the future, but now, in the present, rendering even one's envisioned death acceptable.

If Plath used "Edge" to anticipate or imagine herself dead and laid out, the poem also may depict an attempt to envision detachment from her ego-drama by seeing herself dead to it. In this regard, it is important to remember that the poem focuses not just on the dead woman (and not at all on the *act* of death or suicide), but, especially at the end, on the completion, peacefulness, and indifference of the Moon's perspective. "Edge" would be entirely different were the Moon not in it; for the Moon's presence clearly constitutes more than an ironic commentary by the Mistress of Ceremonies.

The structure of the poem is very like that of certain spiritual exercises or meditations in adopting the perspective of the "witness"—the true, non-egoic, essential Self. In Vedāntic and other traditions, there is the "self as pure witness," as opposed to " 'sheaths' " or "layers of . . . being which arise from a series of false self-identifications";[59] there is "the 'known' " and " 'knowledge,' " "and the knower is the 'I' which constantly accompanies these two; but the witness is the Self which is constant and eternal."[60] The harmonious perspective described by Heim and Noyes may be seen as the sudden apprehension that the Witness is 'I,' and the recognition that the 'I' we thought we were—the selves of the drama; the conscious self, the dreaming self—are only projections, a series of false (inessential) self-identifications. The shock of impending death would dissolve these artificial boundaries and disclose the Witness. One might attempt to achieve the same experience through the well-known spiritual exercise of imagining one's own death.

Plath's poetry reflects that she came to consider success in altering the terms of her being as the "only alternative" to "disintegration on a massive scale" (to use Fingarette's phrase). The terms of this conflict are inherently religious, as they are in the recognition of selfhood as a stigma even while remaining at its mercy, and as they are in the attempt to integrate experiences of selfless ecstasy into mundane life. With this in mind, it should be clear that her suicide cannot be construed as the end of a morbid, tortured, death-loving woman (and, as is clear in comparing her to a poet such as Anne Sexton, the speaker of the late poems does not present herself as sick or neurotic, but as a heroine trapped in "the illusion of a Greek necessity"); it is rather the mark of failure to achieve wholeness in circumstances which made this achievement a matter of life and death. It might be mentioned in this context that her last two poems, both dated February 5, 1963, were "Balloons" and "Edge": in one of these a mother plays with her two children in a realistic domestic setting; the other presents a dead mother and her dead children in a stark symbolic manner.

Toward the end of her life, Plath underwent a religious crisis, undoubtedly precipitated by her domestic crisis, but also quite distinct from it. Although the breakup of her marriage probably made the problem of overcoming the "stigma of selfhood" an urgent one, the need to transcend personal history in a way more radical than that expressed in her poetry as mythic rebirth had long been implicit in her work. Anyone preoccupied with the limitations and apparent inescapability of personal history (concerns evident in "The Disquieting Muses" and "Electra on Azalea Path," and in still earlier poems such as "Lament" and "Full Fathom Five") has a very good chance of coming to be interested in entirely transcending personal history and the self which is its subject.

She had come to consider selfhood a problem; and she had experienced or imagined various states (reflected in "Ariel," "Mystic," "Paralytic") in which a confining selfhood is dissolved in an ecstatic apprehension of a larger identity. Yet while such experiences offer insights, they do not in themselves constitute a way of life that will permanently integrate these insights. This is the problem of the 'dark night of the soul,' acknowledged directly in "Mystic" and implied in "Ariel" and "Paralytic," where the ecstatic experience clearly has no future and will not itself be the state in which the speaker continues to live.

Had Plath survived, it seems likely, given the nature of her concerns at the end of her life, that she would have further developed and further explored the overtly religious themes of some of the last poems, coming more and more to realize her power of what Ted Hughes calls her "free and controlled access to depths formerly reserved to the primitive ecstatic priests, shamans and Holy men, . . ."; and, as in the case of her mythology, evolving a sensibility shaped by several traditions, but with a voice unmistakably her own. The unflinchingness of her gaze, her refusal to compromise the truth, her precision, her intelligence, and her passion—all of these would have qualified her uniquely, in the discovery of her wholeness, to convince us that the achievement is possible.

Notes to Chapters

I. THE MYTHIC NATURE OF THE POETRY

1. Ted Hughes, "Notes on the chronological order of Sylvia Plath's poems," *Tri-Quarterly*, no. 7 (Fall 1966), p. 81.

In a conversation of June 1974, Ted Hughes expressed reservations about his characterization of Lowell's work as "a torture cell walled with family portraits," etc. Perhaps this characterization is less applicable to some of Lowell's later work. Nevertheless, it was particularly useful at the time it was made in distinguishing Plath's poetry—which was being automatically and uncritically labeled 'confessional' (by Lowell, among others)—from that of Lowell and Sexton. And, with appropriate qualification, it continues to have merit.

All subsequent references, in the text or in notes, to conversations with Ted Hughes are to several conversations which took place in June 1974.

2. Lois Ames, Biographical Note to *The Bell Jar*, by Sylvia Plath (New York: Harper & Row, 1971), p. 295.

3. A. E. Dyson in *Critical Quarterly*, cited on the cover of the U.S. edition of *Ariel* (New York: Harper & Row, 1966).

4. Ted Hughes, "Notes on Plath's poems," p. 82.

5. Annette Lavers, "The world as icon—On Sylvia Plath's themes," in *The Art of Sylvia Plath*, ed. Charles Newman (Bloomington: Indiana University Press, 1970), pp. 109, 112, 101.

6. Thomas Szasz, "The Crime of Commitment," *Psychology Today*, March 1969, p. 56.

   David Holbrook, in his article "R. D. Laing & the Death Circuit" (*Encounter*, August 1968, pp. 35–45), treats as items of psychopathology the connection between the themes of false/true self and death/rebirth in Plath's work. And he seems to assume that this is the only way these themes can be taken, overlooking that they are, among other things, the universal terms of religious experience.

7. Ted Hughes, "Notes on Plath's poems," pp. 81–82.

8. See Plath's statement about an "Electra complex" (p. 116).

9. Sylvia Plath, "Ocean 1212-W," *The Listener*, August 29, 1963, p. 313.

10. Herbert Fingarette, *The Self in Transformation: Psychoanalysis, Philosophy, and the Life of the Spirit* (New York: Basic Books, 1963; reprint ed., New York: Harper & Row, Harper Torchbooks, 1965), p. 209.

11. Meerloo, cited by Fingarette, ibid.

II. THE STRUCTURE OF THE IMAGERY

1. A. Alvarez, "Sylvia Plath," *Art of Sylvia Plath*, p. 60.

III. THE CENTRAL SYMBOL OF THE MOON

1. Ted Hughes, "Sylvia Plath," in *Poetry Book Society Bulletin*, no. 44 (February 1965).

2. James Thrall Soby, *Giorgio de Chirico* (New York: Museum of Modern Art, 1955).

   Here is the version (preceded by Plath's epigraph) of "On the Decline of Oracles," published in *Poetry* magazine, September 1959:

   Inside a ruined temple the broken statue
   of a god spoke a mysterious language.
   > —Giorgio de Chirico

   My father kept a speckled conch
   By two bronze bookends of ships in sail,
   And as I listened its cold teeth seethed

With voices of that ambiguous sea
Old Böcklin missed, who held a shell
To hear the sea he could not hear.
What the seashell spoke to his inner ear
He knew, but no peasants know.

My father died, and when he died
He willed his books and shell away;
The books burned up, sea took the shell,
But I, I keep the voices he
Set in my ear, and in my eye
The sight of those blue, unseen waves
For which the ghost of Böcklin grieves.
The peasants feast and multiply

And never need see what I see.
In the Temple of Broken Stones, above
A worn curtain, rears the white head
Of a god or madman. Nobody knows
Which, or dares ask. From him I have
Tomorrow's gossip and doldrums. So much
Is vision good for: like a persistent stitch
In the side, it nags, is tedious.

Straddling a stool in the third-floor window-
Booth of the Alexandra House
Over Petty Cury, I regard
With some fatigue the smoky rooms
Of the restaurant opposite; see impose
Itself on the cook at the steaming stove
A picture of what's going to happen. I've
To wait it out. It will come. It comes:

Three barely-known men are coming up
A stair: this veils both stove and cook.
One is pale, with orange hair;
Behind glasses the second's eyes are blurred;
The third walks leaning on a stick
And smiling. These trivial images
Invade the cloistral eye like pages
From a gross comic strip, and toward

The happening of this happening
The earth turns now. In half an hour
I shall go down the shabby stair and meet,
Coming up, those three. Worth
Less than present, past—this future.
Worthless such vision to eyes gone dull
That once descried Troy's towers fall,
Saw evil break out of the north.

The third stanza accurately describes *The Enigma of the Oracle*. The epigraph to the poem, from de Chirico's "Feeling of Prehistory," appears in this context:

Inside a ruined temple the broken statue of a god spoke a mysterious language. For me this vision is always accompanied by a feeling of cold, as if I had been touched by a winter wind from a distant, unknown country. The time? It is the frigid hour of dawn on a clear day, towards the end of spring. Then the still glaucous depth of the heavenly dome dizzies whoever looks at it fixedly; he shudders and feels himself drawn into the depths as if the sky were beneath his feet; . . . Then like someone who steps from the light of day into the shade of a temple and at first cannot see the whitening statue, but slowly its form appears, ever purer, slowly the feeling of the primordial artist is reborn in me. He who first carved a god, who first wished to *create* a god. . . . Day is breaking. This is the hour of the enigma. This is also the hour of prehistory. The fancied song, the revelatory song of the last, morning dream of the prophet asleep at the foot of the sacred column, near the cold white simulacrum of a god. [Soby, p. 248]

Plath also incorporates into her poem information about Böcklin, which she apparently got from Soby:

Toward the end of his life . . . Böcklin had sat for hours in his garden, paralyzed and near death, but holding to his ears great sea shells so as to hear the roar of an ocean he could no longer visit. [P. 25]

The Enigma of the Oracle, which de Chirico said was intended to evoke the "lyricism of Greek prehistory" (p. 33), is for Plath an image of the romantic yet disturbing, inaccessible past in which she locates her dead father, as well as of the "true" vision which she has lost. She is like a surviving priestess or votary of a dead religion (and probably identifies herself with the figure of the votary in the painting who, turned away from the god, appears to be leaving the temple). A reproduction of this painting appears in Soby's book.

In a letter to her mother dated March 22, 1958, Plath wrote of working on a "series of poems on art" (for *Art News*), saying, "I've discovered my deepest source of inspiration, which is art: the art of primitives like Henri Rousseau, Gauguin, Paul Klee, and De Chirico. I have got out piles of wonderful books from the Art Library . . ." (This, and all subsequent references to Plath's letters are, unless otherwise noted, from *Letters Home: Correspondence 1950–1963*, selected and edited with commentary by Aurelia Schober Plath [New York: Harper & Row, 1975].) Although she wrote a number of poems based on works of art, including "Virgin in a Tree," "Perseus: the Triumph of Wit over Suffering," and "Departure of the Ghost" (Klee), and "Snakecharmer" (Rousseau), it is apparent that only de Chirico evoked her deepest concerns; only in his work did she find a sympathetic echo of her own history.

3. Ardengo Soffici, quoted by Soby, p. 48.

4. Soby, p. 28. The quotation is from de Chirico's autobiography. De Chirico credits Nietzsche with the "innovation" of this "poetry."

5. Sylvia Plath, *The Bell Jar*, p. 154. Subsequent references (to the 1971 Harper & Row edition) will be given in parentheses in the text. Here are other possible echoes of de Chirico:

   I saw the days of the year stretching ahead like a series of bright, white boxes, and separating one box from another was sleep, like a black shade. Only for me, the long perspective of shades that set off one box from the next had suddenly snapped up, and I could see day after day after day glaring ahead of me like a white, broad, infinitely desolate avenue. [P. 143]

   The "white, broad, infinitely desolate avenue," and the "perspective of shades," suggest de Chirico's sensibility as well his prose.

6. Robert Graves, *The White Goddess: A historical grammar of poetic myth*, 3rd ed., amend. and enl. (London: Faber & Faber, 1952), p. 165. Unless otherwise indicated, all references to Graves are to this work, in this edition.

7. Plath's copy of Eliot's *Collected Poems* bears the notation "poet always starting something new, no competition with what has gone before . . ." next to these lines in the *Four Quartets:* "Last season's fruit is eaten / And the fullfed beast shall kick the empty pail. / For last year's words belong to last year's language / And next year's words await another voice" ("Little Gidding," in T. S. Eliot, *The Complete Poems and Plays: 1909–1950* [New York: Harcourt, Brace & Co., 1958], p. 141).

8. Lavers (p. 113n) suggests some associations that Plath's names may have had for her. She mentions that "Plath . . . sounds like the French feminine epithet, *plate,* 'flat'."

9. In the implicit rejection of a natural mother who is "sweet like Mary," Plath perhaps makes a tacit reference to the Roman Catholicism of her own mother.

10. See discussions of "Little Fugue" and the "oracular" yew tree in Chapter VI and "The Moon-Muse" section of Chapter III.

11. In an interview and reading of her poetry for the British Council in association with the Poetry Room in the Lamont Library of Harvard University, recorded on October 30, 1962, Plath remarked, "at one point I was absolutely wild for Auden and everything I wrote was desperately Audenesque" (Peter Orr, general editor, *The Poet Speaks* [New York: Barnes & Noble, 1966], p. 170). In a book of Auden's poems, she had inscribed "I found my god in W. H. Auden."

12. A review of Ted Hughes's play (which also cites some comments he made about it) appeared in *The Listener* shortly after the play was first broadcast. Some of the reviewer's remarks suggest why Plath may have been particularly affected by this work of her husband's:

> . . . Hughes said, . . . that it had come to him in a dream; that he had seen it as a film, and written it down as a radio-play. . . . The plot was . . . a sort of logion of the White Goddess for Mr. Graves to incorporate in the next edition: man is driving up to London at night to meet a girl. . . . he runs over a hare. The hare screams. . . . The scream of the hare sets him thinking of the girl. She wants a red Cadillac, she wants to drain him, she is a succubus. The thought dismisses itself with its own excess . . . pinnacling to

worship her as goddess; . . . [Martin Shuttleworth, "A Poet's Dream," *The Listener*, January 31, 1963, p. 218.]

13. In a conversation of June 1974, Ted Hughes confirmed that Plath knew *The White Goddess* very well, remarking that Graves had had a "terrific effect" on her.

14. Ibid.

15. *Contemporary Poets*, 1970 ed., s.v. "Graves, Robert (Ranke)," by Martin Seymour-Smith.

16. *Letters Home*, letter of October 26, 1960.
    Friends of Plath considered her superstitious. A. Alvarez writes:

    . . . both she and her husband seemed to believe in the occult. . . . both of them talked often enough about astrology, dreams, and magic—enough, anyway, to imply that this was not just a casually interesting subject . . . ["Sylvia Plath: A Memoir," *New American Review*, no. 12 (New York: Simon and Schuster, Touchstone Books, 1971), pp. 29–30. This memoir was reprinted in Alvarez's *The Savage God: A Study of Suicide* (New York: Random House, 1972).]

    Shortly after her marriage, on October 23, 1956, she wrote to her mother about herself and Ted Hughes:

    . . . we shall become a team better than Mr. and Mrs. Yeats—he being a competent astrologist, reading horoscopes, and me being a tarot-pack reader, and, when we have enough money, a crystal-gazer.

    There are many other such references—to being a "seeress," and the like—in her letters to her mother.
    Ted Hughes mentioned, in conversation, that he had probably told Plath that "people born under the dragon's tail [that is, under Scorpio, her birth-sign] were cursed" ("Electra on Azalea Path" appears to allude to this belief).

17. Sylvia Plath, in a letter dated April 19, 1956 (*Letters Home*).

18. *The White Goddess* may also have been a source of the name of the heroine in *The Bell Jar* ("Greenwood"). Graves mentions that children born of May Day orgies were " 'merrybegots' " often "repudiated by their fathers" (p. 396), and lists a number of names

commonly given to such children, including the name Greenwood: "Greenwood and Merriman were of doubtful paternity" (p. 396). Plath's choice of name is appropriate for a girl who 'lost' her father when she was very young, and whose origins are 'mysterious.'

For the same reason there may be a connection with the heroine of Dickens' *Bleak House*, Esther Summerson, who has the same first name as the heroine of *The Bell Jar*, and whose last name likewise marks her as a "greenwood" or illegitimate child. A great deal else about Esther Summerson, particularly the often incredible deadpan ingenuousness with which she tells her story (reflecting a split between what she must, and what she feels it is proper for her, to perceive), suggests Esther Greenwood of *The Bell Jar*. The name "Greenwood," obviously carefully chosen for a number of associations, also translates the name of Plath's grandmother.

The late poem "The Couriers" reads like a riddle, and several of its clues or portents are mentioned in *The White Goddess*. "The Couriers" contains the lines:

> Frost on a leaf, the immaculate
> Cauldron, talking and crackling
>
> All to itself on the top of each
> Of nine black Alps, . . .

Graves quotes an invocation which begins, "Three Ladies came from the East, / One with fire and two with frost" (p. 392). The "immaculate cauldron" is probably the "cauldron of inspiration" (p. 27) which he frequently mentions as belonging to the White Goddess as Muse of poetry. He also says that the Virgin Mary was herself sometimes referred to as "the cauldron or source of inspiration" (p. 391). The "nine black Alps" of Plath's poem may be the "nine precipices of Mount Aroania which overhang the gorge of the Styx" (Graves, p. 367), which are identified with the White Goddess, "Lady of the Nine Heights" (p. 367).

19. Ted Hughes, in conversation, remarked that Plath felt *The White Goddess* "gave shape to what had happened to her."

20. Ted Hughes, "Notes on Plath's poems," p. 87.

21. "I went to the Guinness party and was, to my surprise, called on to read my poem with the regular Guinness winners, which included

Robert Graves, . . ." (*Letters Home,* letter to her mother dated November 5, 1961).

22. See Robert Graves, *Oxford Addresses on Poetry* (New York: Doubleday & Co., 1962). Ted Hughes confirmed that he had the book and that Plath probably read it.

23. In his "Notes on the chronological order of Sylvia Plath's poems," Ted Hughes writes that "The Moon and the Yew Tree" was composed soon after March 1962. This is apparently in error, because her submissions list indicates that she sent out that poem in November 1961, and there is a typescript of the poem dated October 1961.

24. Ted Hughes, "Notes on Plath's poems," pp. 86–87.

25. In "The Dedicated Poet," one of his 1961 *Oxford Addresses on Poetry,* Graves writes:

. . . I must distinguish, . . . between devotees of Apollo and those of the Muse. Apollonian poetry is composed in the forepart of the mind: wittily, . . . always reasonably, always on a preconceived plan, and derived from a close knowledge of rhetoric, prosody, Classical example, and contemporary fashion. . . . The Apollonian allows no personal emotions to obtrude, and no unexpected incident to break the . . . flow of his verse. The pleasure he offers is consciously aesthetic.

Muse poetry is composed at the back of the mind: an unaccountable product of a trance in which the emotions of love, fear, anger, or grief are profoundly engaged, though at the same time powerfully disciplined; in which intuitive thought reigns supralogically, and personal rhythm subdues metre to its purposes. The effect on readers of Muse poetry, with its opposite poles of ecstasy and melancholia, is what the French call a *frisson,* . . . meaning the shudder provoked by fearful or supernatural experiences. [Pp. 19–20]

In another of the Oxford lectures, "The Personal Muse," he writes:

. . . true possession by the Muse . . . does occur sporadically to this day among dedicated poets. [P. 67]

Orthodox Christianity marks a parting of ways between poets who serve the Muse, and non-poets who inherit . . . a mistrust of woman as the temptress: . . . the Muse, so far from being a virgin, presides over physical passion, . . . [Pp. 72–73]

From this obsessive love of an unknown Muse proceed poems of trance, in which the ancient mythical elements assemble thickly. [P. 73]

As I see it, a poet has only one choice: to refrain from exploiting a bovine will-power—from forcing events to adopt intellectually conceived, and therefore unnatural, and therefore disastrous, patterns; and, instead, learn from his Muse how to cultivate an intuitive certitude about the fortunate course of whatever he feels impelled to do. [P. 88]

26. Graves, pp. 199, 210, 374, 172, 97.

27. Ted Hughes, "Notes on Plath's poems," p. 86.
    Whether or not she ever again wrote with uncertainty, the difference between nearly all of her earlier work, and poems such as "Tulips" and "The Moon and the Yew Tree," is obvious. The new speed and sureness were probably in part the fruit of writing disciplines and exercises she had practiced for several years. "Mushrooms," "Poem for a Birthday," and "A Winter Ship" are among the poems which apparently evolved as meditational or improvisational exercises often taken from a list of topics (such as "mushrooms, that they think they are going to take over the world") started by her husband, to which she eventually added some topics of her own (the beginning of the late poems coincides with her abandoning the list). A common procedure, according to Ted Hughes in a conversation of June 1974, was to concentrate on a chosen topic, exploring its associations for a fixed length of time, to "hand it over" to a speaker or persona, and then to put it out of mind until some predetermined time, usually the next day, when she would sit down to write on the subject. This technique combined a deliberate preliminary elaboration of detail with spontaneity in the actual writing of the poem, relying on the unconscious to select and organize the material. The procedure was, in effect, a deliberate stoking of the unconscious. It would also train her in letting another personality take over. In the late poems that personality might be said to be her true self, reigning supralogically.
    For years Plath had used this technique to elaborate assigned

topics into poems of an essentially occasional sort. Topics such as "Surgeon at 2 a.m." and "Wuthering Heights" did not call forth any private reservoirs of association; nor were they relevant to an organizing vision. However, as is apparent from "The Moon and the Yew Tree," the practices which aided in the writing of these poems benefited her later mythology, allowing the expression of it to be the releasing of a unified autonomous impulse. The play of unconscious forces to which she gained access came eventually to be almost involuntary; Alvarez mentions that in June 1962 she described "the new drive to write that was upon her," and that he thought it sounded "like demonic possession" ("Sylvia Plath: A Memoir," p. 18). It is characterized similarly in her writing: "The blood jet is poetry, / There is no stopping it."

28. It is safe to assume that she submitted to a magazine any poem that she found satisfactory. According to her poetry submissions list, which appears to be complete, she sent out "The Moon and the Yew Tree," along with several other poems, in November 1961, and in April 1962 sent out the first of the final burst of poems, including "Little Fugue"; she apparently sent out nothing at all in between. In all of 1961 she sent out fewer new poems than she wrote, and mailed out, in October of 1962.

29. In a letter to her mother dated January 12, 1962, she wrote: "I've felt lazier and lazier . . . I've given up all pretence of working in my study these last weeks; . . ." On December 7, 1961, she had written: "I feel dreadfully lazy . . . I really write terribly little. I remember before Frieda came, I was like this; quite cowlike . . . Then a month or so afterwards I did some of my best poems." Shortly after the birth of her son, in a letter dated March 12, 1962, Plath wrote to her mother, "I have the queerest feeling of having been reborn with Frieda [her daughter]—it's as if my real, rich, happy life only started just about then. I suppose it's a case of knowing what one wants. I never really knew before. . . . I feel I'm just beginning at writing, too."

Ted Hughes, remarking that she "took childbearing in a deeply symbolic way" ("Notes on Plath's poems," p. 84), considers the birth of her first child a turning-point, after which she "was able to turn to her advantage all the forces of a highly disciplined, highly intellectual style of education which had, up to this point, worked mainly against her, but without which she could hardly have gone so coolly into the regions she now entered" ("Notes on Plath's poems," p. 86).

30. "Although the novel was going well, Sylvia complained to a friend that she felt she was doing little work" (Ames, p. 291).

31. The former teacher—and then colleague, when she taught during 1957–58—was Alfred Young Fisher of Smith College, who during her senior year had directed her special studies in poetry writing. He said, in a conversation of spring 1962, that he had recently received Plath's request for the pink memo paper, and that he had just mailed some off to her. Its receipt would coincide with the beginning of the bulk of the late poems; the *Ariel* version of "Elm," as well as "Little Fugue," "Crossing the Water," "Among the Narcissi," and "Pheasant" (all of which date from April 1962), are written on this paper, as are most of her remaining poems. The significance of her request to Professor Fisher is that *she* considered herself not to be writing during this time; whatever other work she was doing was not sufficient. She believed herself to have a "block" and to be in a critical period requiring extraordinary measures— such as trying to stimulate the flow by resorting to one of her fetishes.

32. *Contemporary Authors*, v. 13/14, s.v. "Jackson, Laura (Riding)." The Laura Riding poems in the broadcast that may have some bearing on "Little Fugue" include "The Wind Suffers," "Intelligent Prayer," "The Why of the Wind," and "Autobiography of the Present" (this might be a good subtitle for "Little Fugue"), in which these lines appear:

> Whole is by breaking and by mending.
> The body is a day of ruin,
> The mind, a moment of repair.
> A day is not a day of mind
> Until all lifetime is repaired despair.
> . . .
> Do you remember now, John,
> Our suburban conversation once of bees?
> . . .
> Slowly of honeycombs and swarms
> And angry queens we?
> . . .

Yes, she remembers all that seemed,
All that was like enough to now
To make a then as actual as then,
To make a now that succeeds only
By a more close resemblance to itself.

[*Collected Poems* (New York: Random House, 1938), pp. 182–83.]

33. Aurelia Plath, quoted by Ames, p. 294.

34. Ted Hughes, in conversation, remarked that Graves's "theory that the Muse must never become a wife" had had a particularly strong effect on her.

35. In an unpublished draft version of her commentary for *Letters Home,* Sylvia Plath's mother expressed the opinion that Plath was eager always to put her husband's career ahead of her own as long as she believed in the solidarity and mutuality of their marriage; but when it became clear that her husband was alienated from her, the long-repressed frustration showed itself in a fierce and bitter anger. Plath burned many old manuscripts and concentrated her energies on her children and her writing:

She began at 4 A.M. each morning to pour forth magnificently structured poems, renouncing the subservient female role, yet holding to the triumphant note of maternal creativity in her scorn of "barrenness." [*Letters Home,* p. 483.]

36. Cited by T. S. Matthews in *Great Tom: Notes Towards the Definition of T. S. Eliot* (New York: Harper & Row, 1974), p. 106.

37. From the cover of a paperback edition of *The White Goddess* (American ed., amend. and enl. [New York: Farrar, Straus and Giroux, The Noonday Press, 1966]).

38. Many of the same or related rituals are extensively illustrated by Sir James Frazer in *The Golden Bough,* whose influence on Plath is discussed in the next chapter.

39. In "Ocean 1212-W," a jar or glass coffin encapsulates childhood and, by extension, the childhood self:

My father died, we moved inland. Whereon those nine first years of my life sealed themselves off like a ship in a bottle—beautiful, inaccessible, obsolete, a fine, white flying myth.

The same type of "inaccessible" past appears in "A Life" ("The obsolete house, the sea, flattened to a picture / She has one too many dimensions to enter") and the life itself is sealed off in a glass capsule:

> Touch it: it won't shrink like an eyeball,
> This egg-shaped bailiwick, clear as a tear.

The "bell jar" of Plath's novel is also, of course, a glass coffin.

40. In one of the White Goddess myths, "it is unlucky to see the Moon through glass" (Graves, p. 108).

41. In a discussion of the "whiteness" of the Goddess, Graves says:

Herman Melville in his *Moby Dick* devotes an eloquent chapter to a consideration of the contradictory emotions aroused by the word "white"—the grace, splendour and purity of milk-white steeds, white sacrificial bulls, snowy bridal veils and white priestly vestments, as opposed to the nameless horror aroused by albinos, lepers, visitants in white hoods and so forth— . . . [P. 66]

Graves also speaks of "the pleasant whiteness of pearl-barley, or a woman's body, or milk, or unsmutched snow; . . . [and] the horrifying whiteness of a corpse, or a spectre, or leprosy" (p. 432). "The whiteness of the Goddess has always been an ambivalent concept" (p. 432), and so it is in Plath's poems, in which white sometimes suggests the newness and purity of birth, but at other times the blankness and pallor of death-in-life. In *Three Women*, whiteness is associated with birth but also with death: the pallid woman who, having miscarried, says while looking at the Moon, "How winter fills my soul! And that chalk light / Laying its scales on the windows, . . ." There are also instances of ambivalent whiteness in "Contusion" ("The rest of the body is all washed out, / The color of pearl"), and "The Bee Meeting" ("I am exhausted, I am exhausted— / Pillar of white in a blackout of knives"; "Whose is that long white box in the grove").

42. For greater clarity, the three women are identified not as "First Voice," "Second Voice," and "Third Voice," as they are in the British and American editions of *Winter Trees*, but as they appear in a BBC production script (transmitted June 9, 1968). Here the "Wife" corresponds to "First Voice"; the "Secretary," to "Second Voice";

and the "Girl" to "Third Voice." Each of the three women has an experience which Plath herself had undergone: the birth of a son, a miscarriage, and the birth of a daughter.

43. Plath's first name also has a connection with the White Goddess myths:

> . . . Silvia, the mother of Romulus and Remus, was a Vestal Virgin of Alba Longa . . . The Shepherd-god sends a wolf, . . . to alarm Silvia and then overpowers her in a cave . . . "It was probably a were-wolf. . . . it is likely that your ancient Guild of Lupercal priests originally provided Rome with her were-wolf too. But to speak again of Silvia. The God not only ravished her in a dark cave overshadowed by a sacred grove, but took advantage of a total eclipse of the sun." [Pp. 356–57]

Lupercal is the title of Ted Hughes's second book of poems. This and other of his writings demonstrate his strong interest in Graves.

44. See discussion of "sympathetic magic" (particularly regarding the relation between the protagonist and the Moon) in the discussion of "Daddy" (in the section entitled "Rituals of Exorcism").

45. Sylvia Plath, "The Magic Mirror: A Study of the Double in Two of Dostoevsky's Novels" (undergraduate honors thesis, Smith College, 1955), p. 14.

46. This phrase is from a Tarot book owned by Plath (Basil Ivan Rákóczi, *The Painted Caravan* [The Hague: J. C. Boucher, 1954], p. 64).

47. This last quotation is from "Postscript 1960" in the Noonday paperback edition of *The White Goddess;* the same point is made, though less concisely, in the main body of the *White Goddess* text.
  Other versions of the Gods of the Waxing and Waning Year mentioned by Graves include "the sacred king Adam and the Serpent" (p. 255), and Jesus and the Devil (p. 465).

48. Graves does several times mention the woman poet:

> . . . she should write as a woman, not as if she were an honorary man. The poet was originally the *mystes,* or ecstatic devotee of the Muse; the women who took part in her rites were her representatives, . . . It is the imitation of male poetry that causes the false ring

in the work of almost all women poets. A woman who concerns herself with poetry should, I believe, either be a silent Muse . . . or she should be the Muse in a complete sense; she should be in turn Arianrhod, Blodeuwedd and the Old Sow of Maenawr Penardd who eats her farrow, and should write in each of these capacities with antique authority. She should be the visible moon: impartial, loving, severe, wise. [P. 445]

Graves also discusses the difficulties of the woman poet—which arise because the White Goddess is "anti-domestic." The seventh-century poet Liadan of Corkaguiney, on a traditional circuit of poetic visits, fell in love with a fellow poet, and promised to marry him when her round of visits was over. But then she brooded, "why irrelevantly contemplate the birth of future poets? Why was [he] not content to be a poet himself and live in her poetic company? To bear children to such a man would be a sin against herself; yet she loved him with all her heart . . ." (p. 447). Eventually she "took a religious vow of chastity . . . because she was a poet and realized that to marry [him] would destroy the poetic bond between them" (p. 448).

Graves also mentions that "Cuchulain, who is a poet as well as a hero, has deserted his wife Emer and fallen under the spell of Fand, . . . Emer herself was originally his Muse . . . but marriage had estranged them." Eventually, Cuchulain returns to Emer, but "Emer's victory is as barren as Liadan of Corkaguiney's. An ancient Irish *Triad* is justified: 'It is death to mock a poet, to love a poet, to be a poet' " (p. 448).

49. Another system of 'rival' imagery with certain parallels to the White Goddess myths bears brief mention: the symbolism of the Tarot, which by all accounts Plath took extremely seriously, and in which two male rivals contend for the favors of the Moon (this system too can be inverted). In *The Painted Caravan*, the following appears under the heading "The Moon, Ast the Serpent, or the Card of Dreams":

The threefold nature of the moon has become dramatised in the simple mime of the Harlequinade played by the strolling players of the Gypsy fairs. Colombine is the Lady Moon herself; Pierrot, the Moon youth of Heaven; and Harlequin, the earth powers which compete with the upper air for the attention of the Moon. The success of the sensuous Harlequin brings about an eclipse, but the spiritual love of Pierrot calls the young and virgin Moon to be reborn. [P. 64]

50. This is the "Electra complex" claimed for the heroine in Plath's statement about "Daddy," although in this poem, as in "Electra on Azalea Path," the dominant note is that of mourning, guilt, and bitterness, and not of rivalry. Mother-daughter rivalry is referred to explicitly in "The Beekeeper's Daughter."

51. *The White Goddess* contains several mentions of seven- or eight-year terms. For example, "The Queen of Elfland in *Thomas the Rhymer* was the mediaeval successor of the pre-Celtic White Goddess who carried off the sacred King at the end of his seven years' reign . . ." (p. 430). Graves also mentions a type of Hercules, a co-king, who "reigns alternatively with his twin"; often "The twins' joint reign is fixed at eight years" (p. 126). Graves goes on to mention the "custom of burning a child to death as an annual surrogate for the sacred king," saying that

By the time that the Achaeans had established the Olympian religion in Thessaly . . . the term had been extended to eight, or perhaps seven, years, and a child sacrificed every winter solstice until the term was complete. (Seven years instead of the Great Year of eight seems to be a blunder of the mythographers; but from the Scottish witch-ballad of *True Thomas* it appears that seven years was the normal term for the Queen of Elphame's consort to reign, . . .) [P. 127]

52. In these notes for her novel, she also refers to two films then current: *Last Year at Marienbad* and *Jules and Jim*. In both films, a beautiful, mysterious heroine leaves her husband for a lover (in *Jules and Jim*, this pattern is repeated several times, the two men alternating in the heroine's favor). Both films also involve the theme of freedom, love, and sex in marriage.

Although in her poetry Plath never developed the theme of rivals for 'the other woman,' her notes about the films suggest that the idea of 'rivalry,' and its permutations, was much in her mind at the time she was writing the late poems.

53. This is similar to the heroine's magical identification with the Moon-muse, although the qualities shared, and also their significance, are

not the same as in the case of the rival. For example, the paleness of the Moon is an affirmation of its power; but paleness in the heroine signifies her death-in-life, her subjection to the Moon's 'infection.'

54. The figure of the rival in Plath's myth, like numerous other elements, must have received confirmation from a variety of sources apart from Graves. One of these is likely to have been Mario Praz's *The Romantic Agony*, which contains a long chapter on "La Belle Dame Sans Merci" (other chapters are also relevant to the structure of her myth). This is a type of "fatal woman" who is "always pale." Plath's "white Nike," the marble Victory with her "moon-glow" (and the rival generally conceived) is a type of "belle dame"—"sans merci," mercy-less, without kindness, like the Moon (therefore opposite in spirit to Dame Kindness).

55. Plath transcribed this passage at the end of a page otherwise devoted to quotations from Jung (see also p. 74).

56. "The Magic Mirror," p. 3. In this context it might also be noted that, in Plath's brief outline for her novel, rival says to heroine: "I shall drive you mad."
    Plath also says, in "The Magic Mirror," that

    . . . the appearance of the Double is an aspect of man's eternal desire to solve the enigma of his own identity. By seeking to read the riddle of his soul in its myriad manifestations, man is brought face to face with his own mysterious mirror image, an image which he confronts with mingled curiosity and fear. This simultaneous attraction and repulsion arises from the inherently ambivalent nature of the Double, which may embody not only good, creative characteristics but also evil, destructive ones. In the most complete sense of the word, the Double is the form given to any and all personifications of man's ego in both the psychic and the physical world. [P. 1]

57. Graves mentions that, for the Cypriots, the God of the Year "is himself and his other self at the same time, king and supplanter, victim and murderer, poet and satirist— . . . elsewhere, . . . he was represented as twins, . . . poets are aware that each twin must conquer in turn, in an agelong . . . war . . . for . . . the White Goddess, . . ." (p. 444).

58. In the following list of examples (which is not exhaustive), implicit descriptions are given without quotation marks; material from drafts of the poem appears in brackets, material from the final version without brackets; in each pair of opposites, the first characteristic is an attribute of the heroine. The examples are vulnerable ≠ invulnerable; real ≠ ["not real"]; ["yellow"] ≠ "white"; mother ≠ "Nike," ["mannequin"]; "Navel cords, . . . Shriek from my belly like arrows" ≠ "knitting, . . . Hooking itself to itself" (i.e., like knotted navel cords, a thwarting of nature); "I scratch like a cat" ≠ ["You move on wheels"]; domestic ≠ exotic; ["I am not wild"], ["serviceable as burlap"] ≠ ["O rare thing"], ["The bones are perfect, of course"]; ["thick with babies"] ≠ "womb of marble"; ["queen of turnips"] ≠ ["goddess of autos"], "White Nike"; ["my ecstasies are wordless"] ≠ "you confess everything."

59. The Moon-related deathliness of the rival is similarly portrayed in poems such as "Childless Woman," where the barren woman's breasts are "gleaming with the mouths of corpses"; and "Thalidomide" (originally called "Half-Moon"), where the Moon governs travesties of motherhood: a "luminosity," the Moon is linked, through the word-play on 'monstrosity,' with the malformation of children.

60. Robert Graves, *King Jesus* (New York: Funk & Wagnalls, Minerva Press, 1946), pp. 16, 288. Ted Hughes mentioned in conversation that Plath had read this book. It is in any case likely that she would have read all of Graves's work pertaining to the White Goddess myths.

61. C. G. Jung, *The Collected Works of C. G. Jung,* ed. Sir Herbert Read, Michael Fordham, Gerhard Adler, trans. R. F. C. Hull, vol. 17: *The Development of Personality,* Bollingen Series XX (New York: Pantheon Books, 1954). For "The Development of Personality," see pp. 167–186 (the phrase cited is from p. 183); for "Marriage as a Psychological Relationship," see pp. 189–201.

In late 1962, Plath was also rereading Blake, Yeats, and Lawrence, among others, and some of the same concerns probably dictated this reading. In Blake and Lawrence, numerous remarks about marriage are underlined or asterisked, and in several cases annotated with dates. Lawrence's poem "The Mess of Love," for example, appears on a page on which she wrote "October 22, 1962." A number of

232 Notes to Page 74

the lines about marriage which she annotated pertain to the roles of heroine, husband, or rival. Lawrence's "Walk Warily" reads in part: ". . . the Sunderers . . . the swift ones / the ones with the sharp black wings / and the shudder of electric anger . . . the knife-edge cleavage of the lightning / . . . cleave us forever apart . . . / and separate heart from heart, . . . / with the white triumphance of lightning and electric delight . . ."; this suggests Plath's "white Nike" (a white winged victory—or "triumphance"), "Streaming between my walls? / . . . blue lightning . . ." The draft of Plath's "The Other" also contains the lines "Cold glass, how you insert yourself / Between heart & heart!"

In her volume of Yeats's *Collected Plays*, a number of the plays are underlined in a fashion which makes clear she read (or reread) them during the same period. Next to one of the speeches in *The Unicorn from the Stars*, she wrote the date "November 13, 1962" and "The prophecy—true?" (she refers to this prophecy in a letter of November 19). The previous play in the volume, similarly annotated, is *The Hour-Glass*. Three of the lines she underlined in that play have been used as the epigraph to the present book.

Perhaps she felt spurred to reread Yeats when early in November she found a flat in a London house where he had once lived: "it is utter heaven . . . and it's Yeats' house, which right now means a lot to me" (Ames, p. 293). Two months earlier, in September, she had visited Yeats country in Ireland.

62. Here are some possible echoes: " 'The *stars of thine own fate* lie in thy breast' "; and ". . . the way of the soul in search of its *lost father* . . . leads to the *water*, to *the dark mirror* that reposes *at its bottom*. . . . This water is no figure of speech, but a living symbol of the dark psyche" (italics added).

Compare this with "Sheep in Fog":

> They threaten
> To let me through to a heaven
> Starless and fatherless, a dark water.

And with "Words":

> While
> From the bottom of the pool, fixed stars
> Govern a life.

And "Child":

> Pool in which images
> Should be grand and classical
>
> Not this troublous
> Wringing of hands, this dark
> Ceiling without a star.

(The material quoted from Jung is from "Archetypes of the Collective Unconscious" in *The Basic Writings of C. G. Jung,* ed. and with an Introduction by Violet Staub de Laszlo, Modern Library [New York: Random House, 1959], pp. 290, 300.)

63. Jung, "Marriage as a Psychological Relationship" in *The Development of Personality,* p. 198.

64. Ibid.

65. Ibid., pp. 198–99.

66. Graves, in his chapter "The Single Poetic Theme," has an extensive discussion of "La Belle Dame Sans Merci" (see also note 54, p. 230).

67. Jung, "Archetypes of the Collective Unconscious" in *The Basic Writings of C. G. Jung,* pp. 312, 309, 313, 312, 310.

68. Ibid., p. 314.

69. Jung, "Marriage as a Psychological Relationship" in *The Development of Personality,* p. 199.

70. Graves, Noonday Press edition of *The White Goddess* (1966), pp. 490–91. This remark, from his "Postscript 1960," makes plain the connection Plath may have made between the White Goddess and the "anima" type.

71. Even the name of her husband's sister, Olwyn Hughes, reinforces the mythic quality of Plath's life—"Olwen" is a Welsh name of the White Goddess mentioned more than a dozen times by Graves (the Hugheses are of Welsh descent).

72. Conversation with Ted Hughes.

IV. THE DYING GOD AND THE SACRED MARRIAGE

1. Plath cites *The Golden Bough* three times in "The Magic Mirror." Her personal library includes the one-volume edition of *The Golden*

Bough, inscribed to her from her mother, and dated Christmas 1953; the book is heavily annotated and underlined.

2. *The White Goddess* is organized around views similar to those expressed by Frazer, who wrote:

> . . . we may conclude that a great Mother Goddess, the personification of all the reproductive energies of nature, was worshipped under different names but with a substantial similarity of myth and ritual by many peoples of Western Asia; that associated with her was a lover, or rather series of lovers, divine yet mortal, . . . we may surmise that the Easter celebration of the dead and risen Christ was grafted upon a similar celebration of the dead and risen Adonis, . . . The type, created by Greek artists, of the sorrowful goddess with her dying lover in her arms, resembles and may have been the model of the *Pietà* of Christian art, . . . [Sir James George Frazer, *The Golden Bough: A Study in Magic and Religion,* 1 vol. abr. ed. (New York: Macmillan Co., Macmillan Paperbacks, 1963), pp. 385, 401.]

3. The distinction is Frazer's: "the ebbing tide . . . [is] *a real agent* as well as *a melancholy emblem* of failure, of weakness, and of death" (p. 40; italics added). The tide (like the Moon-muse) can both cause and symbolize a certain condition.

4. Ibid., pp. 207–08. (This is the chapter from which Plath quoted in "The Magic Mirror.")

5. Ibid., pp. 163, vii, 687, 686.

6. "Dionysus was not the only Greek deity whose tragic story and ritual appear to reflect the decay and revival of vegetation. . . . the old tale reappears in the myth of Demeter and Persephone. . . . [which is] identical with the Syrian one of Aphrodite . . . and Adonis, . . . of Cybele and Attis, . . . of Isis and Osiris. . . . [In these] a goddess mourns the loss of a loved one, who personifies the vegetation, . . . the Oriental imagination figured the loved and lost one as a dead lover or a dead husband lamented by his leman or his wife [and] Greek fancy embodied the same idea in the tenderer and purer form of a dead daughter bewailed by her sorrowing mother" (Frazer, p. 456).

7. Both Frazer and Graves give many instances of this type of dying god/mourning goddess myth. Tammuz (Adonis) was

. . . the youthful spouse or lover of Ishtar, the great mother goddess, . . . every year Tammuz was believed to die, passing away
. . . to the gloomy subterranean world, and . . . every year his
divine mistress journeyed in quest of him "to the land from which
there is no returning, to the house of darkness, . . ." [P. 379]

8. The quotation is from Ted Hughes, "Notes on Plath's poems," p.
84. Several years earlier there was a reference to the sacred marriage
grove in a version of "All the Dead Dears," which was included in
"Two Lovers and a Beachcomber," a manuscript submitted by
Sylvia Plath to Cambridge University as part of her English Tripos.
Here the father is represented in Dionysian emblems:

> A man who used to clench
> Bees in his fist
> And out-rant the thundercrack,
> That one: not known enough: death's trench
> Digs him into my quick:
> At each move I confront his ready ghost
>
> Glaring sunflower-eyed
> From the glade of hives,
> Antlered by a bramble-hat,
> Berry-juice purpling his thumbs: o I'd
> Run time aground before I met
> His match.
>
> [Cambridge MS, pp. 57–58]

9. Possibly this line echoes the "Fire Sermon" section of Eliot's *The
Waste Land:* " 'My feet are at Moorgate, and my heart / Under my
feet' " (Eliot, *Complete Poems*, p. 46). The lines in both poems appear in contexts which suggest the debasement or distortion of myth
and custom, particularly those relating to marriage and sexuality.

10. From Plath's response to Peter Orr's question, "Do your poems tend
now to come out of books rather than out of your own life?" Her
full reply was:

No, no: I would not say that at all. I think my poems immediately
come out of the sensuous and emotional experiences I have, but I
must say I cannot sympathize with these cries from the heart
that are informed by nothing except a needle or a knife, or whatever it is. I believe that one should be able to control and manipu-

late experiences, even the most terrifying, like madness, being tortured, this sort of experience, and one should be able to manipulate these experiences with an informed and an intelligent mind. I think that personal experience is very important, but certainly it shouldn't be a kind of shut-box and mirror-looking, narcissistic experience. I believe it should be *relevant,* and relevant to the larger things, the bigger things such as Hiroshima and Dachau and so on.

[*The Poet Speaks,* pp. 169–70]

V. "POEM FOR A BIRTHDAY" AND THE IMAGERY OF METAMORPHOSIS

1. Ted Hughes, "Notes on Plath's poems," p. 85. (See also note 27, p. 222, for a description of one of her "exercises.")

   Nearly every poem in the "Birthday" series involves at least one of the themes on her list of topics, including "flute-notes from a reedy pond," "person walking through enormous dark house," "change of vision of a maenad, as she goes under the fury," "the stones of the city—their patient sufferance (requisitioned as they are)," "owl mobbed by birds"; and perhaps also, less obviously, "roots, roots, roots," "the hibernants," "ants," and "bird in unexplored valley." Unlike the topic "mushrooms, that they think they are going to take over the world," these themes are transformed to serve her biographical purposes. Quite possibly they were not even specifically marked out for the "Birthday" poems, but fell into place spontaneously. Doubtless, too, the concentrated effort to break down the discursive public persona—which inhibited, if it did not nearly strangle, some of her earlier poems—also helped these set themes to bear fruit.

2. Ted Hughes, "Notes on Plath's poems," p. 85.

3. Theodore Roethke, *The Collected Poems of Theodore Roethke* (New York: Doubleday & Co., 1966), p. 156.

4. Ibid., p. 72.

5. Ted Hughes, "Notes on Plath's poems," p. 85.

6. Ibid., p. 86.

7. Ibid.

8. "It is probable that Sylvia already had a version of *The Bell Jar* in her trunks when [in 1957] she returned to the States" (Ames, p. 287).

9. Ibid., p. 286.

10. A review published when *The Colossus* first appeared observed that

   Miss Plath tends to be elusive and private in a way, as if what the poems were "about" in a prose sense were very much her own business. [From the *Times Literary Supplement*, quoted in *The Art of Sylvia Plath*, p. 285.]

   Although this is not true of all the poems in *The Colossus*, it applies accurately to many of them, and particularly to much of "Poem for a Birthday." This probably helps explain why, in the American edition of *The Colossus* published two years later, all of the "Birthday" poems except "Flute Notes from a Reedy Pond" and "The Stones" were omitted at the request of the publisher, a judgment with which Plath concurred ("Knopf wanted me to . . . leave out about ten poems, especially those in the last ["Poem for a Birthday"] sequence. Well, by a miracle of intuition I guessed (unintentionally) the exact ten *they* would have left out—they wanted me to choose independently" (*Letters Home*, letter to her mother, May 1, 1961).

11. Not only a celebration of her former psychic rebirth of 1953 (written on the occasion of her twenty-seventh birthday), but the anticipation of a literal birth, would have been in Plath's mind—though this latter is a private level of meaning. While working on the poem she was pregnant with her first child—thus about to give birth to a new self, to be reborn. The poem for "a" birthday obviously had several meanings for her, and perhaps this accounts for her use of the indefinite article.

12. Some of Plath's observations about similar imagery in Dostoevsky may be relevant here. In discussing *The Double*, she says of Golyadkin's urge to hide in darkness or shadow, "This instinct to hide in the dark . . . reiterates Golyadkin's desire to be anonymous (therefore irresponsible and detached) and unseen (therefore nonexistent or dead)" ("The Magic Mirror," p. 25). Also: "The death wish . . . is a severe intensification of his desire to hide in the dark . . ." (pp. 13–14). "Dark House" and other poems in the series may have been

influenced by Dostoevskian imagery (see also his *Notes from Underground*). Compare the following lines from Plath's "Dark House":

> This is a dark house, very big.
> I made it myself,
> Cell by cell from a *quiet corner*, . . .
> . . .
> It is *warm* and tolerable
> In the bowel of the root. . . .

and "The Beast":

> I've married a *cupboard of rubbish.* . . .
>
>   [all italics added]

with the following passage from *The Double*:

What he must try to think of, was some *quiet little corner* which, if not altogether *warm*, would at least be convenient and concealed . . . earlier . . . he had spent over two hours . . . standing between a *cupboard* and some old screens amidst all sorts of . . . *rubbish*. [F. M. Dostoyevsky, *The Double*, trans. George Bird (Bloomington: Indiana University Press, 1958), p. 233; italics added.]

The suicide scene in *The Bell Jar* might also be read in light of Plath's remarks about Golyadkin.

13. "All-mouth" is apparently Plath's version of a character in "Mantis and the All-Devourer," one of the folktales collected by Paul Radin (*African Folktales*, Bollingen Series [Princeton University Press, Bollingen Paperbacks, 1970]). Compare "The All-Devourer licked up the meat and the bushes with it" (Radin, p. 94) with Plath's "All-mouth licks up the bushes / And the pots of meat."

14. *Century Dictionary and Cyclopedia*, 1906 ed., s.v. "firefly."

15. Ibid., s.v. "larva."
    In conversation, Ted Hughes confirmed the likelihood of Plath's awareness of this and other such etymologies, saying that the meanings of such words were "commonplace" to her; he also remarked that she was a "well-read entomologist."

16. The image of the bean tree is used for a similar purpose. Before the father's death, it produced "fingers of wisdom"; after he died,

the leaves became "dumb." Variations on this theme occur widely in Plath's early poems. In "On the Decline of Oracles," her oracular vision has gone "dull" and "worthless," and the once-heroic world resembles "a gross comic strip."

17. "A red tongue is among us" seems to refer to All-mouth (in "Dark House") and to Radin's All-Devourer, who, like the father in "Maenad," is called "the Old Man" (p. 93)—although the phrase is of course common. The epithet also appears in *The Golden Bough*. In both contexts, "the Old Man" is a godlike figure or surrogate.

18. Possibly, when Ted Hughes jotted down the topic "change of vision of a maenad, as she goes under the fury," he had in mind (as Plath probably does in her poem) Graves's remark that "No poet can hope to understand the nature of poetry unless he has had a vision of the Naked King crucified to the lopped oak, and watched the dancers, red-eyed from the acrid smoke of the sacrificial fires, stamping out the measure of the dance, their bodies bent uncouthly forward, with a monotonous chant of: 'Kill! kill! kill!' and 'Blood! blood! blood!' " (p. 446).

Graves also writes, "An English or American woman in a nervous breakdown of sexual origin will often instinctively reproduce in faithful and disgusting detail much of the ancient Dionysiac ritual. I have witnessed it myself in helpless terror" (pp. 449–50).

19. Radin, p. 43; italics added.

20. A similar contrast appears in "Full Fathom Five": "Father, this thick air is murderous. / I would breathe water." Also compare "I've married a cupboard of rubbish" with "My hours are married to shadow," which appears in "The Colossus" in a similar context. "The Beast" also contains a reference to Radin: "The sun sat in his armpit" echoes "The Sun and the Children," in which the Sun is a man whose light comes out of his "armpit." Plath's image therefore presents the "bullman" as even mightier than the Sun.

21. A similar theme occurs in other early poems:

> . . . o I'd
> Run time aground before I met
> His match.

> ["All the Dead Dears"]

O ransack the four winds and find another
Man who can mangle the grin of kings:
The sting of bees took away my father . . .
                    ["Lament," Cambridge MS, p. 52]

22. In "The Magic Mirror," Plath discusses Golyadkin's characteristic empathy with low forms of life. He hides in "a litter of rubbish" which serves as his "mousehole"; he thinks of himself as an insect and is followed by an abject, homeless dog who looks at him with "timid comprehension," implying a kind of brotherhood between them (in "The Beast," "Fido Littlesoul" is "the bowel's familiar"). Plath says, "All these humiliating similes arise from Golyadkin's meek side and indicate [his] inherent tendency to degrade his ego; yet, in his constant emphasis on such self-abasement there is a suggestion of the Underground Man's paradoxical 'voluptuous pleasure' in disgrace" ("The Magic Mirror," p. 13).

23. *Century Dictionary*, s.v. "chrysalis."

24. Ibid., s.v. "pupa," "nymph," "chrysalis."

25. Ted Hughes's note suggests that it may have been written slightly earlier than the poems obviously indebted to Radin ("Notes on Plath's poems," p. 85).

26. *Encyclopaedia Britannica*, 1968 ed., s.v. "caddis fly." The "mummified" pupae which are to be born recall the "mummy's stomach" ("Who"), which also implies a resurrection. Possibly some other insect is alluded to in Plath's hymn to metamorphosis—some caddis flies are also called may-flies; the "lamp-headed nymphs" might be an aquatic type of firefly (Lampyridae). But, from the context, it seems more likely that the poem remains focused on the caddis fly, following it through a complete cycle of metamorphosis.

27. *Century Dictionary*, s.v. "imago."

28. The "black-sharded lady" appears to be the "mother of beetles." (A 'shard' is the wing-cover of a beetle.) The epithet "mother of beetles" comes from a Zulu tale collected by Radin—"Untombine, the Tall Maiden," in which a monster, "Unomabunge" ("mother of beetles"), devours a king's daughter. The monster is eventually slain, and the daughter disgorged—'reborn' from this "mother." (Probably this is a source of the request, in "Who," for a "Mother

of otherness" to "Eat me"—to devour her so that she can be reborn.) Similarly, in "Witch Burning," the persona has been under the spell of a malevolent maternal force. All of the mothers referred to in "Poem for a Birthday" have a certain ambiguous hostility to the persona and seem to represent the world in which the persona lives after her father's death.

29. Images of the mutual alienation of body and mind appear frequently in *The Bell Jar*. For example:

> . . . the skin of my wrist looked so white and defenseless . . . It was as if what I wanted to kill wasn't in that skin or the thin blue pulse that jumped under my thumb, but somewhere else, deeper, more secret, and a whole lot harder to get at. [P. 165]

30. Apparently Plath fuses Radin's "City Where Men Are Mended" with the phrase, suggested by her husband, about "the stones of the city" (see note 1 of the present chapter).

31. A girl has accidentally been killed, and her mother, a good, generous woman, takes the bones to "the city where men are mended." Along the way she undergoes various tests which prove her goodness, and as a result the daughter is flawlessly repaired. The mother's jealous co-wife competes by actually murdering her own daughter (she pounds her to death in a mortar, which probably suggested to Plath the "mother of pestles" named in "The Stones"), so that she can take the bones to the same city. The tests which proved the goodness of the first mother reveal the badness of the second, whose daughter, mended accordingly, receives only half a body— one arm, one leg, and so on.

   This tale may also illuminate the line "Mother of otherness / Eat me" ("Who"). One of the tests undergone by each of the mothers is a series of encounters with various pots of food, each of which invites the mothers to "Eat me." The proper response is to decline. The bad mother not only gobbles up each potful of food, but rudely tells it, "do you need to invite me to eat you?" (p. 252).

32. In her depiction of this theme, Plath may also have been echoing Eliot, whose work had a considerable influence on her—she had studied it in college, heavily annotating her volume of his poems. At the time she wrote "The Stones," "Ash-Wednesday" had undoubtedly been recently in her mind, since a phrase from it, "the

devil of the stairs," is the title of a manuscript of poems she had sent out several months earlier, in the autumn of 1959. "Ash-Wednesday," like "The Stones," also deals with death, resurrection, and spiritual rebirth—though to different purpose. It contains the lines:

> Under a juniper-tree the bones sang, scattered and shining
> We are glad to be scattered, we did little good to each other,
> . . .
> Forgetting themselves and each other, united
> In the quiet of the desert.
>
> [*Complete Poems*, pp. 62–63]

Like these bones, the stones of Plath's poem speak:

> I became a still pebble.
> The stones of the belly were peaceable,
>
> The head-stone quiet, jostled by nothing.
> Only the mouth-hole piped out,
> Importunate cricket
>
> In a quarry of silences.

Like the cricket mouth in "The Stones," in "Ash-Wednesday" "the bones sang chirping" (*Complete Poems*, p. 62). One of Plath's many annotations to the poem reads, "ego dispersed gladly relinquishes self"—an attitude toward the ego or self which may be found in some of her last poems.

33. Ted Hughes, "Notes on Plath's poems," pp. 83, 84, 85.

34. The bald nurse who has power over life and death also appears in "The Tour," a late poem which suffers from a maniacal jauntiness:

> . . . don't trip on the nurse!—
>
> She may be bald, she may have no eyes,
> . . .
> She's pink, she's a born midwife—
> She can bring the dead to life . . .

The Moon in "Barren Woman" is also connected with a nurse and with birth and death (as also with fertility and barrenness). In a gesture which ambiguously suggests both protection and the imprinting of a mark, the Moon "lays a hand" on the barren woman's forehead.

35. There is a similar ambiguity and tentativeness in *The Bell Jar*. At the end of the novel, as Esther enters the room to be interviewed for release from the hospital, she walks in "as by a magical thread" (p. 275). This still-necessary mental crutch resembles a pathological symptom exhibited by Miss Norris, a co-patient of Esther's:

> She . . . lifted her feet over the door-sill and into the dining room as though stepping over an invisible shin-high stile. [P. 215]

Plath could easily have ended "The Stones" with a more dramatic image of rebirth, such as that of a newborn baby, for which she had prepared by her earlier use of fetal imagery (the "stones of the belly"). The image of the vase shows a more literal regeneration. Similarly, *The Bell Jar* ends with Esther feeling that she has been "retreaded," although a number of more absolute images of rebirth had been used earlier. After her hot bath, for example, she feels "pure and sweet as a new baby" (p. 22).

36. Ames, p. 286.

37. Although, as Ted Hughes points out, there are "metamorphoses" in her late poetry ("Notes on Plath's poems," p. 81).

VI. THE MYTHIC BIOGRAPHY IN THE LATE POETRY

1. The poems discussed under the above heading, under each of the subheadings ("Rituals of Exorcism," "Rituals of Death," "Rituals of Rebirth") in the next chapter, and in Chapter IX, "Beyond Drama," are discussed in each section in order of composition.

2. *Webster's New Twentieth Century Dictionary*, 2nd. ed., s.v. "fugue."

3. Both thematically and in terms of imagery, there may be a connection with Eliot, particularly with the *Four Quartets* and with "Ash-Wednesday," in which he speaks of "voices shaken from the yew-tree" (*Complete Poems*, p. 66). In the *Quartets*, the symbol of the yew entails themes similar to those treated in "Little Fugue":

> We die with the dying:
> See, they depart, and we go with them.

We are born with the dead:
See, they return, and bring us with them.
[="Little Gidding," *Complete Poems*, p. 144]

Her annotation reads: "We live by memory of the past (the dead) and we are born again by memory of events in the past . . ." A little later, she also notes: "time *not* unredeemable—past *can* exist in present; present can always be a fresh beginning—"

For Eliot, the yew is associated with both life and death (Plath's annotation to part of "The Dry Salvages" reads, "human part of pattern of death & birth: *yew tree*"). The element of reconciliation is, however, notably absent in the yew tree symbolism of "Little Fugue": although the tree connects death, life, and the present, it does so in a grotesque and horrifying way. The yew trees have a similarly grotesque combination of meanings in "The Munich Mannequins" (in the childless womb, "the yew trees blow like hydras," and this is doubly significant because though they represent a barren woman, the trees are supposed to be "the tree of life and the tree of life"); and there is the same ambiguity in "The Moon and the Yew Tree," where the "message" (either from the dead, or that of death itself) is "blackness and silence."

4. This image offers a good example of a relation between Plath's life and her poetry. In July 1962, after the incident which provides the basis' for her more occasional poem "Words heard, by accident, over the phone" (the words were spoken by Plath's rival), Plath actually ripped out the telephone. Knowing this, one might think that the image in "Daddy" is merely 'occasional.' Perhaps she used the image of a telephone "off at the root" that had once connected her to her father because she had ripped out a telephone in an incident involving her husband. But even so, it is also worth considering that her rage toward her father's proxy took the form it did because of the symbolic significance the telephone already held for her, as is evident in "Little Fugue," written several months before the phone incident, where the black yew tree functions as a telephone through which a dismaying connection is maintained. The same function of a medium to the dead is served by the telephone in "Daddy," where Daddy's foot (his root) and the telephone root become identified, and where the voices are worms coming out of the wormholes of the ear-piece. Now that "The black telephone's off at the root, / The voices just can't worm through."

5. It is worth noting that in the paintings of Francis Bacon, Plath may have encountered a visual equivalent to many of her themes and images, particularly those of catastrophe, emotional crippling, and violence.

Ted Hughes mentioned in conversation that Plath had been strongly affected by an exhibition of Bacon's work which she visited (in his recollection, probably around 1960 or 1961). This may, among others, have been a show held in London by Bacon's gallery (the Marlborough) in the spring of 1960. There was also a show held between May 24 and July 1, 1962, at the Tate Gallery. Quite possibly Plath saw that show, too.

Like Plath's, Bacon's imagery is shocking, violent, dehumanized (unlike her, however, his work does not seem to relate such images to a vision of transcendence). In some paintings it is difficult to distinguish a living person from a carcass ready for the meat-hook. The figures in his domestic interiors, and the interiors themselves, often appear wounded, or themselves to resemble wounds. Persons and objects are distorted, grotesque, or disintegrating as the result of an unseen holocaust.

"Berck-Plage," which Plath began writing at the end of June 1962, may well have been written after a visit to the Tate Gallery exhibition which crystallized for her several disturbing past experiences. The first three sections of the poem, which focus on a "hospital . . . for the disabled" (Ted Hughes, "Notes on Plath's poems," p. 87), are strikingly Baconian in spirit; and the death and funeral described later in the poem are also in sympathy with his vision.

A passage in "Berck-Plage" echoes, with eerie accuracy, images in Bacon's "Three Studies for a Crucifixion," demonstrating, if not a direct influence, at least an affinity of spirit. In these paintings, blood-red walls and a brilliant orange floor provide the background against which appear, as if invisibly spotlighted, figures of disturbing grotesqueness: a man is lying on a striped mattress which, together with the walls, is spattered with blood. The man has suffered some terrible violence, and if he is alive, it is only marginally so. In another of the series, a man hangs, cut open and upside-down, his ribcage prominently exposed: a 'side' of man, similar to a side of beef. Likewise:

This is the side of a man: his red ribs,

The nerves bursting like trees, . . .
. . .
On a striped mattress in one room
An old man is vanishing.

["Berck-Plage"]

Other of Bacon's motifs that Plath may have found compelling are that of a mouth opened in a horrifying scream and that of a thin white rectangle sketched around a solitary figure, as if it were enclosed in a glass case.

6. The passage appears on the reverse side of an unfinished poem which she apparently wrote shortly after the birth of her son, in winter 1962. It is clear she was using an old draft of *The Bell Jar* as scrap paper. The passage may date from months before "Little Fugue" was written. On November 20, 1961, shortly after receiving a Eugene F. Saxton grant to work on *The Bell Jar*, she wrote to her mother:

Don't worry about my taking on anything with the Saxton. Just between the two of us . . . I finished a batch of stuff this last year, tied it up in four parcels and have it ready to report on bit by bit as required.

7. Graves's *King Jesus*, which he refers to in his chapter on the lame god ("The Bull-Footed God"), gives an elaborate account of the ritual laming of Jesus (it is one of the necessary tokens of his kingship).
   Dionysus is another important god of this type. According to Graves, his name likely means " 'The Lame God of Light' " (p. 328). Dionysus' lameness is a "bull-foot," and thus he is a "bull-god." This may be a source for the representations of her father in "Poem for a Birthday" as Dionysus (his implied identity in "Maenad") and "bullman" (in "The Beast").

8. Translation quoted by Hans Magnus Enzensberger in "In Search of the Lost Language," *Encounter*, September 1963, p. 45. It is quite possible, given her interest in contemporary German literature, that Plath knew Günter Eich's poem.
   She considered the Nazi holocaust a part of her personal background, as is apparent from her reply to a question put to her by Peter Orr:

ORR: You say, Sylvia, that you consider yourself an American, but when we listen to a poem like 'Daddy,' which talks about Dachau and Auschwitz and *Mein Kampf*, I have the impression that this is the sort of poem that a real American could not have written, because it doesn't mean so much, these names do not mean so much, on the other side of the Atlantic, do they?

PLATH: Well now, you are talking to me as a general American. In particular, my background is, may I say, German and Austrian. On one side I am a first generation American, on one side I'm second generation American, and so my concern with concentration camps and so on is uniquely intense. And then, again, I'm rather a political person as well, so I suppose that's what part of it comes from. [*The Poet Speaks*, p. 169]

9. All of the Enzensberger quotations in this paragraph are from pages 44 and 45 of his article.

10. "Daddy" and "Little Fugue" may have been influenced by Paul Celan's "Fugue of Death," from which Enzensberger quotes ("a master from Germany death comes with eyes that are blue" [p. 48]).

Enzensberger laments the popularity of the Teutonic stereotype and the ease with which things Germanic are described in terms of it. He protests the British stereotype of German writing:

What the Germans have written, are writing, or will write is first of all "Teutonic." . . . my suspicion [is] that among the literary sources of this notion we must number a famous standard work on Germany, to wit *Dracula*. [P. 50]

"Daddy" deliberately invokes these stereotypes, presenting the story as a parodied 'Teutonic' drama. The Dracula-Nazi figure is an inspired fusion.

11. "The Magic Mirror" is much concerned with the theme of parricide and its reversal. Plath relates these themes to *The Double* and *The Brothers Karamazov*, and also to Kafka's story "The Judgment," in which a father 'sentences' his son to death. The themes are also interplayed throughout her poetry. In her mythology the father, by dying, sentences his daughter to death-in-life or to death (as a means of symbolically rejoining him); and to reverse the sentence, she must in turn condemn him, as in "Daddy" ("Daddy, I have had to kill you").

According to a former roommate of hers, Plath said of her father:

"He was an autocrat . . . I adored and despised him, and I probably wished many times that he were dead. When he obliged me and died, I imagined that I had killed him." [Quoted by Nancy Hunter Steiner in *A Closer Look at Ariel: A Memory of Sylvia Plath*, with an Introduction by George Stade (New York: Harper & Row, Harper's Magazine Press, 1973), p. 45.]

12. Quoted by M. L. Rosenthal in "Sylvia Plath and Confessional Poetry," *The Art of Sylvia Plath*, p. 70.

13. Ibid.

14. Ovid, *The Metamorphoses*, trans. Mary M. Innes (London: Penguin Books, 1955), p. 375.

VII. RESOLUTIONS OF THE MYTH

1. When Plath said that "Daddy" was about "a girl with an Electra complex" (that is, with the female version of an Oedipus complex), she gave a clue to what may be a play on words in the poem. "Oedipus" means "swell-foot," and therefore the speaker's identification of herself as a "foot" may be a private way of saying "I am Oedipus" and incorporating an allusion to the Electra complex into the poem.

2. Alvarez, "Sylvia Plath," p. 66.

3. The biographical basis for this identification is evident in *Letters Home*. Shortly after marrying Ted Hughes, she wrote ecstatically to her mother:

He is better than any teacher, even fills somehow that huge, sad hole I felt in having no father. [November 29, 1956]

The glorification of Ted Hughes in her outpouring of letters makes immediately apparent what form a reversal of attitude would take:

. . . I have fallen terribly in love, which can only lead to great hurt. I met the strongest man in the world, . . . brilliant poet . . . a large, hulking, healthy Adam, . . . with a voice like the thunder of God—a singer, story-teller, lion and world-wanderer, a vagabond who will never stop. . . . [April 17, 1956]

Ted is incredible, . . . a huge Goliath. [April 29, 1956]

In unpublished letters she writes of him as a mythical hero or divinity from another age: an Adam who is both violent and creative, a possessor of strength and genius, who would breed supermen.

It is obvious that many qualities of this omniperfect husband/god could equally well characterize an omnipotent devil, and in fact part of Plath's presentation of him is as a reformed or reformable destroyer. She describes him, in unpublished letters written shortly after they first met, as someone whose best nature has been hidden behind a mask of ruthlessness and cruelty; as a conqueror of people, used to devastating women. She casts herself as his match, the woman who will tame him, smooth his edges, and save him from being a cynical recluse. And she feels she has discovered her own best self in the process of helping him to find his.

The excessive glorification of her husband is discomfittingly redolent of fascist sensibility. Doubtless Plath—at least at the time— would have been horrified at the suggestion, but the 'gods,' both father and husband, manifest themselves in "Daddy" in precisely this form. No wonder the husband-identified-with-father appears as a Nazi and a fascist—he was originally worshipped as a (fascist) god, as an ideal of adolescent longing and, except for the last few letters, her depiction of him to her mother is a torrent of superlatives, in a mood of simultaneous exaltation and submission.

Some of Susan Sontag's observations on fascist art apply to Plath's creation, in her letters, of the character of her husband—for the letters are to an appreciable extent a literary creating of characters, determinedly evoking her life on paper in order to share it, and usually in the best light possible, with her mother. Sontag writes:

Fascist aesthetics include but go far beyond the rather special celebration of the primitive . . . They also flow from (and justify) a preoccupation with *situations of control, submissive behavior, and extravagant effort; they exalt two seemingly opposite states, egomania and servitude.* The relations of domination and enslavement take the form of a . . . grouping of people/things around an all-powerful, hypnotic leader figure or force. . . . Fascist art glorifies surrender; it exalts mindlessness: it glamorizes death. [From Susan Sontag, "Fascinating Fascism," a review of *The Last of the Nuba,* by Leni Riefenstahl, and *SS Regalia,* by Jack Pia, in *New York Review of Books,* February 6, 1975, p. 26. Italics added.]

Even taking into account the usual excesses of early love, and that Plath met and married Ted Hughes when she was in her early twenties, the combination of "egomania and servitude" in her description of the relationship is extraordinary:

. . . I am strong in myself and in love with the only man in the world who is my match . . . [April 23, 1956]

I am coming into my own; . . . how best I can be for a woman, . . .

I feel that all my life, all my pain and work has been for this one thing. . . . I see the power and voice in him that will shake the world alive. Even as he sees into my poems and will work with me to make me a woman poet like the world will gape at; . . . [May 3, 1956]

He is the most brilliant man I've ever met . . . I could never get to be such a good person without his help. He is educating me daily, setting me exercises of concentration and observation. [August 2, 1956]

. . . I can't for a minute think of him as someone 'other' than the male counterpart of myself, always just that many steps ahead of me intellectually and creatively so that I feel very feminine and admiring. [September 11, 1956]

During this period she also writes, in unpublished letters, that she feels exalted doing dishes and preparing his meals; that there is no woman like her, no man like him, and no one else in the world whole and strong enough to be the other's match.

The typical concern of the fascist sensibility with "physical perfection" (Sontag, p. 26) also figured importantly in Plath's values. Even before she met Ted Hughes, she considered health a prime requirement in a man, and she later exulted, in an unpublished letter, that her high demands for health, creativity, and faithfulness had been fulfilled.

Clearly she perceived her husband as (to use Sontag's words) "an all-powerful, hypnotic leader figure or force" (he did literally hypnotize her, to relax her for sleep); and too, he suggested to her a glamorous symbol of death. After their first encounter Plath wrote to her mother of just having met "the only man I've met yet here who'd be strong enough to be equal with" and that she "wrote my best poem about him afterwards" (March 3, 1956). She explained the poem (identified in an unpublished letter as "Pursuit"):

It is, of course, a symbol of the terrible beauty of death, and the paradox that the more intensely one lives, the more one burns and consumes oneself; death, here, includes the concept of love, and is larger and richer than mere love, which is part of it. [March 9, 1956]

But significantly, in the end, in "Daddy"—in the poetry—so that she can escape the devil-gods, the adored fascists, Plath's heroine claims "I think I may well be a Jew," thereby negating her complicity by redefining herself as the extremest victim and exacting a commensurate revenge.

4. Frazer says:

If we ask why a dying god should be chosen to take upon himself and carry away the sins and sorrows of the people, it may be suggested that in the practice of using the divinity as a scapegoat we have a combination of two customs . . . the result would be the employment of the dying god as a scapegoat. He was killed, not originally to take away sin, but to save the divine life from the degeneracy of old age; but, since he had to be killed at any rate, people may have thought that they might as well seize the opportunity to lay upon him the burden of their sufferings and sins, in order that he might bear it away with him to the unknown world beyond the grave. [Pp. 667–68]

"Stings," like "Daddy," contains a divine scapegoat figure:

A third person is watching.
He has nothing to do with the bee-seller or with me.
Now he is gone

In eight great bounds, a great scapegoat.

This scapegoat is probably a composite father/husband (see also the discussion of "Stings" on p. 150). In a draft of the poem, the scapegoat is "black as the devil," which even more closely identifies him with the "devil" and the "black man" of "Daddy." (According to Frazer, the scapegoat was sometimes conceived as a black devil; he mentions "A man, painted black to represent the devil" [p. 651].)

Beyond this, the "third person" may possibly allude ironically to *The Waste Land*: "Who is the third who walks always beside you?" (Eliot, *Complete Poems*, p. 48). Although Plath's phrase echoes Eliot's, and at least through him refers to Christ's visitation of the two disciples on the road to Emmaus, Plath surely did not intend the third man to represent Christ, as has been suggested by Ingrid Melander (*The Poetry of Sylvia Plath: A Study of Themes*, Gothenberg Studies in English 25 [Stockholm: Almqvist & Wiksell, 1972]).

5. By the time "Tulips" was written, she had clearly developed much of the technique, imagery, and themes (such as the logic of sympathetic magic) of the late poems.

6. The belief Frazer mentions, that "a barren wife infects her husband's garden with her own sterility" is the sort of contagion that occurs in *Three Women*, in which the Secretary has been infected by the Moon's sterility and by that of the men with whom she works. Men, who cannot bear children, have the disease of "flatness," for they create only negations of and abstractions about life rather than life itself. This disease can (through the mediumship of the Moon) be caught from men, and it is therefore also an inversion or parody of conception. Referring to her miscarriage, the Secretary says:

> I watched the men walk about me in the office. They
>   were so flat!
> There was something about them like cardboard, and
>   now I had caught it, . . .

7. "Medusa" (the name of the genus of jellyfish) is synonymous with "Aurelia" (the name of Plath's mother):

> **aurelia** . . . A genus of . . . *Hydromedusoe*, . . . The name is synonymous with *Medusa* regarded as a genus . . . The adult state of any medusa, . . . [*Century Dictionary*, s.v. "aurelia"]

8. Stigma:

> A place or point on the skin which bleeds periodically or at irregular intervals during some mental states. . . . *pl.* In the *Rom. Cath. Ch.*, marks said to have been supernaturally impressed upon the bodies of certain persons in imitation of the wounds on the crucified body of Christ . . . [*Century Dictionary*, s.v. "stigma"]

9. There are several echoes of Dylan Thomas in Plath's poetry. In her interview with Peter Orr, she says, "In America, in University, we read—what?—T. S. Eliot, Dylan Thomas, Yeats, that is where we began" (*The Poet Speaks*, p. 169). Sylvia Plath, like Thomas, was

born on October 27, a coincidence which she no doubt found meaningful.

10. It might be noted that, just as the portrait in "Daddy" by no means represents the full truth of Plath's feelings for her father (or even the 'facts' about him), it is a reductive absurdity to suppose that "Medusa" represents what Plath 'really' felt about her mother— just as it would be absurd to say of a boy in an Oedipal phase that he *really* wants to murder his father.

Mythic rebirth for Plath evidently entailed rejecting the past as it was embodied in her parents; that is, asserting independence from the paternal ("Daddy") and the maternal ("Medusa") aspects of her history. In accomplishing such exorcism, she activates (unconscious) motifs through the creation of figures of mythic horror, and here real characteristics are indispensable for much the same reason that a fingernail clipping or a strand of hair belonging to the real person must be attached to an effigy.

In the case of her mother, the need to exorcise may reflect not a lack but an excess of gratitude: it may be just that aspect of the relationship—the intolerable burden of gratitude, the need to compensate a parent for sacrifices made—that is rejected; for such a debt may come to seem hopeless and interminable. Several of Plath's letters suggest that this was the case. In 1953 (not long before her breakdown), she wrote to her brother:

You know, as I do, and it is a frightening thing, that mother would actually kill herself for us if we calmly accepted all she wanted to do for us. She is an abnormally altruistic person, and I have realized lately that we have to fight against her selflessness as we would fight against a deadly disease. . . .

After extracting her life blood and care for 20 years, we should start bringing in big dividends of joy for her, . . . [May 12, 1953]

The realization may eventually come that certain obligations are both unasked-for and undischargeable. That Plath had pondered issues of parental sacrifice and filial gratitude is reflected in her transcription of this passage from Jung's essay "The Development of Personality":

. . . parents set themselves the fanatical task of always "doing their best" for the children and "living only for them." This clamant ideal effectively prevents the parents from doing anything about their own development & allows them to thrust their "best" down their children's throats. This so-called "best" turns out to be the very things the parents have most badly neglected in themselves. In this way the children are goaded on to achieve their parents' most dismal failures, and are loaded with ambitions that are never fulfilled.

It appears that one of Plath's devices for compensating her mother was, particularly through her letters, the sharing of her life—especially her joyous marriage. That her mother witnessed Plath's traumatic discovery in July 1962 meant that Mrs. Plath herself became a repository of terrible knowledge. Plath was "overexposed, like an X ray" before her mother—who could now 'see through' the illusion of her marriage.

On October 9, 1962, a week before writing "Medusa," Plath wrote to her mother:

. . . I haven't the strength to see you for some time. *The horror of what you saw and what I saw you see last summer is between us* and I cannot face you again until I have a new life; . . . [Italics added.]

The remark that the "horror . . . is between us" is strikingly echoed in "Medusa": "Off, off, eely tentacle! / There is nothing between us." The canceling of the humiliating past is obviously a necessary preface to rebirth ("a new life").

On October 16, the day "Medusa" was written, Plath said in a letter to her mother:

. . . it would be psychologically the worst thing to see you now . . . [I want] To make a new life. . . . I must not go back to the womb . . .

And on October 18 she expressed her concern to her brother that their mother

. . . identifies much too much with me, and you must help her see how starting my own life . . . here—not running, is the only sane thing to do.

The wish to have a new life, and not to retreat to the womb, not to be identified with her mother, is the wish, expressed in "Medusa," to be completely born—to sever the "umbilicus." (The "root" pulled out in "Daddy" is the counterpart of the umbilicus in "Medusa.")

11. See Robert Lowell, Foreword to the U.S. edition of *Ariel* (New York: Harper & Row, 1966), p. ix. Although Lowell says she becomes "one of those super-real, hypnotic, great classical heroines" in her late poetry, he clearly means this more metaphorically than literally (to explain how she is "not another 'poetess' "). He does not see her poetry as mythic: "Everything in these poems is personal, confessional, felt" (p. vii).

12. Ibid., p. viii.

13. The biographical parallel to this reading has been confirmed by her letters (she uses the very words "clean break"). A week before writing the poem, she wrote to her mother:

    It is the uncertainty, week after week, that has been such a torture. . . . Since I made the decision [to seek a legal separation], miraculously, my own life, my wholeness, has been seeping back. [September 24, 1962]

    And, shortly before that:

    . . . I want a clean break, so I can breathe and laugh and enjoy myself again. [August 27, 1962]

    "A Birthday Present" was written on September 30. On October 9, she wrote "The shock to me has been an enormity," and that she had only suddenly in the last days learned that what she had long believed was a delusion.

    Just such paralyzing uncertainty which prevents her from breathing, and the desire for release into wholeness through the resolution of uncertainty, are presented in the poem.

14. The Gate of Ivory is "the semi-transparent gate of the house of Sleep, through which dreams appear distorted so as to assume flattering but delusive forms," while the Gate of Horn "is of transparent horn, through which true visions are seen by the dreamer" (*Century Dictionary*, s.v. "gate"). The "diaphanous" veils of falseness quite accurately represent the distorting semitransparency of the Gate of Ivory. Plath alluded to the same myth in "Flute Notes from a Reedy Pond":

    Puppets, loosed from the strings of the puppet-master,
    Wear masks of horn to bed.

The pupae, in their transparent "masks of horn," are dreaming true dreams—of the adult (true) forms into which they will shortly emerge. Their dreams must be true, because in their present pupal phase they exactly resemble their adult selves; they only lack animation.

The association of falseness, false hope, or deception with whiteness and translucency or opacity is a recurrent pattern in the late poetry (the clouds in "Little Fugue"; or, from "The Rival": "Your dissatisfactions . . . / Arrive through the mailslot with loving regularity, / White and blank, expansive as carbon monoxide"). These negative white images, associated with the false self or death-in-life, are also associated with the death-in-life aspect of the Moon-muse, whose whiteness can indicate coldness, sterility, blankness.

Variations of the contrary association, of truth with clarity or transparency, are also to be found throughout her work (balloons are "Guileless and clear"). However, images of transparency (like images of whiteness) are not univocal. The bell jar, and other forms of encapsulation, are also transparent. The glass of a bell jar indicates the false self, but also allows that self to perceive the true world as true, though unreal for her: "To the person in the bell jar, blank and stopped as a dead baby, the world itself is the bad dream" (p. 267). The image of the mirror is sometimes associated with truth (see "Mirror": "I am silver and exact. I have no preconceptions"); but it can also disguise its true nature (see "Purdah").

15. Apparently a reference to a terroristic technique of kidnappers and others.

16. Ted Hughes confirmed, in conversation, that Plath knew *Ivan Ilyitch*. He said it was one of her favorite stories, which "she was always promoting."

17. "Ivan Ilyitch's chief torment was a lie,—the lie somehow accepted by everybody, that he was only sick, but not dying, . . . And this lie tormented him: . . . they . . . preferred to lie to him about his terrible situation, and went and made him also a party to this lie. This lie, this lie, it clung to him, . . . tending to reduce the strange, solemn act of his death to the same level as visits, curtains, sturgeon for dinner . . . This lie surrounding him, and existing in him, more than all else poisoned Ivan Ilyitch's last days. . . . panic seemed to seize . . . [his family] lest suddenly this ceremonial lie should

somehow be shattered, and the absolute truth become manifest to all." (Count Lyof N. Tolstoi, *Ivan Ilyitch and Other Stories*, trans. Nathan Haskell Dole [London: Walter Scott, 1889], pp. 62, 64, 73.)

18. Ibid., pp. 56–58.

Ivan Ilyitch also contains the image of a "black sack," which Plath takes up elsewhere in her work. Tolstoy first uses the image in connection with the "ceremonial lie" which suffocates Ivan Ilyitch:

It seemed to him that they were forcing him cruelly into a narrow black sack, . . . [P. 75]

Later, the same image is used to describe his death-throes (and also his final acceptance of death):

Three whole days, during which for him there was no time, he struggled in that black sack wherein an invisible, invincible power was thrusting him. . . . He felt that his suffering consisted, both in the fact that he was being thrust into that black hole, and still more that he could not make his way through into it. [P. 87]

Finally, however, he

. . . was hurled through the hole, and there at the bottom of the hole some light seemed to shine upon him. It happened to him as it sometimes does on a railway carriage when you think that you are going forward, but are really going backward, and suddenly recognize the true direction. . . . Ivan Ilyitch fell through, saw the light, and it was revealed to him that his life had not been as it ought, but that still it was possible to repair it. [P. 88]

He reconciles himself to his family, and to death, and finds transcendence:

In place of death was light! [P. 89]

Plath uses the "black sack" to describe Esther Greenwood's breakdown in *The Bell Jar*, where it presents an image of the false self:

. . . I was so scared, as if I were being stuffed farther and farther into a black, airless sack . . . [P. 144]

In Tolstoy, the black sack transforms itself into a tunnel leading to light. Similarly, Esther, who has never before skied, plummets suicidally down a hill:

. . . through year after year of doubleness and smiles and compromise, . . . People and trees receded on either hand like the
dark sides of a tunnel as I hurtled on to the still, bright point at
the end of it, . . . [P. 108]

In "The Jailor," the image stands for death-in-life as well as un-
consciousness:

> Seven hours knocked out of my right mind
> Into a black sack . . .

And in "Daddy," the daughter nearly dies,

> But they pulled me out of the sack,
> And they stuck me together with glue.

Still another echo appears in "By Candlelight":

> . . . the sky . . .
> The sack of black! It is everywhere, tight, tight!

Although Plath does not specifically allude to the "black sack" in
"A Birthday Present," the apparent references elsewhere in her
work suggest a strong sympathy with Tolstoy's themes; and "A
Birthday Present" contains a general thematic resemblance. Just as
lies and the fear of death force Ivan Ilyitch into a black sack (the
death-in-life he eventually penetrates to find light), so the veils
smother the heroine in "A Birthday Present."

19. Russell Noyes, Jr., "The Experience of Dying," *Psychiatry* 35 (May
1972): 178.

20. Cited by Russell Noyes, in "Dying and Mystical Consciousness,"
Journal of Thanatology 1 (January-February 1971): 31.

21. There is perhaps an echo of Iphigenia here:

> . . . Silent, unflinching,
> I offer my neck to the knife.

[Euripides, *Iphigenia in Aulis*, in *Euripides IV*, trans. Charles R.
Walker (New York: Washington Square Press, 1968), p. 296.]

The priest-king according to Frazer is also sometimes a "magician."

Frazer gives a chilling example of ritual self-sacrifice and transcendence:

This province has a king over it, who has not more than twelve years to reign from jubilee to jubilee. His manner of living is in this wise, that is to say: when the twelve years are completed, on the day of this feast there assemble together innumerable people, and much money is spent in giving food to Bramans. The king has a wooden scaffolding made, spread over with silken hangings: and on that day he goes to bathe at a tank with great ceremonies and sound of music, after that he comes to the idol and prays to it, and mounts on to the scaffolding, and there before all the people he takes some very sharp knives, and begins to cut off his nose, and then his ears, and his lips, and all his members, and as much flesh off himself as he can; and he throws it away very hurriedly until so much of his blood is spilled that he begins to faint, and then he cuts his throat himself. And he performs this sacrifice to the idol, and whoever desires to reign another twelve years and undertake this martyrdom for love of the idol, has to be present looking on at this: and from that place they raise him up as king. [P. 320]

22. The envisioned rebirth defeated in this poem is, however, finally accomplished in "Stings."

23. Rosenthal, p. 70.

Ted Hughes remarked, in conversation, that the figures of the two men are based in part on two Americans who had visited him, hoping to persuade him to make a reading tour of the United States —a prospect which he says Plath thought might be death to their marriage.

It is also, in this connection, worth mentioning Francis Bacon's painting, *Two Americans*, which was shown in his 1962 Tate Gallery exhibition. The two men in the picture, dressed in business-wear, look as cadaverous—they are practically decomposing—as anyone could wish.

Perhaps, too, Plath had in mind a line from Coleridge's *The Rime of the Ancient Mariner* (part III):

> And is that Woman all her crew?
> Is that a Death? and are there two?
> Is Death that woman's mate?

24. This line also appears in *Three Women* in a context which relates death to completeness. It is spoken by the Secretary who has miscarried. The moon, overlooking the scene, has a sympathetic connection with the speaker:

> There is the moon in the high window. It is over.
> How winter fills my soul!

"Perfection"—completeness—is, in *Three Women,* associated with death (the completed life or history) and also with the unborn child (the unlived life or history):

> The face of the unborn one that loved its perfections,
> The face of the dead one that could only be perfect
> In its easy peace, could only keep holy so.

25. Sir Paul Harvey, ed., *The Oxford Companion to Classical Literature* (Oxford: Oxford University Press, Clarendon Press, 1962), p. 109.

26. There are elsewhere in Plath's poetry other possible references to *Antony and Cleopatra.* In the final lines of "Fever 103°," the speaker becomes a "pure acetylene Virgin," all "heat," "light," and fire. Cleopatra says:

> I am fire and air; my other elements
> I give to baser life.
>
> [V.ii.292–93]

Possibly Plath felt an ironic private connection with the play because in it a wound is spoken of in terms of her husband's initials:

> I had a wound here that was like a T,
> But now 'tis made an H.
>
> [IV.vii.7–8]

27. Compare, "There would be a nobility then, there would be a birthday." Cleopatra several times refers to her intended suicide as "noble."

28. Because in "Edge" the children are dead, implicitly through the agency of their mother and in the absence of their father, there might appear to be a parallel to *Medea.* But this would be a serious misreading of the spirit of the poem and the meaning of the dead children. The children must be dead in order for the woman's history to be perfected, for she regards them as extensions of herself; that is why she speaks of folding them "*back* into her body."

29. Both "Edge" and "Balloons" are dated February 5, 1963—a week before Plath's death—and there is no indication of which poem came first. These were apparently the last two poems she wrote, and

the last she submitted to a magazine. (Nearly all of the late poems took their final form within a day or two of being written, and they were usually sent out soon after. "Edge" and "Balloons" were both sent out the day they were composed.)

30. A draft of the poem speaks of leaving behind the "dead men" (the drones) and the "nurseries," as well as the "wax house." This implies that home, children, and husband (and perhaps father) are all identified with drudgery and suppression of the true self.

31. A stanza excised from the final version of "Stopped Dead," but included in Plath's recording of October 30, says, "You see, I see a sort of a twig / That might just hold me, but not you, you're too big." This narrow escape is dropped in favor of a more miraculous and mythic resolution.

32. The second interpretation is supported by Ted Hughes's remark that the poem incorporates an experience of his, a near-fatal mishap involving himself and an uncle.

33. Alvarez, "Sylvia Plath: A Memoir," pp. 23, 21, 22.

34. Alvarez (in "Sylvia Plath: A Memoir") suggests that the third death in the poem refers to an automobile accident Plath had a few months previously:

It had been no accident; she had gone off the road deliberately, seriously, wanting to die. But she hadn't, . . . The car crash was a death she had survived, . . . [P. 21]

The seriousness of the crash has been disputed by Ted Hughes, but in any case, the third death within the poem is generalized to represent the ability of Lady Lazarus to renew herself, to be miraculously reborn even after having been 'killed' by men.

35. "The pure gold baby / That melts to a shriek" appears to echo Blake's "The Mental Traveller" (Plath, a little more than three months before her death, had been rereading Blake; see also note 24, p. 273):

> And if the Babe is born a Boy
> He's given to a Woman Old,
> Who nails him down upon a rock,
> Catches his shrieks in cups of gold.
>
> . . .

. . . from the fire on the hearth
A little Female Babe does spring.

And she is all of solid fire
And gems & gold, that none his hand
Dares stretch to touch her Baby form, . . .
[Geoffrey Keynes, ed., *Poetry and Prose of William Blake* (London: Nonesuch Press, 1972), pp. 111–12.]

The Blakean dialectic of infancy and old age is echoed still more clearly in a line from Plath's early draft: "You age, & I am new."

36. Franz Kafka, "A Hunger Artist," in *The Penal Colony: Stories and Short Pieces*, trans. Willa and Edwin Muir (New York: Schocken Books, 1948), p. 246.

37. Ibid., p. 255.

38. Quoted by Martin Greenberg in *The Terror of Art: Kafka and Modern Literature* (New York: Basic Books, 1968), p. 90. Many of Greenberg's observations about Kafka can be applied to Plath.

Plath's desire for a new life and the difficulty of achieving it are plain from several of her letters:

I must make a life all my own as fast as I can . . . the flesh has dropped from my bones. [October 9, 1962]

. . . writing like mad— . . . Terrific stuff, as if domesticity had choked me. [October 12, 1962]

Just now I am a bit of a wreck, bones literally sticking out all over and great, black shadows under my eyes from sleeping pills, a smoker's hack . . . [October 12, 1962, to her brother and his wife; all other quotations in this note are from letters to her mother]

. . . I am a genius of a writer; I have it in me. I am writing the best poems of my life; they will make my name. [October 16, 1962]

. . . I need time to breathe, sun, recover my flesh. [October 18, 1962]

I *must* . . . get myself back to the live, lively, always learning and developing person I was! I want to study, learn history, politics, languages, travel. I want to be the most loving and fascinating mother in the world. London, a flat, is my aim, and I shall, in spite of all the obstacles that rear, have that; . . . I [shall have] the Salon that I will deserve. I am *glad* this happened and happened *now*. I shall be a rich, active woman . . . [October 23, 1962]

She continued in this vein a few days later:

. . . I shall be a knockout. My haircut gives me such new confidence, . . .

Living apart from Ted is wonderful—I am no longer in his shadow, and it is heaven to be liked for myself alone, knowing what I want. I may even borrow a table for my flat from Ted's girl— . . . I envy them nothing. [November 7, 1962]

39. Perhaps in this "Purdah" echoes Virginia Woolf:

Women have served all these centuries as looking-glasses possessing the magic and delicious power of reflecting the figure of man at twice its natural size. . . . Whatever may be their use in civilised societies, mirrors are essential to all violent and heroic action. . . . That serves to explain in part the necessity that women so often are to men. . . . The looking-glass vision is of supreme importance because it charges the vitality; it stimulates the nervous system. Take it away and man may die, like the drug fiend deprived of his cocaine. [*A Room of One's Own* (New York: Harcourt, Brace & World, Harbinger Books, 1957), pp. 35–36.]

40. "Getting There" contains a similar image:

There is mud on my feet,
Thick, red and slipping. It is Adam's side,
This earth I rise from, and I in agony.

Graves mentions, in *The White Goddess*, that Adam probably means "red" and that Eve is a White Goddess:

In the *Genesis* story of Adam and Eve the iconotropic distortion is . . . very thorough. Clearly Jehovah did not figure in the original myth. It is the Mother of All Living [Eve], conversing in triad, who casts Adam out . . . because he has usurped some prerogative of hers— . . . The curse in *Genesis* on the woman . . . is obviously misplaced: it must refer to the ancient rivalry decreed between the sacred king Adam and the Serpent . . . the Serpent will sting Adam's sacred heel, each in turn bringing the other to his annual death. [P. 255]

After her marriage, in the summer of 1956, Plath kept her new status a secret from the authorities at her college. During this period, on October 8, 1956, she wrote to her mother:

It is the longest I have ever been away from Ted and . . . we have mystically become one. I can appreciate the legend of Eve coming from Adam's rib as I never did before; the damn story's true! . . . Away from Ted, I feel as if I were living with one eyelash of myself only. It is really agony.

41. Graves mentions numerous variations on this theme. See also pp. 315, 330, 331. Clytemnestra is related to Lady Macbeth and Cleopatra, whom Graves also considers male-destroying embodiments of the White Goddess.

42. Eileen Aird, *Sylvia Plath* (New York: Harper & Row, Barnes & Noble Books, 1973), p. 85.

43. *Oxford Companion to Classical Literature*, p. 241.

44. Gary Kissick, "Plath: A Terrible Perfection," review of *Ariel*, in *The Nation*, September 16, 1968, p. 247.

45. Aeneas made his journey armed with a golden bough. Frazer says that

According to the public opinion of the ancients the fateful branch [in the Nemi ritual] was the Golden Bough which . . . Aeneas plucked before he essayed the perilous journey to the world of the dead. [P. 3]

46. As mentioned earlier (note 61, p. 231), Plath had been rereading Lawrence while writing her last poems, and there are many echoes of his work in hers. In "Tortoise Shout," for example, much underlined in her copy of Lawrence's poems, the tortoise-scream (during sex) is

A death-agony,
A birth-cry . . .

Plath may have echoed these lines in "Stopped Dead":

A squeal of brakes.
Or is it a birth cry?

"Tortoise Shout" also includes the lines "I remember . . . running away from the sound of a woman in labour, something like an owl whooing" (Vivian de Sola Pinto and Warren Roberts, ed. and intr., *The Complete Poems of D. H. Lawrence* [New York: Viking Press, 1971], p. 366). In *The Bell Jar*, Plath describes a woman in labor: "all the time the baby was being born she never stopped making this unhuman whooing noise" (p. 72).

Also compare the end of "Tortoise Shout" (the last three stanzas of which Plath underlined):

> Torn, to become whole again, after long seeking
>   for what is lost,
> The same cry from the tortoise as from Christ, the Osiris-
>   cry of abandonment,
> That which is whole, torn asunder,
> That which is in part, finding its whole again
>   throughout the universe.
>
> [*Complete Poems*, p. 367]

with the end of "Burning the Letters":

> The dogs are tearing a fox. This is what it is like—
> A red burst and a cry
> That splits from its ripped bag and does not stop
> With the dead eye
> And the stuffed expression, but goes on
> Dyeing the air,
> Telling the particles of the clouds, the leaves, the water
> What immortality is. That it is immortal.

47. Eliot, *Complete Poems*, pp. 119, 127.

In other ways, too, "Getting There" echoes Eliot:

> The wounded surgeon plies the steel
> That questions the distempered part;
> . . .
>   Our only health is the disease
> If we obey the dying nurse
> Whose constant care is not to please
> But to remind of our, and Adam's curse,
> And that, to be restored, our sickness must grow worse.
>
>   The whole earth is our hospital.
>
> ["East Coker," *Collected Poems*, pp. 127–28]

The following lines, also from the *Four Quartets* (*Collected Poems*, p. 142), may illuminate not only "Getting There" but other poems (such as "Little Fugue"):

> There are three conditions which often look alike
> Yet differ completely, flourish in the same hedgerow:
> Attachment to self and to things and to persons, detachment
> From self and from things and from persons; and,
>   growing between them, indifference
> Which resembles the others as death resembles life,
> Being between two lives—unflowering, between
> The live and the dead nettle. This is the use of memory:
> For liberation—not less of love but expanding
> Of love beyond desire, and so liberation
> From the future as well as the past. Thus, love of a country
> Begins as attachment to our own field of action
> And comes to find that action of little importance
> Though never indifferent. History may be servitude,
> History may be freedom. See, now they vanish,
> The faces and places, with the self which, as it could,
>   loved them,
> To become renewed, transfigured, in another pattern.
>
>   ["Little Gidding"]

VIII. DEATH, REBIRTH, AND TRANSCENDENCE

1. As has been suggested, it is severely distorting to view Plath's poetry as an expression of mental illness (as, for example, have David Holbrook, in "R. D. Laing & the Death Circuit" and elsewhere, and Jan B. Gordon in " 'Who Is Sylvia?' The Art of Sylvia Plath," *Modern Poetry Studies* 1 [1970]: 6–33). The tendency to do so appears to be particularly tempting in the case of Plath's theme of death and rebirth (and the related theme of death-in-life and life-in-death). While this motif may fit a 'schizoid' scheme, it is also universally present in myth and literature, and it belongs to the conventional language of religious experience, where the death of one aspect of self is identified with the birth or revelation of another aspect ("he that loseth his life for my sake shall find it" Matthew 10:39). The desire to 'die into' mystical experience might, from the psychopathological point of view, appear an ominous symptom—

it has in fact been viewed as infantile regression. But such psycho-pathological categories shrink and distort what they intend to explain. (See also note 3 of the present chapter.)

Care must likewise be taken in labeling certain images as, say, 'typically schizophrenic.' It might be remarked, for example, in the case of a painter such as de Chirico—whose images might readily be used as illustrations of perceptual dysfunctions or hallucinations symptomatic of certain mental illnesses, but who is not popularly thought of as an example of this or that syndrome—that had he Plath's well-publicized history of mental breakdown, attempted suicide, and suicide, it might well become irresistible to perceive his work primarily in terms of the apparently psychopathological dimension. And this would certainly be a dismissive attitude.

The Jungian analyst John Weir Perry, in "Reconstitutive Process in the Psychopathology of the Self" (*Annals New York Academy of Sciences* 96 [1962]: 853–76), outlines "the interplay of certain themes of imagery in the unconscious psyche," and the themes he describes strikingly resemble many of Plath's. He has found that these are not peculiarly fantasies of the disturbed, but are universally present, a part of the structure of the psyche. Perry finds a characteristic sequence of imagery "in the deep turmoil of the schizophrenic process," and he asks:

. . . can we look for its appearance in some other form in human experience? . . . yes, [it] can be found. Moreover, the ritual (with its accompanying myth) that resembles it is the principal and central rite of the civilizations of remote antiquity, and parallels the image-sequence step for step. I am referring to that ritual pattern of divine kingship . . .

It appears that the imagery itself is not abnormal in these sequences, for we find the same forms and the same . . . images in the unconscious of various kinds of patients, from those nonpathological to those profoundly disturbed. [Pp. 859, 866]

2. Russell Noyes, "The Experience of Dying" and "Dying and Mystical Consciousness" (both cited earlier). Also, "The Experience of Dying from Falls," including a translation of "Remarks on Fatal Fall" by Albert von St. Gallen Heim, trans. and commentary by Russell Noyes, Jr., and Roy Kletti, *Omega* 3 (February 1972): 45–52.

3. Noyes, "Dying and Mystical Consciousness," p. 25; "Experience of Dying," p. 181. In "Dying and Mystical Consciousness" (p. 35),

Noyes remarks that one study of "deathbed observations" revealed that "Moods were so heightened in some cases that patients claimed they wished to 'die into' this kind of experience rather than continue living without it." One would not call such 'death-wishes' morbid.

4. Ibid., pp. 181, 178.

5. Noyes, "Experience of Dying," p. 174. The mystical experiences while dying are in all significant aspects parallel to the mystical experiences described by William James in *The Varieties of Religious Experience,* which Plath had closely read—her copy of the book is heavily annotated.

6. Heim, "Fatal Fall," p. 50.

7. Ibid., p. 51.

8. Noyes, "Experience of Dying," p. 180.

9. Ibid., p. 177.

10. Ibid., p. 183.

IX. BEYOND DRAMA

1. In Plath's "A Lesson in Vengeance" (pub. 1959), William James is evidently the source of her material on the Christian mystic Suso:

> . . . Suso's
> Hand hones his tacks and needles,
> Scourging to sores his own red sluices
> For the relish of heaven, relentless, dousing with prickles
> Of horsehair and lice his horny loins, . . .

In his chapter on "Saintliness," James quotes from Suso's third-person autobiography:

He wore for a long time a hair shirt . . . until the blood ran from him, . . . an undergarment . . . into which a hundred and fifty brass nails, pointed and filed sharp, were driven, and the points of the nails were always turned towards the flesh. . . . tormented also by noxious insects [lice] . . . brass tacks, . . . When . . . the wounds had healed, he tore himself again and made fresh wounds.

James adds:

. . . he made himself a cross with thirty protruding iron needles and nails. . . . he pointed them . . . with a file, . . . his self-scourgings— [*The Varieties of Religious Experience: A Study in Human Nature* (New York: Collier Books, 1961), pp. 246–47.]

2. Ibid., p. 311. James is quoting from the memoirs of Malwida von Meysenbug.

3. Richard De Martino, "The Human Situation and Zen Buddhism," in *Zen Buddhism and Psychoanalysis,* by D. T. Suzuki, Erich Fromm, and Richard De Martino (New York: Harper & Row, Harper Colophon Books, 1970), p. 154; italics added.

4. Christmas Humphreys, *The Way of Action: A Working Philosophy for Western Life* (Baltimore: Penguin Books, Pelican Books, 1971), pp. 57, 183.

5. The lines

> Not you, nor him
> Nor him, nor him . . .

may be an allusion to the end of the Brihadāranyaka Upanishad, which "culminates in the famous description of Brahman as 'Not, Not' (*neti neti*)": "Brahman . . . is *neti neti*, not this, not that; it is the negation of everything that is thinkable" (Eliot Deutsch and J.A.B. van Buitenen, *A Source Book of Advaita Vedānta* [Honolulu: University Press of Hawaii, 1971], pp. 23, 308).

Ted Hughes confirmed, in conversation, that Plath knew the Upanishads, or at least Yeats's versions of them, and had been absorbed in them in late 1962. Yeats's version of the Brihadāranyaka Upanishad contains the lines:

That Self described as "not this, not that" cannot be grasped, nor destroyed, nor captured, nor afflicted. [*The Ten Principal Upanishads,* Put into English by Shree Purohit Swami and W. B. Yeats (New York: Macmillan Co., 1937), p. 147.]

And also:

They describe Spirit as "Not this; not that." The first means: "There is nothing except Spirit"; the second means: "There is nothing beyond Spirit." They call Spirit the "Truth of all truths." [P. 129]

6. Rosenthal, p. 62.

7. "The name 'fire of heaven,' by which the midsummer fire is sometimes popularly known, . . ."; "the 'fire of heaven' . . . made on St. Vitus's Day" (Frazer, pp. 746–47).

8. The aspect of punishment was elaborated in a stanza which Plath read for her October 30, 1962 recording, but which she later excised from the poem:

> O auto-da-fé!
> The purple men, gold crusted, thick with spleen
>
> Sit with their hooks and crooks and stoke the light.

The speaker's burning fever leads her to imagine being burned at the stake during the Inquisition.

9. *Interpreter's Dictionary of the Bible*, 1962 ed., s.v. "Ariel."

10. *Illustrated Bible Dictionary*, 1908 ed., s.v. "Ariel." "Ariel" as "lion of God" may also mean "a hero, a valiant warrior" (*Catholic Biblical Encyclopedia*, 1956 ed., s.v. "Ariel").

11. *Encyclopedia Judaica*, 1971 ed., s.v. "Ariel."

12. *Catholic Encyclopedia*, s.v. "Ariel."

13. *Century Dictionary*, s.v. "holocaust."
    Robert Graves says of Isis that "Her absolute power was proved by a yearly holocaust in her honour as 'Lady of the Wild Things,' in which the totem bird or beast of each society was burned alive" (p. 386). The image of holocaust in "Mary's Song" has a similar meaning:

> It is a heart,
> This holocaust I walk in,
> O golden child the world will kill and eat.

14. This line may echo James Wright's "Dead riches, dead hands" ("Having Lost My Sons, I Confront the Wreckage of the Moon: Christmas, 1960"), which Plath might have known. Wright's sensibility and technique in this poem (the image of the moon, the way in which words are repeated and lines broken up) suggest that Plath may have found in Wright a kindred spirit.

15. Godiva's name—'Godgifu' ('God's gift') is parallel to the epithet "God's lioness."

16. *Century Dictionary*, s.v. "stasis."

17. The red "eye" is a "heart" in an earlier draft. The "cauldron of morning" may for Plath also have been associated with her destiny as poet—a common emblem of the White Goddess as Muse is her cauldron of poetic inspiration, mentioned many times by Graves. This too implies the subordination of the self by something larger.

18. A similar image in "Love Letter" also suggests that the 'suicide' of the dew is to be taken as the surrender of a burdensome selfhood. The speaker in "Love Letter," having once been like a stone onto which snowflakes would fall, melt, and freeze, describes her awakening from this hibernation as an ascension:

> And I slept on like a bent finger.
> The first thing I saw was sheer air
> And the locked drops rising in a dew
> Limpid as spirits. . . .
>
> . . .
>
> From stone to cloud, so I ascended.

The following passage from Graves's *King Jesus* is also germane:

> . . . the Essenes . . . believe in the resurrection of the soul which, they say, is united to the body as to a prison, and which when free from the bonds of the flesh mounts upwards shining and joins the cluster of shining souls which give the Sun its wonderful brightness; . . . [P. 209]

Here the very illumination of the Sun derives from the souls which have flown into it.

A related image appears in "Getting There":

> I shall count and bury the dead.
> Let their souls writhe in a dew,
> Incense in my track.

Here the souls, still "dew," have not yet evaporated and become one with their source.

Similarly, the speaker's description of herself as an arrow flying into the sunrise resembles a line in Yeats's version of the Mundaka

Upanishad, "the personal self [is] the arrow, impersonal Self the target. Aim accurately, sink therein" (*The Ten Principal Upanishads,* p. 53).

There are various other sources from which this image of ecstasy would have gained support—including Plotinus and other philosophers.

19. Lavers, pp. 106, 129–30.

20. Ingrid Melander, too, somewhat misses the import of the experience described in "Ariel":

In "Ariel" the persona feels one with the horse, one with the landscape—a seemingly ideal state of unity in which the "beautiful fusion with the things of this world" ("Ocean 1212-W" . . .) may presumably be restored. The deep irony about the situation is, however, that in order to attain that ideal state, she will have to free herself from the shackles of life:

> White
> Godiva, I unpeel—[Pp. 100–01]

Though Melander does admit that the end of the poem "may also include the notion of possible rebirth," she thinks it "is probably an expression of the idea of death as triumph" (p. 101).

21. James, p. 28n.

22. A similar characterization of God as blank and vacuous occurs in "Lyonnesse" (originally part of the poem called "Amnesiac") where he is an amnesiac: "The white gape of his mind was the real Tabula Rasa."

23. Ted Hughes, "Notes on Plath's poems," p. 88.
    'Ecstasy' (a standing outside of oneself) is

A state in which the mind is exalted or liberated as it were from the body; a state in which the functions of the senses are suspended by the contemplation of some extraordinary or supernatural object, or by absorption in some overpowering idea, most frequently of a religious nature; entrancing rapture or transport . . . "The Neoplatonists . . . regarded the condition of *ecstasy* as not only transcending but including all, . . ." [*Century Dictionary,* s.v. "ecstasy"]

24. Two weeks before Plath wrote "Years," Peter Orr asked her about writers who had influenced her. She replied, "Now I again begin to go backwards, I begin to look to Blake, for example" (*The Poet Speaks*, p. 170).

   Plath's distinction between eternity in a negative sense (the jealous stasis) and a positive sense also appears to echo Blake ("Energy is Eternal Delight"), who contrasts an abstract principle of eternity (to which the "great Stasis" and boring eternity are comparable), which is "in love with the productions of time," with "infinity" (eternity experienced in time).

25. This image may echo Yeats's "An aged man is but a paltry thing, / A tattered coat upon a stick, unless / Soul clap its hands and sing, . . . For every tatter in its mortal dress, . . ." ("Sailing to Byzantium," in *The Collected Poems of W. B. Yeats*, defin. ed. [New York: Macmillan Co., 1956], p. 191).

26. Sacramentally eating the "important" people parodies the "eating the god" ritual (which Frazer discusses extensively), a practice which, though related to totemism, seems to be more central to the poem than is totemism, for one is generally not supposed to eat one's totem, though one does eat the god. These two elements may be combined in the image of the farmers who, gilded like pigs, resemble the animals (their totems) which they bring to slaughter. And perhaps she means to suggest that in a world devoid of sacred value the habitual taboo on eating or killing one's totem (in which one's life is, or once was, invested) is overturned, and one kills it for profit. If so, this is an image of insane self-destruction. (There is also a private level of meaning in the poem, particularly with respect to the totem; see note 32.)

27. Sir Richard Burton's *Arabian Nights*, quoted by Penzer in an appendix to Somadeva, *The Ocean of Story*, 10 vols., ed. N. M. Penzer, trans. C. H. Tawney (London: Chas. J. Sawyer, 1924), 1: 217.

28. These lines of Plath's might echo the last few lines of Lawrence's "The Ship of Death" (see p. 163).

29. W. B. Yeats and Shree Purohit Swami, translators, "Famous Debates in the Forest" (Brihadāranyaka Upanishad) in *The Ten Principal Upanishads*, p. 153.

   The theme of "Getting There" may possibly owe something to

The Tibetan Book of the Dead, a guide for the soul after death—either to rebirth or to a transcendence of the cycles of rebirth (Ted Hughes has confirmed that Plath had read this book).

30. Shankaracharya, *Upadeshasāhasrī,* in *Advaita Vedānta,* p. 127.

31. Brihadāranyaka Upanishad, ibid., p. 31; "Summary," ibid., p. 312.

32. "Totem" provides a good example of Plath's poetic process. There is a private level here, which the meaning of the poem does not require the reader to know. Ted Hughes remarked in conversation that he and she had had a private joke that the hare was one of his totems. He said he had once upset her when he jugged a hare, which he cut in pieces and placed in a bowl; and that the afterbirth of her son was later deposited in this same bowl. The hare-totem was also associated (through her name, Assia) with Plath's rival. (This private association may figure in "Kindness," in the line "A rabbit's cry may be wilder / But it has no soul." See also the quotation from a review of Ted Hughes's radio play, note 12, p. 218.) The cobra, too, carries an association with Plath's rival, who had once given her a wooden toy snake. On this level, the "loneliness" in the cobra's eye resembles that of "the silver limbo of each eye / Where the child can never swim"; and could also refer to Plath's own loneliness caused by the 'Serpent'-rival. But these and many other details from private life clearly do not enter into the meaning of "Totem." Instead, the personal level fuels the impersonal, providing concrete images which express the most universal themes, even as they are private emblems of what drives her to investigate such themes. The private is not the ultimate level of meaning but part of something extraneous to the poem which nevertheless helped make a successful poem possible. Her own mythology finally becomes a scaffolding that is not only unobtrusive but altogether outside the poem, although one of the sources of the poem's energy.

33. James, pp. 143, 254.

34. The chapter on "Saintliness" apparently provided material to which Plath had referred in "A Lesson in Vengeance" (discussed earlier, in note 1, p. 268).

Compare the paralytic's withdrawal and the idea that acts "blacken the heart like vultures" with these remarks of James's:

The saintly person becomes exceedingly sensitive to inner inconsistency or discord, and mixture and confusion grow intolerable. [Pp. 233–34]

When the craving for moral consistency and purity is developed to this degree, the subject may well find the outer world too full of shocks to dwell in, and can unify his life and keep his soul unspotted only by withdrawing from it. That law which impels the artist to achieve harmony in his composition by simply dropping out whatever jars, or suggests a discord, rules also in the spiritual life. [P. 238]

(In the draft of the poem, Plath speaks of "disharmonies" falling away.)

35. Ibid., p. 233.

36. James, p. 221. This, according to James, is one of the universal features of saintliness.

37. A number of Plath's images reflect that she was more than superficially acquainted with Hinduism and Buddhism. (Her familiarity with these literatures was confirmed by Ted Hughes, in conversation.) In "Insomniac" (probably written in 1961), she refers to sleeping pills as:

> Those sugary planets whose influence won for him
> A life baptized in no-life for a while, . . .

The term she coins—"no-life"—is modeled on a conventional Buddhist terminology, for example: no-mind, no-action, no-relation, no-soul. Plath invents "no-life" to suggest a state not of enlightenment or awakening, but of insensibility and stupor.

An ironic reference occurs in the line "Even in your Zen heaven we shan't meet" ("Lesbos"). The point is that even in the most radical and complete state of enlightenment, where all opposites are reconciled, the speaker and her friend will still not "meet," so irreconcilable is their "venomous" opposition. Plath's usage is quite precise. It would, by contrast, be meaningless to say, "Even in your Christian heaven we shan't meet" because there would be nothing particularly significant about not meeting there.

The self-identification of the man in "Paralytic" as a buddha; his discarding of all wants and desire; and, in a draft of the poem, the reference to these as "jewels without value": these are in Hindu and Buddhist contexts common representations of enlightenment.

Noyes's observations on the connection between rebirth and the experience of dying; poems such as "Stopped Dead" ("A squeal of brakes. / Or is it a birth cry?"); and the line "I am learning to let go": all are illuminated by the following remark on Buddhist enlightenment:

If you want to get at the unadulterated truth of egolessness, you must once for all *let go your hold* and fall over the precipice, when *you will rise again newly awakened* and *in full possession of the* four *virtues* of eternity, bliss, freedom, and purity, *which belong to the real ego.* What does it mean to let go of your hold on the precipice? Suppose a man has wandered out among the remote mountains, where no one else has ever ventured. He comes to the edge of a precipice unfathomably deep, . . . he can neither advance nor retreat, death is looking at him in the face. His only hope lies in holding on to the vine which his hands have grasped; . . . If he should by carelessness let go his hold, his body would be thrown down to the abyss and crushed to pieces, bones and all.

It is the same with the student of Zen. When he grapples with a koan single-handedly he will come to see that he has reached the limit of his mental tension, and he is brought to a standstill. Like the man hanging over the precipice he is completely at a loss what to do next. Except for occasional feelings of uneasiness and despair, it is like death itself. All of a sudden he finds his mind and body wiped out of existence, together with the koan. This is what is known as 'letting go your hold.' As you become awakened from the stupor and regain your breath it is like drinking water and knowing for yourself that it is cold. It will be a joy inexpressible. [D. T. Suzuki, *Essays in Zen Buddhism,* Second Series (London: Luzac and Co., 1933; reprint ed., London: Rider and Co., 1950, 1958), p. 100.]

The Chinese terms used in connection with the moment of breakthrough or enlightenment mean

. . . "one out-bursting cry." The moment is thus: "the bursting of the bag," . . . "a sudden bursting," "the bursting of the bamboo with a crack," "the breaking up of the void," etc. [Suzuki, p. 120]

A similar image is used to this effect at the end of "Burning the Letters," which speaks of "A red burst and a cry / That splits from its ripped bag" and that "goes on / Dyeing the air, / Telling the particles of the clouds, the leaves, the water / What immortality is. That it is immortal." The poem ends with an image of transcendence, even if it originates in the expression of a transcendent outrage and pain. Suffering and anger, but also mortality itself, are transformed through the speaker's identification with the fox. Although killed, with a "dead eye [I]," its cry stains the universe, telling that it (the self merged into the universe) is immortal. (See also note 46, page 265, on Plath and Lawrence.)

38. W. B. Yeats and Shree Purohit Swami, translators, "Famous Debates in the Forest," in *The Ten Principal Upanishads*, pp. 154–55.

39. "Just as a small patch of cloud, by obstructing the vision of the observer, conceals, as it were, the solar disc extending over many miles, similarly ignorance, though limited by nature, yet obstructing the intellect of the observer, conceals, as it were, the Self which is unlimited and not subject to transmigration. Such a power is this power of concealment. It is thus said:—"As the sun appears covered by a cloud and bedimmed to a very ignorant person whose vision is obscured by the cloud, so also That which to the unenlightened appears to be in bondage is my real nature—the Self— Eternal Knowledge." (Sadānanda, from Vedāntasāra, in *Advaita Vedānta*, p. 296.)

40. James, pp. 299–300.

41. *The Encyclopedia of Philosophy*, 1967 ed., s.v. "John of the Cross, St.," by Ninian Smart.

42. Fingarette, pp. 307, 320. Also: "As we are often told, Nirvana and this world are one" (p. 211).

43. Virginia Woolf, *The Years* (New York: Harcourt, Brace & World, Harvest Books, 1965), pp. 381–82, 426–28, 432–35.

44. Aird, p. 67.

45. Joseph Maréchal, "On the Feeling of Presence in Mystics and Non-Mystics," quoted by Louis Dupré, "The Mystical Knowledge of the Self and its Philosophical Implications," *International Philosophical Quarterly*, 14 (December 1974): 508.

46. Harriet Rosenstein's interpretation of "Mystic" suffers from the 'confessional' terms in which the poem is read:

For the wife in "Mystic," no relief has come. Still "the air is a mill of hooks— / Questions without answer." Her passion extinguished, her faith in its resurrection annulled, she asks: "Once one has been seized up / . . . and used, / Used utterly, in the sun's conflagrations, / What is the remedy?" It is not meditation; thought simply multiplies the griefs and confusions: "Is there no way out of the mind?" ["Reconsidering Sylvia Plath," *Ms.* Magazine, September 1972, p. 98.]

This reading does not make sense of the poem ("Is there no great love, only tenderness?" certainly does not apply to the extinction of the 'wife's' passion).

47. Joyce Carol Oates, review of *Winter Trees*, by Sylvia Plath, in *New York Times Book Review*, November 19, 1972, p. 14.

48. Joyce Carol Oates, "The Death Throes of Romanticism: The Poems of Sylvia Plath," *Southern Review*, n.s., 9 (July 1973): 520.

49. *The Poet Speaks*, p. 172.

50. Plath, "Magic Mirror," p. 1.

51. Otto Rank, "The Double as Immortal Self," in *Beyond Psychology* (New York: Dover Publications, 1958), p. 76.

52. Other of Rank's observations which show the ambiguity of the double motif:

Originally, the double was an identical self (shadow, reflection), promising personal survival in the *future;* later, the double retained together with the individual's life his personal *past;* ultimately, he became an opposing self, appearing in the form of evil which represents the perishable and mortal part of the personality . . . [Pp. 81–82]

He discusses stories of twins as versions of double mythologies. This suggests how one part of the self can die and the other survive:

Hence, in twin-mythology the typical motif of fratricide turns out to be a symbolic gesture on the part of the immortal self by which it rids itself of the mortal ego. [P. 92]

The twin or hero who survives at the expense of his twin or another surrogate

. . . is constituted by a fusion of the two separate selves, the mortal and immortal, in one and the same personality; he has, so to speak, absorbed his original double, be it shadow or twin, into a doubled self which has, as it were, two lives to spare. [P. 95]

Some of Rank's observations might also be related to manifestations of false and true selves in Plath's work—particularly in *The Bell Jar* (the structure of which, with its multiple images of counterfeit and genuine roles, or selves, is probably indebted to Dostoevsky's *The Double*). According to Rank, the double theme sometimes appears as an "almost pathological loss of one's real self through a super-imposed one" (p. 70). The relation between the true and false selves in some of Plath's work (and that between heroine and rival) might be viewed as variations on a theme of this sort.

53. Sources for the association of the Moon with mind include astrology, where the Moon represents subjective aspects of personality or fate, and the symbolism of the Tarot. A description of the Moon card in a Tarot book owned by Plath might be compared with the import of the Moon in "Edge":

Fertilizing dew saying "peace, be still" falls from her beams . . . [if the card is well-placed] then will come sweet peace, voluptuous dreams, celestial visions, the fertilization of creative ideas falling with the dew, calmness of mind, assuagement of the passions and of the nameless terrors and hideous phantoms of the deep . . . [Rákóczi, *The Painted Caravan*, p. 61]

Another book on the Tarot says:

The intellectual light is a reflection . . . The face of the mind directs a calm gaze upon the unrest below . . . the message is: Peace, be still; and it may be that there shall come a calm upon the animal nature, while the abyss beneath shall cease from giving up a form. [Arthur Edward Waite, *The Pictorial Key to the Tarot* (New York: University Books, 1959), pp. 142–43.]

54. D. T. Suzuki, *Mysticism: Christian and Buddhist. The Eastern and Western Way* (New York: Harper & Row, Perennial Library, 1957), pp. 30, 32.
     This is also the "Self . . . self-luminous" of Vedānta (*Advaita Vedānta*, p. 310).

55. Annette Lavers says that "Shine, glitter, mirrors, which are or cause reflections, like the moon, are always used in a derogatory manner" (Lavers, p. 121). But derogatory meanings express only one aspect of the Moon-muse: in "Purdah," both mirrors and moon are reflectors which represent subjection to someone else (the sun), yet even in such a case, the moon also represents liberation, because the sun-god dies and the moon triumphs over him.

56. The image of unspoiled, original Self may also appear in "Brasilia," where the baby is a "mirror." In "Mirror," the mirror has the nature of a true reflector: "I am silver and exact. I have no preconceptions"; "I am not cruel, only truthful." (Having "no preconceptions" is, in a sense, an attribute of a pure or enlightened mind.) In the poem, both Moon and mirror affect how the speaker appears to herself and to others. The Moon is, in this context, a 'liar' because its light softens and romanticizes what it illuminates.

   Whether or not Plath intended a connection between mind-moon and mirror, she would have encountered it in one of the sources mentioned. Other possible sources are Graves, who in *The White Goddess* mentions the mirror of Marian—a mermaid sea-goddess—as representing the injunction to 'know thyself' (p. 393), and Yeats, who mentions "The Spirit, the Self that is in all selves, the pure mirror" ("The Holy Mountain," in *Essays and Introductions* [London: Macmillan & Co., 1961], p. 461).

57. Fingarette, pp. 333–34.

58. *The Cloud of Unknowing*, intr. and trans. by Ira Progoff (New York: Dell Publishing Co., Delta Books, 1957), pp. 161–63.

59. *Advaita Vedānta*, p. 310.

60. Sureshvara, *Naishkarmya Siddhi*, in *Advaita Vedānta*, p. 226.

Selected Bibliography of Sources Cited
from the Work of Sylvia Plath

I. BOOKS

(British editions are given in brackets)

Ariel. Foreword by Robert Lowell. New York: Harper & Row, 1966. [London: Faber and Faber, 1965.]

The Bell Jar. Biographical Note by Lois Ames. New York: Harper & Row, 1971. [London: Faber and Faber, 1963.]

The Colossus and Other Poems. New York: Alfred A. Knopf, 1962. [London: William Heinemann, 1960, as *The Colossus.* London: Faber and Faber, 1967, as *The Colossus.*]

Crossing the Water. New York: Harper & Row, 1971. [London: Faber and Faber, 1971.]

Winter Trees. New York: Harper & Row, 1972. [London: Faber and Faber, 1971.]

II. SHORT NONFICTION

"Ocean 1212-W." *The Listener,* August 29, 1963, pp. 312–13.

III. DRAMA

Three Women. BBC Production Script of June 9, 1968 rebroadcast. [First transmitted August 19, 1962. A slightly different version is printed in *Winter Trees.*]

IV. UNPUBLISHED WORKS

"The Magic Mirror: A Study of the Double in Two of Dostoevsky's Novels." Undergraduate honors thesis, Smith College (Northampton, Massachusetts), 1955.

"Two Lovers and a Beachcomber." Part II, English Tripos, Newnham College, Cambridge University, 1957.

V. CORRESPONDENCE AND INTERVIEWS

Interview. In *The Poet Speaks,* pp. 167–172. General Editor Peter Orr. New York: Barnes & Noble, 1966.

Letters Home: Correspondence 1950–1963. Selected and edited with commentary by Aurelia Schober Plath. New York: Harper & Row, 1975.

VI. POEMS

Page references are given first to the U.S. and then (in parentheses) to the British editions of Plath's books. "Poem for a Birthday" ("Who"; "Dark House"; "Maenad"; "The Beast"; "Flute Notes from a Reedy Pond"; "Witch Burning"; "The Stones") was published under that title in its entirety only in the British editions. (British editions of *Ariel, Winter Trees,* and *Crossing the Water* also differ slightly from the U.S. editions.) Some elsewhere uncollected poems are published by The Rainbow Press (London) in limited editions: *Crystal Gazer and Other Poems* (1971); *Lyonnesse* (1971); *Pursuit* (1973). The Cambridge MS is in the English Faculty Library in Cambridge, England (No. 134). Some of the poems recorded for the British Council in association with the Poetry Room in the Lamont Library of Harvard University are found on two recordings: *The Poet Speaks* (Argo Record Co. Ltd., London, 1965), on which appear "Lady Lazarus," "Daddy," and "Fever 103°" (and part of an interview with Peter Orr); and on *Treasury of 100 Modern American Poets* (Vol. 18) produced by Arthur Luce Klein, edited by Paul Kresh (Spoken Arts Records), on which appear "The Applicant," "Lady Lazarus," "Stopped Dead" (erroneously listed as "Stop Dead"), and "Medusa."

"All the Dead Dears." *The Colossus,* pp. 29–30 (27–28). Cambridge MS, pp. 57–58.

"Amnesiac." *Winter Trees,* pp. 19–20.

"An Appearance." *Winter Trees,* p. 10. (*Crossing the Water,* p. 23.)

"The Applicant." *Ariel,* pp. 4–5 (14–15). Also appears on *Treasury of 100 Modern American Poets.*

"Apprehensions." *Winter Trees,* p. 3.

"Ariel." *Ariel,* pp. 26–27 (36–37).

"The Arrival of the Bee Box." *Ariel,* pp. 59–60 (63–64).

"Balloons." *Ariel,* pp. 79–80 (80–81).

"Barren Woman." Published as "Small Hours." *Crossing the Water*, p. 28 (46).

"The Beast." *Crossing the Water*, p. 52. (*The Colossus*, pp. 83–84.)

"The Beekeeper's Daughter." *The Colossus*, pp. 73–74 (75).

"The Bee Meeting." *Ariel*, pp. 56–58 (60–62).

"Berck-Plage." *Ariel*, pp. 20–25 (30–35).

"A Birthday Present." *Ariel*, pp. 42–44 (48–50).

"Brasilia." *Winter Trees*, pp. 11–12 (13).

"Burning the Letters." *Pursuit.*

"By Candlelight." *Winter Trees*, pp. 29–30 (28–29).

"Child." *Winter Trees*, p. 18 (12).

"Childless Woman." *Winter Trees*, p. 34 (16).

"The Colossus." *The Colossus*, pp. 20–21 (20–21).

"Contusion." *Ariel*, p. 83 (84).

"The Courage of Shutting-Up." *Winter Trees*, pp. 8–9 (20–21).

"The Couriers." *Ariel*, p. 2 (12).

"Crossing the Water." *Crossing the Water*, p. 56 (14).

"Cut." *Ariel*, pp. 13–14 (23–24).

"Daddy." *Ariel*, pp. 49–51 (54–56). Also appears on *The Poet Speaks*.

"Dark House." *Crossing the Water*, p. 50. (*The Colossus*, pp. 81–82.)

"Death & Co." *Ariel*, pp. 28–29 (38–39).

"The Death of Mythmaking." *Poetry* 94 (September 1959): 370.

"The Detective." *Winter Trees*, pp. 13–14.

"The Disquieting Muses." *The Colossus*, pp. 58–60 (58–60).

"Edge." *Ariel*, p. 84 (85).

"Electra on Azalea Path." *Hudson Review* 13 (Autumn 1960): 414–15. *Lyonnesse*, pp. 12–13.

"Elm." *Ariel*, pp. 15–16 (25–26).

"Event." *Winter Trees*, p. 16. (*Crossing the Water*, p. 43.)

"The Eye-Mote." *The Colossus*, pp. 12–13 (14–15).

"Face Lift." *Crossing the Water*, pp. 5–6 (17–18).

"Faun." *The Colossus*, p. 17 (18). See also "Metamorphosis."

"The Fearful." *Pursuit. The Observer*, February 17, 1963.

"Fever 103°." *Ariel*, pp. 53–55 (58–59). Also appears on *The Poet Speaks*.

"Flute Notes from a Reedy Pond." *The Colossus*, pp. 80–81 (84–85).

"For a Fatherless Son." *Winter Trees*, p. 33 (33).

"Full Fathom Five." *The Colossus*, pp. 46–48 (46–47).

"Getting There." *Ariel*, pp. 36–38 (43–44).

"In Midas' Country." *London Magazine* 6 (October 1959): 11. *Lyonnesse*, p. 14.

"In Plaster." *Crossing the Water,* pp. 16–17 (30–32).

"Insomniac." *Crossing the Water,* pp. 10–11 (21–22).

"The Jailor." *Encounter,* October 1963, p. 51.

"Kindness." *Ariel,* p. 82 (83).

"Lady Lazarus." *Ariel,* pp. 6–9 (16–19). Also appears on *The Poet Speaks* and *Treasury of 100 Modern American Poets.*

"Lament." *New Orleans Poetry Journal* 1 (October 1955): 19. Cambridge MS, p. 52. *Crystal Gazer,* p. 27.

"Last Words." *Crossing the Water,* p. 40 (63).

"Lesbos." *Ariel,* pp. 30–32. (*Winter Trees,* pp. 34–36.)

"A Lesson in Vengeance." *Poetry* 94 (September 1959): 371.

"A Life." *Crossing the Water,* pp. 54–55 (53–54).

"Little Fugue." *Ariel,* pp. 70–71 (71–72).

"Love Letter." *Crossing the Water,* pp. 27–28 (44–45).

"Lyonnesse." *Winter Trees,* pp. 31–32 (30).

"Mad Maudlin." Cambridge MS, p. 26. See also "Maudlin."

"Maenad." *Crossing the Water,* p. 51. (*The Colossus,* pp. 82–83.)

"Mary's Song." *Ariel,* p. 45. (*Winter Trees,* p. 39.)

"Maudlin." *Crossing the Water,* p. 43. See also "Mad Maudlin."

"Medusa." *Ariel,* pp. 39–40 (45–46). Also appears on *Treasury of 100 Modern American Poets.*

"Metamorphosis." Cambridge MS, p. 30. See also "Faun."

"Mirror." *Crossing the Water,* p. 34 (52).

"The Moon and the Yew Tree." *Ariel,* p. 41 (47).

"Moonrise." *The Colossus,* pp. 64–65 (66–67).

"The Munich Mannequins." *Ariel,* pp. 73–74 (74–75).

"Mushrooms." *The Colossus,* pp. 37–38 (34–35).

"Mystic." *Winter Trees,* pp. 4–5 (26–27).

"The Net Menders." *The New Yorker,* August 20, 1960, p. 36.

"Nick and the Candlestick." *Ariel,* pp. 33–34 (40–41).

"On the Decline of Oracles." *Poetry* 94 (September 1959): 368–69.

"The Other." *Winter Trees,* pp. 21–22 (22–23).

"Ouija." (*The Colossus,* pp. 52–53.)

"Paralytic." *Ariel,* pp. 77–78 (78–79).

"Pheasant." *Winter Trees,* p. 28. (*Crossing the Water,* p. 13.)

"Poem for a Birthday." (*The Colossus,* pp. 80–88.)

"Poppies in July." *Ariel,* p. 81 (82).

"Poppies in October." *Ariel,* p. 19 (29).

"Purdah." *Winter Trees,* pp. 40–42 (17–19).

"The Rabbit Catcher." *Winter Trees,* pp. 35–36 (25).

"The Rival." *Ariel*, p. 48 (53).

"The Rival." Section omitted from the *Ariel* version. *Pursuit*.

"A Secret." *Pursuit*. Also on recording from Lamont Poetry Room, Harvard University, recorded October 30, 1962.

"Sheep in Fog." *Ariel*, p. 3 (13).

"Small Hours." *Crossing the Water*, p. 28 (46). See also "Barren Woman."

"Stings." *Ariel*, pp. 61–63 (65–67).

"The Stones." *The Colossus*, pp. 82–84 (86–88).

"Stopped Dead." *Winter Trees*, p. 17 (24). Also appears on *Treasury of 100 Modern American Poets*.

"The Surgeon at 2 A.M." *Crossing the Water*, pp. 30–31 (48–49).

"The Swarm." *Ariel*, pp. 64–66. (*Winter Trees*, pp. 37–38.)

"Thalidomide." *Winter Trees*, pp. 23–24 (31–32).

"Totem." *Ariel*, pp. 75–76 (76–77).

"The Tour." *Winter Trees*, pp. 37–39. (*Crossing the Water*, pp. 61–62.)

"Tulips." *Ariel*, pp. 10–12 (20–22).

"Two Campers in Cloud Country." *Crossing the Water*, pp. 32–33 (50–51).

"Who." *Crossing the Water*, pp. 48–49. (*The Colossus*, pp. 80–81.)

"Wintering." *Ariel*, pp. 67–68 (68–69).

"Witch Burning." *Crossing the Water*, p. 53. (*The Colossus*, pp. 85–86.)

"Words." *Ariel*, p. 85 (86).

"Words heard, by accident, over the phone." *Pursuit*.

"Years." *Ariel*, p. 72 (73).

Selected Bibliography of Other Works

Aird, Eileen. *Sylvia Plath*. New York: Harper & Row, Barnes & Noble Books, 1973.

Alvarez, A. "Sylvia Plath." In *The Art of Sylvia Plath*, pp. 56–68. Edited by Charles Newman. Bloomington: Indiana University Press, 1970.

————. "Sylvia Plath: A Memoir." *New American Review*, no. 12. New York: Simon and Schuster, Touchstone Books, 1971, pp. 9–40.

Ames, Lois. Biographical Note to *The Bell Jar*, by Sylvia Plath. New York: Harper & Row, 1971.

Blake, William. *Poetry and Prose of William Blake*. Edited by Geoffrey Keynes. London: Nonesuch Press, 1972.

Burton, Sir Richard. *Arabian Nights*. Quoted in Penzer, appendix to Somadeva, *The Ocean of Story*, 10 vols., edited by N. M. Penzer, translated by C. H. Tawney, 1: 217. London: Chas. J. Sawyer, 1924.

The Cloud of Unknowing. Introductory commentary and translation by Ira Progoff. New York: Dell Publishing Co., Delta Books, 1957.

Contemporary Authors, v. 13/14. S.v. "Jackson, Laura (Riding)."

Contemporary Poets, 1970 ed. S.v. "Graves, Robert (Ranke)," by Martin Seymour-Smith.

De Martino, Richard. "The Human Situation and Zen Buddhism." In D. T. Suzuki, Erich Fromm, and Richard De Martino, *Zen Buddhism and Psychoanalysis*, pp. 142–171. New York: Harper & Row, Harper Colophon Books, 1970.

Deutsch, Eliot, and van Buitenen, J. A. B. *A Source Book of Advaita Vedānta*. Honolulu: University Press of Hawaii, 1971.

Dostoyevsky, F. M. *The Double*. Translated by George Bird. Bloomington: Indiana University Press, 1958.

Eliot, T. S. Excerpts from the poetry of T. S. Eliot are from his volume *Collected Poems 1909–1962,* and are reprinted by permission of Harcourt Brace Jovanovich, Inc.; copyright, 1936, by Harcourt Brace Jovanovich, Inc.; copyright © 1943, 1963, 1964 by T. S. Eliot; copyright 1971 by Esme Valerie Eliot.

Enzensberger, Hans Magnus. "In Search of the Lost Language." *Encounter,* September 1963, pp. 44–51.

Fingarette, Herbert. *The Self in Transformation: Psychoanalysis, Philosophy, and the Life of the Spirit.* New York: Basic Books, 1963; reprint ed., New York: Harper & Row, Harper Torchbooks, 1965.

Frazer, Sir James George. *The Golden Bough: A Study in Magic and Religion.* 1 vol. abr. ed. New York: Macmillan Co., Macmillan Paperbacks, 1963. Copyright 1922 by Macmillan Publishing Co., Inc., renewed 1950 by Barclays Bank Ltd.

Gordon, Jan B. " 'Who Is Sylvia?' The Art of Sylvia Plath." *Modern Poetry Studies* 1 (1970), pp. 6–33.

Graves, Robert. *King Jesus.* New York: Funk & Wagnalls, Minerva Press, 1946.

———. *Oxford Addresses on Poetry.* New York: Doubleday & Co., 1962.

———. *The White Goddess: A historical grammar of poetic myth.* London: A. P. Watt & Son.

———. *The White Goddess: A historical grammar of poetic myth.* First American, amend. and enl. ed. New York: Farrar, Straus & Giroux, Noonday Press, 1966.

Heim, Albert von St. Gallen. "Remarks on Fatal Fall." Translated and with commentary by Russell Noyes, Jr., M.D., and Roy Kletti, "The Experience of Dying from Falls," *Omega* 3 (February 1972), pp. 45–52.

Holbrook, David. "R. D. Laing & the Death Circuit." *Encounter,* August 1968, pp. 35–45.

Hughes, Ted. "Notes on the chronological order of Sylvia Plath's poems." *Tri-Quarterly,* no. 7 (Fall 1966), pp. 81–88.

———. "Sylvia Plath." *Poetry Book Society Bulletin,* no. 44 (February 1965).

Humphreys, Christmas. *The Way of Action: A Working Philosophy for Western Life.* Baltimore: Penguin Books, Pelican Books, 1971.

James, William. *The Varieties of Religious Experience: A Study in Human Nature.* New York: Collier Books, 1961.

Jung, C. G. *The Basic Writings of C. G. Jung.* Edited and with an introduction by Violet Staub de Laszlo. Modern Library. New York: Random House, 1959.

———. *The Collected Works of C. G. Jung.* Edited by Sir Herbert Read, Michael Fordham, Gerhard Adler, translated by R. F. C. Hull. Vol. 17: *The Development of Personality.* Bollingen Series XX. New York: Pantheon Books, 1954.

Kafka, Franz. *The Penal Colony: Stories and Short Pieces.* Translated by Willa and Edwin Muir. New York: Schocken Books, 1948.

Kissick, Gary. "Plath: A Terrible Perfection," review of *Ariel,* by Sylvia Plath. *The Nation,* September 16, 1968, pp. 245–47.

Lavers, Annette. "The world as icon—On Sylvia Plath's themes." In *The Art of Sylvia Plath,* pp. 100–35. Edited by Charles Newman. Bloomington: Indiana University Press, 1970.

Lawrence, D. H. *The Complete Poems of D. H. Lawrence.* New York: Viking Press, 1971.

Lowell, Robert. Foreword to *Ariel,* by Sylvia Plath. New York: Harper & Row, 1966.

Maréchal, Joseph. "On the Feeling of Presence in Mystics and Non-Mystics." Quoted in Louis Dupré, "The Mystical Knowledge of the Self and its Philosophical Implications," p. 508. *International Philosophical Quarterly* 14 (December 1974), pp. 495–511.

Matthews, T. S. *Great Tom: Notes Towards the Definition of T. S. Eliot.* New York: Harper & Row, 1974.

Melander, Ingrid. *The Poetry of Sylvia Plath: A Study of Themes.* Gothenberg Studies in English 25. Stockholm: Almqvist & Wiksell, 1972.

Noyes, Russell, Jr., M.D. "Dying and Mystical Consciousness." *Journal of Thanatology* 1 (January–February 1971), pp. 25–41.

———. "The Experience of Dying." *Psychiatry* 35 (May 1972), pp. 174–84.

———, and Kletti, Roy. "The Experience of Dying from Falls." *Omega* 3 (February 1972), pp. 45–52.

Oates, Joyce Carol. "The Death Throes of Romanticism: The Poems of Sylvia Plath." *Southern Review,* new series, 9 (July 1973), pp. 501–22.

———. Review of *Winter Trees,* by Sylvia Plath. *New York Times Book Review,* November 19, 1972, pp. 7, 14.

Orr, Peter, Gen. Ed. *The Poet Speaks.* New York: Barnes & Noble, 1966.

The Oxford Companion to Classical Literature. Edited by Sir Paul Harvey. Oxford: Oxford University Press, Clarendon Press, 1962.

Perry, John Weir. "Reconstitutive Process in the Psychopathology of the Self." *Annals New York Academy of Sciences* 96 (1962), pp. 853–76.

Plath, Aurelia Schober, sel., ed., comm. *Letters Home: Correspondence 1950–1963,* by Sylvia Plath. New York: Harper & Row, 1975.

Radin, Paul, sel., ed., intr. *African Folktales.* Bollingen Series. Princeton University Press, Bollingen Paperbacks, 1970.

Rákóczi, Basil Ivan. *The Painted Caravan.* The Hague: J. C. Boucher, 1954.

Review of *The Colossus. Times Literary Supplement,* August 18, 1961, p. 550. Quoted in Charles Newman, Ed. *The Art of Sylvia Plath,* p. 285. Bloomington: Indiana University Press, 1970.

Riding, Laura. *Collected Poems.* New York: Random House, 1938.

Roethke, Theodore. "I'm Here": "I'm Here," copyright 1956 by Theodore Roethke, from *The Collected Poems of Theodore Roethke.* Reprinted by permission of Doubleday & Company, Inc.

Rosenstein, Harriet. "Reconsidering Sylvia Plath." *Ms.* Magazine, September 1972, pp. 44–51; 96–99.

Rosenthal, M. L. "Sylvia Plath and Confessional Poetry." In *The Art of Sylvia Plath,* pp. 69–76. Edited by Charles Newman. Bloomington: Indiana University Press, 1970.

Shuttleworth, Martin. "A Poet's Dream," review of "Difficulties of a Bridegroom," by Ted Hughes. *The Listener,* January 31, 1963, pp. 217–218.

Smart, Ninian. "John of the Cross, St." In *Encyclopedia of Philosophy,* edited by Paul Edwards. New York: Macmillan Publishing Co., 1967.

Soby, James Thrall. *Giorgio de Chirico.* New York: Museum of Modern Art, 1955.

Sontag, Susan. "Fascinating Fascism," review of *The Last of the Nuba,* by Leni Riefenstahl, and *SS Regalia,* by Jack Pia. *New York Review of Books,* February 6, 1975, pp. 23–30.

Steiner, Nancy Hunter. *A Closer Look at Ariel: A Memory of Sylvia Plath.* Introduction by George Stade. New York: Harper & Row, Harper's Magazine Press, 1973.

Suzuki, D. T. *Essays in Zen Buddhism,* second series. London: Luzac and Co., 1933; reprint ed., London: Rider and Co., 1950, 1958. Reprinted by permission of Hutchinson Publishing Group, Ltd.

———. *Mysticism: Christian and Buddhist. The Eastern and Western Way.* New York: Harper & Row, Perennial Library, 1957.

Szasz, Thomas. "The Crime of Commitment." *Psychology Today,* March 1969, pp. 55–57.

Tolstoi, Count Lyof N. *Ivan Ilyitch and Other Stories.* Translated by Nathan Haskell Dole. London: Walter Scott, 1889.

Waite, Arthur Edward. *The Pictorial Key to the Tarot.* New York: University Books, 1959.

Woolf, Virginia. *A Room of One's Own.* New York: Harcourt, Brace & World, Harbinger Books, 1957.

———. *The Years.* Copyright, 1937, by Harcourt Brace Jovanovich; copyright 1965, by Leonard Woolf. Reprinted by permission of the publishers.

Yeats, W. B. *The Collected Poems of W. B. Yeats.* Definitive edition. New York: Macmillan Co., 1956.

———. *Essays and Introductions.* London: Macmillan & Co., 1961.

———, and Purohit Swami, Shree. *The Ten Principal Upanishads.* New York: Macmillan Co., 1937.

Index

Sontag, Susan, 249–50 n.3
Soul, separable, 80–81, 125, 136–42,
    152–53; in "Stopped Dead," 138,
    152–53
  double as, 137, 206
  and Moon, 138, 157; in "Purdah," 157
  as queen bee, 138–42
  and transcendence, 169
Spider, image of, 190
Stasis, 9, 183
Stevens, Wallace, 19–20
"Stings," 10, 11, 12, 17, 48, 139, 141,
    148–51, 173, 175, 176, 251–52 n.4,
    261 n.30
"The Stones," 90, 95, 101–7, 137, 236 n.1,
    237 n.10, 241 n.30, 31, 241–42 n.32.
    243 n.35
"Stopped Dead," 138, 151–54, 157, 169,
    171, 261 n.31, 32, 264 n.46, 276 n.37
"Strange Case of Dr. Jekyll and Mr.
    Hyde" (Stevenson), 71
Suffering, 158, 175–77, 179, 180, 185–87,
    192–93, 270 n.8
Suicide, 11, 12, 166–68, 208. *See also*
    Breakdown, psychic; Plath, Sylvia
  in *The Bell Jar*, 238 n.12
  Cleopatra and, 145–47, 166, 260 n.27
  of "dew," in "Ariel," 184, 271–72 n.18
  "Edge" as suicide note, 208–9
  Plath's, and interpretation of her
    work, 1, 129–30, 136, 147–48, 166–67
"Suicide Off Egg Rock," 104
Sun, symbolism of, 199–200
Sun-god, 50, 51, 54, 62, 119, 156–57,
    280 n.55
"Surgeon at 2 a.m.," 137–38, 223 n.27
Suso, 268–69 n.1
"The Swarm," 139
Szasz, Thomas, 5

Tarot, 41, 219 n.16, 227 n.46, 228–29 n.49,
    279 n.53
Telephone imagery, 112, 129, 244 n.4
The Tempest (Shakespeare), 180–81
"Thalidomide," 231 n.59
Thomas, Dylan, 128, 252–53 n.9
Three Studies for a Crucifixion (Bacon),
    245 n.5
Three Women, 35, 47, 58–59, 70, 72–73,
    104, 226 n.41, 226–27 n.42, 252 n.6,
    259–60 n.24
The Tibetan Book of the Dead, 274 n.29
Tithonus, 191
Tolstoy, Leo, 132–34, 256 n.16, 256–57
    n.17, 257–58 n.18
"Tortoise Shout" (Lawrence), 264–65 n.46
"Totem," 172, 176–77, 187–92, 196,
    273 n.26, 28, 274 n.32
Totems, 138, 152, 205, 273 n.26, 274 n.32
"The Tour," 242 n.34

Transcendence, 3, 5, 13, 43, 134, 143,
    145, 148, 192, 200; in "Edge," 205,
    207–9; in "Getting There," 163–65.
    See also Rebirth; Selfhood (ego),
    dissolution of, and transcendence
  and ecstasy: in "Ariel," 180–85, 271–72
    n.18; in "Mystic," 199; in "Years,"
    186–87
  eternity, and time, 202, 186–87, 273
    n.24; in "Years," 185–87
  imminent death, apprehension of, and,
    167–72, 209, 268 n.3, 5, 276 n.37
  Moon and, 204–9
  mystical experience, transitoriness of,
    and, 196–99, 202–4, 210; in "Mystic,"
    196–99, 202–4, 210
  of past. *See* Past, transcendence of
  and purification, 178–83, 199
  through suffering: in "Fever 103°,"
    180; in "Paralytic," 192–93; in
    "Years," 185–87
  sun as symbol of, 199–200
Transparency *vs* opacity, 131, 255–56 n.14
True self, 5, 10. *See also* True/false selves
  rebirth of, and "Getting There," 158–60
  rebirth of, and killing of male figure(s),
    11–13, 108–9, 125, 151, 182; in
    "Lady Lazarus," 118–20, 154–55; in
    "Purdah," 19, 156–58
  rebirth of, and triumph over male
    figure(s), in "Stings," 149–50
  soul, separable, as, 137, 157, 169
  as "still point," 163–65
True/false selves. *See also* False self;
    True self
  breakdown and, 77, 90–107
  conflict of, 10–13, 15–18, 36, 105–7,
    125, 138, 142; and "A Birthday
    Present," 130–36; in "Medusa,"
    126–28; in "Poppies in July," 17–18;
    in "Poppies in October," 15–17; in
    "Purdah," 156–57; in "Stings,"
    148–51
  and death/rebirth. *See* Death/rebirth,
    true/false selves and
  and double, 77, 279 n.52
  and metamorphosis, 94–95
  split, and death of father, 9–11, 13, 55,
    112, 117
"The Truth," 130
Truth/falseness, 130–35, 256–57 n.17
  transparency *vs* opacity and, 255–56
    n.14
"Tulips," 16, 17, 44, 126, 193, 200,
    222 n.27, 252 n.5
Two Americans (Bacon), 259 n.23
"Two Campers in Cloud Country," 159
"Two Lovers and a Beachcomber,"
    235 n.8